THE FARM

THE FARM
published by *Risen Angel Publishing*

Information:
Risen Angel Publishing
British Columbia, Canada
risenangel@live.ca

Twice fallen, once risen –
All is darkness, and filled with death.
A new beginning to an old solution,
Always hoping for absolution.

Thrice fallen, twice risen –
Never finding a way out of prison.
All is torment and sickening strife,
Once again I find this life.

How long must I remain –
Left alone here to go insane;
All I have left is pain,
Left alone here once again.

Once fallen I never rise;
Life on earth is my demise.
In some way is this surprise?
No, laughing angel in my eyes.

What's all this falling?
I never fell,
Yet look around me,
I'm in hell.

Table of Contents

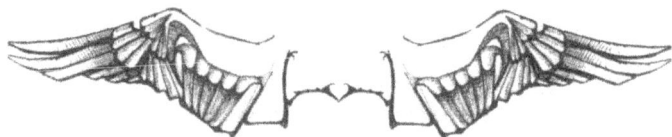

Introduction

W hat a couple of drinks means to me. For a moment I feel like a god. The whole world is brighter and my vision clearer. Then it suddenly fades, and I am left empty, lost, and alone. I am overwhelmed by an urge to continue pouring the intoxicating liquid down my throat. All reason and clarity of mind disappears. If I stop at this point, I am destined to immediate and excruciating pain which consumes my mind and physical body.

My skin aches and I want to tear the flesh from my bones, clawing away until the feeling subsides. Only this feeling of agony does not pass; it endures – putting my flesh through the throes of torment. I begin to hear a voice screaming inside my head, and it isn't God.

I know the way to free myself, and it comes in the form of a glass pipe with a white stone inside of it. Within five seconds of inhaling its smoke, my agony is gone and I am existing in a silent world, but I have chosen evil and the price will be exacted of me.

I spend every cent I have in my pocket, wallet, and bank. When I am finished with that, I exhaust all credit, and sell anything of value. There is no longer any pleasure – only a need remains. I must continue using, and will continue, for days, until I exhaust all avenues of acquiring the drug.

I wander the streets until there is nothing left of me except the desire for one more high. I pursue it even after the effects stop working. There is a black hole inside me, a darkness that can never be filled. From sheer exhaustion, and from the wounds I have inflicted upon myself, I collapse into a bed or upon the floor and sleep.

If I survive the night, I awake in its incessant grip. I must use again. Soon the demons come, and begin their torture of my afflicted soul.

There is only one freedom from this, and it is given by Jesus Christ. He alone has the power to lift the curse from me, heal my wounds, restore my heart, and give me new life. There is no other way. He asks for all of me: my heart, mind, body, and soul. I will give him anything because the freedom he has given me is priceless. There is nothing I can do earn it, nothing I can trade in exchange for it. I will never abuse this gift, because in my life, one drop of evil means a flood.

Does it ever rain only a single drop of water?

Zero Hour

Chapter ONE

Dreams fill my night, and I awaken several times, speaking to someone I can't see. After two days of endless drug use, I am exhausted, and finally fall asleep. This morning I have no energy and my muscles ache. I have persevered through this day, continuing onward in spite of the pain.

Memories resurface and flash before my eyes. Nearly all are times I would rather forget – it seems like it has happened to another person.

I know nothing. I have no resistance.

Saturday

Dreams fill my night, and I awaken several times in the darkness. The night is not long enough, and the dreams end too quickly. I am changed. The dream proves it, and God seals his instruction.

I am living in a dormitory with five other men. Apparently, this is the intake building. It's a separate facility from the rest of the farm. All the people I live with are right off the street, or a recent relapse.

There are staff who run the house, but everyone calls them *leadership*. I don't really understand what that means, but I am trying to figure it out. We are segregated from the rest of the farm, and isolated from the men who are in The Program, but tonight we are attending one of their meetings.

The speaker I listen to at the meeting last night is powerful, and at the end of message I am on my knees with my hands in the air. I have never done this in front of other people, but I have no fear of holding back. I have given everything. What else remains? I am broken, my body is sick, and pain follows me throughout the day.

What can I do except await healing?

Sunday

I awake early in the darkness, and my mind is filled with worry. What is this place? What is The Program like? Can I do it? No one has talked to me about The Program. I am walking blind. I can't see where I am going. It is difficult.

The church service was long, but the message was good. The preacher was talented, and knew the scriptures well. I am distracted by the state of my being, and unsure of myself around other people. My body refuses to obey me, and waves of nausea pass over me.

Monday

I feel alright today. Most of the physical pain has passed and I begin to feel alive – reborn. I always pass through this phase when I emerge from addiction, although usually it takes much longer to complete.

I am reading *the word* again, as I once did, and the text is revealed to me with speed and ease. It is not hidden as it once was. All these changes are new and exciting, but I still have unease within me. I have been rejected for so long, by so many, that it has left a deep wound within me. I hope it will heal in time.

Tuesday

This morning, we were given another taste of The Program. All of us ascended the pathway up the mountain, emerging into an upper field that has been converted into a greenhouse area. Not just one. I think there are nine industrial greenhouses. There are plants *everywhere*.

I spent the morning working in one of the greenhouses. I was at peace, working with the plants, and delving into the soil. On our way down the mountain, we stopped at the barn, where they keep all of the animals. Apparently, they raise the animals for slaughter, which is sad because I felt myself connecting with them. I was quite at home in the dimly lit barn, standing in the hay, and walking the dirt floor. I did not want to leave.

I have always had an attachment to living creatures. I could never understand why people so callous with the other creatures that share this earth with us. I've always seen the beauty in nature, and know that I am a part of it. I am not separate from this earth; I am made up from the soil I walk on.

Human beings are another story. I have been hurt deeply in the past, and I do not allow myself to attach. I shield myself. It is the only way to protect my heart. My life has been given to God, and I am following him with all my heart, which is why it is so important to keep it protected.

Wednesday

Every day in the afternoon, our house does *chores*. There is a list of things that need to be done, from mopping the floors and sweeping the sidewalks, to wiping the tables and washing the dishes. The guys like to put worship music on while we work. Apparently, the most requested is Jesus Culture. It's okay. I am amazed by this girl who sings with such passion. Did I have the passion once in the past? Have I lost it? Will it return?

I long to have a purpose, and direction for my life. I have been wandering around, lost in the darkness, consumed by pain and hatred. I have been hurting myself, and my family, by continuing in this life of addiction. I've walked further away from God than ever before. I even stopped praying. I gave up hope of ever being free, and resigned myself to dying in my addition.

Thursday

In order to stay here on the farm, and enter the first phase of The Program, I have been asked to sign a one-year commitment. It disturbs me. I am signing away my life, and agreeing to blindly follow all of the rules they have yet to lay out.

During the interview process, they made it seem nearly impossible. Any infraction of the rules, they can throw me out of the program, and I will be homeless. I thought they wanted to help me, not hurt me. They told me nothing of The Program, but insisted that I sign their contract. Refusal is not an option. If I don't sign the paperwork, I have to leave the farm.

The intake facility is only for the first seven days.

They say this paperwork is my commitment to God. They used some obscure verse from one of the gospels to justify it, and basically told me I'm going to suffer, die, and burn in hell, if I break the contract. They didn't use those words, of course, but the meaning was implied. I'm not an idiot.

There are a lot of so-called 'Christian' organizations that are offering help to people coming out of addiction. I been betrayed by many of them. I've been thrown out so many times that I've lost count, and every time, I've been sent to the street. The irony is that I was never homeless while using drugs. It is only when I came to the Lower Mainland for recovery that I ended up on the street. All because of these 'Programs' and 'Christians' who are 'helping me.'

This place seems different than any other I've been to, so I'm going to take chance, place my trust in God, and pray for a good outcome. What else can I do? My life is in utter ruin, my body destroyed, my emotions frayed, and my mind fragmented.

God did not bring me here to hurt me. I believe he will heal me, and restore what has been taken. Human beings are fallible, sinful, and untrustworthy. God is completely true, and can be trusted with my life. I've decided to keep my eyes focused on Christ, and take a step of faith.

Saying that, I never forget the enemy, trying to destroy my life.

Friday

My mind is filled with memories of women from my past – all of the women I've had sex with, over the years. I can see them clearly inside my mind, and it is frustrating. No matter how much sex I had, I was never satisfied. My relationships fell apart, over and over again. Now, they are a torment, laughing inside my mind.

The inundation of memory persisted for an hour. and then faded away. I continually tried to refocus my mind on the ways of God, but the mental discipline took all the strength I had. These memories rise up within me as accusations and temptations. I hear a voice inside my mind, telling me that I am not good enough, and that I will always fail.

I pray God reveals my sin to me, and forgives me for it.

Saturday

This has been a long day, and I'm tired. I hope to sleep through the whole night. I have been waking up early and laying in the darkness. I have vivid dreams, and sometimes I can't return to sleep. I find myself in meditation and prayer until the morning, watching the sun rise.

Sunday

I awake early, and lay in the darkness of my room. The dreams of last night have left a bitter taste in my mouth, and I am calling out to God with my heart. He answers. Once again, I have begun to awaken spiritually, and I find solace in God's presence. Even after everything I've done, he does not withhold himself from me.

Church service, and the worship before, were a positive experience. It took a little while to get into worship, but eventually God opened my heart, and I began to sing. It is the first time in months that I have used my voice to worship in song. I inflicted so many wounds upon myself that I wasn't sure if I could heal from them. However, God is faithful, and he is already beginning to work in my life.

Tonight, all the people in my house gathered in the living room. We just sat together and talked about our lives. This place is beginning to feel like home, and the people around me, family. This is a new life I have been given, and I am thankful for each day I live. It is like walking out into the sunshine, after living in darkness for a long time.

Monday

My sleep has been restless for over a week. I keep hoping this night will be the last, and my sleep pattern will be restored. I am still waking up early in the darkness, and laying there until it is time to rise. Why is this happening?

I played ball hockey for the first time in years today. My lungs burn with fire, and I realize how out of shape I have become – just one more thing destroyed by my addiction. I pray God heals me in time. I have turned my life over to God, completely. I have held nothing back, and have repented of my past. In turn, he has freed me from addiction, and given me a new life.

Tuesday

We worked all day in a cloud on the top of a mountain. I couldn't help but think of God, and how he appeared to Israel. I couldn't see the valley or mountains, only a white blanket of nothingness that lay just outside the trees.

My body is sore, but I know it is because of the good things I have done, and not the bad – for once in my life. I used to punish myself physically with drug use. It took its toll. Thank God I am free today. I feel thankful, hopeful, and convinced I am making the right choice. God has brought me here, and I pray he continues to lead me in his pathway.

Wednesday

I worked all day, and stayed up late last night. My mind is in a good place, and God has allowed me to memorize scripture again. My heart is turned toward God, and my mind centered in him. I want to go to sleep. I want to run to him in prayer, close my eyes, and search for his voice in my dreams. I am waiting. The noise around me is loud, and I am having a hard time concentrating. I need sleep.

Thursday

I haven't spoken to my family recently. I've cut off all contact because of the shame I feel around my addiction. I thought about calling them yesterday, but couldn't bring myself to pick up the phone. Today, my mother called. I don't know how she found me.

I believe God knew my heart, and spoke to my mother. Things like this have happened before in my life, but each time it seems new. I hope I never lose the awe I have of God, and the love I have for him. Sometimes, I feel small and insignificant. Why is God mindful of me? Who am I that he is interested in my life?

Recently, I have come to understand, in a small way, the love God has for me. I am overwhelmed at the memory of how he showed me. He gave me a taste of what it is to truly love. I pray he continues to reveal himself and his character to me.

Friday

I am in class right now, singing. I really enjoy the classes, and they end too quickly. I could listen to *the word* being preached all day long, and not grow tired of it. Something inside of me wakes up when I hear it. I want to fill my heart and mind with its living water.

I find myself constantly meditating on scripture, keeping my mind focused on God. While I do this, my past has no power and Satan has no room to cast his accusations. I have been a Christian for a long time, yet each day feels new, and each word inspires me. My belief has grown in the fires of addiction. God has changed me, and I never noticed it happening. I thought I suffered for nothing, but it is not true.

Saturday

Watched "The Passion" and cried. The horror and torture that Jesus went through is hard to understand, and even harder to watch on the screen. I want to pray and sleep. I feel messed up. What should I do? How can I please God? He suffered and died for us. I don't want to write anything else tonight. I am ashamed of the way I have lived, knowing what Christ has done for me. He gave me life, and I have taken it for granted. I fell into sin, letting it rule my life and guide my actions.

No more – never again. The time has come for me to stand against the evil in my life.

Sunday

Tonight, the farm put on its annual Christmas play. Many visitors came to our secluded farm, and brought joy with them. It was amazing. During one solo I almost cried. I felt like I was in church. I was among people, but had no shame driving me away into hiding.

This entire day has been beautiful. Going to the barn, and seeing the animals, lifted my spirit. It always does. I think it is because they accept me, they don't judge, and they don't talk about wanting to leave, or how good the old life was.

Please God, help me stand up for what is right.

Monday

I got a hat-trick in ball hockey this morning. I felt excited to be alive. I love playing the game. I do the best I can, but don't usually score. That's okay. It's not about winning for me. I play for the love of the game.

I had a dream last night which disturbed me. I had just finished reading the verses that talk about Jesus as a judge. I was scared. I have done a lot of wrong in my life, but instead of condemning me, he spoke to me about my heart.

Today was a good day, and I'm thankful.

Tuesday

I had using dreams last night, which I consider a trial. When I wake in the morning I am faced with a choice: condemn myself, or claim forgiveness – which Jesus died to give me. Today I stood in the promises of God, and did not allow the night to destroy the day. Have I done the right thing? I believe so, but the truth will come out in the dreams tonight. I don't want to write. My mind is unfocused and having difficulty concentrating. I am tired, I suppose.

Wednesday

I am tired; exhausted. I left the farm today to travel across the land. We went to a retirement home to pick up some donated dressers. I felt useful and at peace. The environment felt caring and loving, with a sense of sadness – grief and loss mixed with hope. People die in this building, yet the residents are smiling and secure. I get the feeling that they know something that I do not. I am grateful that I was chosen to go because I enjoy serving in a meaningful way. Being out in the world, however, angered me deep inside. I hate it – I hate what I see, I hate what I sense.

Nothing appeals to me; mankind's marvels seem to me a sickness, a disease spreading across the earth – consuming the goodness and casting all into darkness. I can't see myself living in the world. I see no way to make peace with the emotions inside of me. Even as a child I felt this pain. I didn't understand it then, and couldn't find the words to describe it.

I truly am an alien to this world, of this I have no doubt. Nothing makes sense to me. How could the people stray so far? There are times that I want to see it all destroyed, saving only a remnant. The cities are where I feel the worst revulsion. I sense the evil around me, I see the corruption hanging as a dense cloud of air – it all feels wrong inside, like the creation has become twisted, distorted, and changed from its original intention.

It becomes all that much clearer when I withdraw from it for a time. A man standing in a haze doesn't realize it is there until he walks a few miles, turns around, and stares at where he once stood.

Satan's great lie keeps all the people in ignorance. They willingly go to their destruction. I feel alone, like I am the only one who can sense what is coming. Many of the people surrounding me are blind, and it has been this way my entire life.

Thursday

The farm has a rule. No one is allowed to go anywhere alone. In order to police this, they put people into *partnerships*, each one consisting of a *senior* and *junior partner*. These pairings are supposed to provide security and accountability, but usually they are a source of conflict and stress. Two people fresh out of addiction, each one trying to seize the reigns of the arrangement. It is a constant power struggle, and control issue.

To avoid resentments building to the point of explosion, *leadership* switches the *partners* on a weekly basis. If a partnership is working well, they usually leave it unchanged.

In order to keep things fresh, they switch up the partnerships, and move people from room to room. Today, I lost one *partner* and gained another.

I have no idea why they move people around so much here. It is strange. Just when I fall into a routine, they switch up my life. I have lived a life of constantly moving from place to place, and I don't want to do it anymore.

I suppose I will learn something, and gain some knowledge, but right now my mind is clouded with disturbing thoughts. I have a hard time seeing God's plan when I am focused on my own life. Class was enlightening and counseling was honest. *I can't believe I told him about the demon in our first conversation.*

Friday

We are in class, watching a sermon. I am loving this preaching, but the computer system crashes, and I miss the end of the message.

It's too bad because he had some good things to say. He was talking about some of my favorite verses in The Prophets. It is refreshing to hear the truth preached with understanding, and something inside me responds.

Someone just came in and addressed the class. He confesses a relapse, and asks for help. He shows courage and humility, facing his fear and allowing us to share in his pain. I feel accepted, and loved. He is showing me his heart, and there is nothing more that I could ask of him. I know that God has gifted him with musical ability, perseverance, and strength. If he continues to stand in humility, and keeps searching, I'm sure God will reveal himself.

It is these moments of honesty, where men show their true selves (in weakness and strength) that I begin to feel a sense of belonging. I have felt like a man wandering, searching for his lost people, continually rejected and despised by the world. I don't know if I am saying this right. When Paul speaks of 'the brethren' my heart stirs – I seek this kind of relationship with people: people who are of God, chosen, called, seeking – *whatever.*

I am so tired. It has been a long week and I am ready for the extra two hours of sleep.

Another night; another dream: a day inside the night. I am considering beginning to journal my dreams again. God is speaking and I don't want to lose the knowledge he is giving me. I want to have it so I can reflect and see the connections; but, neither do I want to be consumed by the visions.

Saturday

Today we were dragged to a fundraising church service. The farm finds a church to host these events from time to time. They have a banquet and invite potential donors. They parade us out on the stage, and play to the emotions of the crowd in order to solicit funds. I was overwhelmed by the amount of people who showed up.

The hardest part for me to accept is the deception the farm has pulled over our eyes. They present it to the residents as a Christmas party, but really it is a fundraiser. I didn't want to be there to begin with. I'm dealing with a lot of issues from my past addiction, and I am really uncomfortable with being around people right now.

When I saw the donation envelopes placed on every single chair in the church, I became angry. I felt betrayed and used. This night was never about caring for the residents. It was all about the money. I've been at other recovery houses where they have done this. It's disgusting the way these places use the client's addiction in order to raise more money. They try to evoke pity from the people, just like the commercials for starving African children. *Look at the drug addicts, how pathetic they are, can't you do something to help?*

The truth is that many of us are brilliant people, bordering on genius, but addiction has enslaved us, and robbed us of the life we could have had.

Sunday

My mind is stressed out, and messed up. The days have caught up with me and my heart is frozen. I need God to awaken the things inside of me that have fallen asleep. I need to let go of whatever is blocking me from coming completely into his presence.

People are leaving the farm and struggling, listening to the deception of their minds. I have been there in the past, but I am no longer blind. What can I do to help? What would you have of me? Tell me, and I will do it. Teach me, and I will obey your word.

I am nothing, Lord – you are everything.

Monday

I found a hardness in my heart. It has developed over the last few days. I've started to lose compassion for the people around me. I've begun to focus on their faults rather than how I can serve them. I went to God in prayer, and read the gospel of John, but it wasn't enough, so I admitted the weakness to my companions and asked for their help.

Once I walked through this, God immediately lifted the ice from my heart, and I was able to once again love my brother. I feel embarrassed that I need the help of other people. I want to be able to rely on only myself and God, but apparently he wants me in relation with others.

Tuesday

I am extremely tired. I didn't get the six hours of free time this weekend because of the Christmas banquet, and then kitchen duty. I usually rest during this time and it revitalizes me – without it I am suffering. I almost fell asleep in class this morning.

I feel lifted up right now. Class has just finished and the message spoke to me clearly. Draw near to God, and he will draw near to you. This is why I came to this place. I understood that it would give me a chance to do what I have wanted to for a long time – withdraw from the world and seek God with all my heart and time.

God, please help me to go forth and sin no more; strengthen me in your word and in faith. Teach me your ways and give me the power to walk with you always. I am struggling. I keep thinking that I have done something wrong and that is why you hide your face from me. Sometimes I think it is a test. I know your presence and without it I am empty – I feel alone, irritable, and angry. If I miss a single day of your voice, my world is shattered.

I know you will never leave or forsake me, so therefore it must be something inside of me that is broken.

Now that I have written this I will have to share it with my *journal group*, but these words are for God, not for them.

So much I feel that I must hide, and an unwillingness to trust that you will work all things to my good. Please, forgive me.

Wednesday

We did *warfare* early. It is a strange concept, this gathering together at the end of the night to pray. They need to make it exciting, so they call it *warfare*. I am going to sleep, exhausted. Thank you for the night off. It came at exactly the right time.

People keep leaving. I spent the entire morning working with someone, and then at lunch he got kicked out. It seems like every time I open up to someone, they walk away. This makes it difficult to continue building relationships, but I am doing it anyway.

I was so tired that I didn't write my journal before bed, so I am writing it now, at two in the morning. My pen just died, so good night.

Thursday

I've spent the last while crying in front of the people in my house. In prayer my heart hurt so much that I couldn't contain it: watching my brothers scream and yell at each other, the pain in their hearts, and the pain they are inflicting on each other.

My house asked to lay hands on me, and pray over me, and I consented. I don't like people touching me, but today it helped the process of breaking my heart before God. *I am rending my heart, Lord. Thank you for walking beside me.*

I feel raw and sad, like the slightest thing will send me into tears, sorrow. I don't feel these things because of trauma or past memories, I feel them because I know God's love for me. I am learning to love the people that God has placed in my life. He is teaching me and the lesson is painful.

If we are created in God's images and we have emotions, I suppose that God has them as well. I am reasonably sure that he can feel hurt just like us, and if this situation is hurting me then I imagine it hurts God as well.

We hurt ourselves, and God cries.

I am honest in my journal, but I hold back saying what I truly want to. No one would understand where I am coming from. Every day we read our daily journal entry aloud in something called *journal group*, and once a week we have to submit our journal to *leadership* for review. The *leader* reviewing the journal is expected to write a comment, and attach it to the journal. It is pretty much an invasion of privacy, but I'm sure they have their reasons. I don't think the *leader* who read my journal this week understood anything, and I'm disappointed. If they can't handle a small taste of what I need to say, how will they handle the rest of my experience and knowledge?

I think I've written six books and two volumes on dreams – countless pages filled with words, all written and waiting for the right person to appear, read the work, and understand the message. In the last three years I have written my personal history four times, each focused on a different area of my life. Two years I dedicated to the recording of visions and dreams that God started revealing to me.

A journal sometimes seems like a waste of time, an inconvenience that interferes with the larger picture. A journal is something that I kept as a child, in between the times I was writing love letters and poetry for whatever girl I was in love with at the moment.

Writing has a significant place in my heart and my life. For a long time, it was my only form of expression: it was, and is, my voice. Verbally I am not talented. I struggled for a long time, learning how to speak.

When I allow someone into the sanctuary of my thoughts I do not appreciate them tracking mud over the threshold. In my opinion it is better for a man to stay out than to come inside and misunderstand.

Perhaps if they read the first eight volumes, I might give more weight to their comments. Besides, I'm not giving an accurate description of my life in the brief captured thoughts that these people consider a journal entry.

When I was younger I would come home from school, lock myself in my room and write for several hours. Later, I carried a journal and a pen, writing at every opportunity. Now it is reduced to five minutes a day, unless I want to sacrifice sleep (like I am right now) in order to explain myself. Why can't people just take it for what it is rather than criticizing? I feel tired and deflated, trapped in explaining trivial things. I suppose if I entered in the scripture references every time I write it would make it easier for others to understand what I am saying, because as I write, verses enter my mind. However, I never have been one for remembering the correct address; *the word* is more of a living entity – it *speaks* to me inside my mind.

I want to scream, but it would be pointless. How many pages can I write and get away with reading it in *journal group*? If I write six and read two, am I wasting my time? I pray that the next person who reads my journal gets more out of it than the last. Perhaps they should read the very first entry: I wrote that while I was still high on my first day.

A demon was tormenting me, taunting me and laughing because I chose to use that day. Since that day I have been healed, delivered, and set free. God has removed all craving, obsession, and compulsion to use. I am physically and psychologically free from an addiction that has taken the last twenty years of my life.

Ten years of that I spent in a self imposed prison cell of darkness and psychosis. I can't even begin to describe the agony that I went through – all this because I believed a lie that Satan whispered in my ear.

That seed destroyed my field, and turned the soil bitter – nothing could live on the land. Yet God did not leave me, and I walked through the fire virtually unscathed. Wounded surely, but alive; and my spirit still resting in his hands.

I have seen so many unearthly things to have retained a normal (whatever that is) perception of the world. If my view appears askew, please consider this thought.

I grew up blind, but not knowing that I was any different than anyone else. The day I received my glasses, I saw the world for the first time, and I have never been able to see it the same again.

Friday

It is Christmas weekend, and I am away from my family for the third year in a row. I was raised with family traditions and at this time of year we all gathered together. I have left this behind in order to be here. I have sacrificed this in obedience to the Lord. He has called, and I am here in response to that call. I have finally emerged from the darkness.

I really do not want to write tonight. Last night I stayed up late, and didn't have much of a chance to read. I read every day because my spirit craves *the word*. I have developed a taste for it. I have read the bible several times, and I want to keep reading. I get something new out of it each time – a new message, or a verse will speak to me. I meditate on its principles and examine my own life to see if I am living according to its words. It is my guide book and history lesson. It reveals the character of God, who I am seeking.

I feel failure. I thought I would be home this Christmas. I had my heart set on it. God has saved my life, and it is the greatest gift I have been given this year. Anyway, this is not about me. It is about the Lord of my life, and what he has planned for me. I give my life in service. I have severed myself from the world. It must be this way.

Saturday

Today I was given another gift. My heart was broken and sad this morning. My view on the day was miserable, but then everything changed. I had a dream about forgiveness. God was speaking to me. After sharing it in *journal group*, someone invited me to come and worship. I hesitated, but finally accepted. I am so glad that I did because the next hour and a half lifted my spirit.

I have always found that worshipping God with a guitar in my hands gives me access to parts of my spirit that I can't get to normally. God poured out his blessings upon me, teaching me rhythms and melody that on my own I would have struggled with. I loved singing with my brother and my heart is glad. Christmas is about the birth of Jesus Christ, and today we honoured God. It is what we are supposed to do.

I got *chored* for it, but I count it pure joy. I know I did the right thing, and if people can't understand it then that is their problem. Some people get so focused in on the problem that they lose sight of the bigger picture; besides, it is better to serve God than obey man.

Now, to speak about this morning: I have an appointment with God every morning. Someone rescheduled the daily devotion and it interfered with my appointment, so I chose to seek God rather than obey man. Twice in one day.

30 Days

Chapter TWO

P eople keep losing it in my house; one person in particular – over and over again. Nothing even happened this morning to provoke a fight, yet one broke out anyway. Now everyone is affected and more arguments are spreading through the house. All of this caused by one person, who brought a violent evil spirit into this house, and to top it all off, this is Christmas morning. Happy Birthday, Jesus.

I had an amazing dream last night. Clear and powerful, but I don't know what to think of it. I met and fell in love with a girl. The first time I saw her, we were alone, and we got close. The next time we met she was with her friend, talking about a scandal – the scandal was us, but she didn't know.

When her friend left, we had sex. I looked into her eyes, and told her I loved her. Her eyes lit up brightly as she smiled. I woke up and prayed to God. I was confused. Is this dream from God or Satan?

Maybe time will reveal the answer, as for now I take it for what it is: a good dream. Anyway, it is breakfast time and I am hungry. I usually don't write my journal first thing in the morning, but a fight broke out, I was upset, and I needed to talk about it here in these pages.

Monday

I don't want to write. I've been angry for most of the day. It's not a total loss. There were some inspiring moments. I had a chance to speak with the lead pastor of the farm, and the founder of the ministry. I was touched by the pastor's compassion, and the founder's intelligence. Both seemed to truly care about the people here.

These moments carry me through the struggles I have. In these moments, I remember God has blessed me with, and know that he is watching over me. If I focus on the bad things rather than the good, my day quickly goes down hill. I am trying to rise above the crap that is attempting to sink me beneath its waves.

I've had several conversations with people about my problems, and each person has brought different areas to my attention. It's a holiday, so they've cancelled class, and we're going to watch a movie. Sometimes democracy is the cause of stupidity, as is revealed in the choice of tonight's film. I'm stuck here watching it because no one can go anywhere alone. Sigh.

Tuesday

I dream of naked girls running around. Strange. Where do these dreams come from? From deep inside of me? From all the images I have seen in my life? Now they come alive in my sleep, and to what avail? To tempt me perhaps. I don't know.

In addition to a daily journal entry, we are required to write about a childhood memory. There are no rules as to what kind of memory. We simply must write about something. I am having a difficult time remembering my childhood. I look inside my mind, but nothing is there. Hold on, I just remembered one. Maybe more will come to me.

I am angry, but not as much as usual. Unfortunately, all my emotions are still raging just beneath the surface, and one incident could set me off. I prayed last night about the anger I have, how it makes me feel dirty and wrong inside. I hope God heals whatever it is inside of me that is broken.

Someone just walked up to me as I was writing, and told me I can't put my feet on the table. I've been here a month and no one told me about this rule. People can't just make up rules whenever they want. This is retarded.

Wednesday

Hockey was a lot of fun today. I wasn't expecting to play, but I am glad that I did. All of my anger from yesterday is gone, except for the irritation of finding unflushed urine in the toilet this morning. Can't people flush the toilet? We are all grown men. Our mothers aren't going to flush it for us. It gets left for the next unsuspecting soul who comes along.

We have been off work over the Christmas weekend, but we are returning today. I feel conflicted. I enjoy the time off, but I also enjoy the feeling of accomplishment work brings. I'll have to finish this later because I have to go now.

Thursday

I just murdered my girlfriend. I tied her up and threw her body in the ocean. She refused to die, and rose up again, so I hit her with a frying pan until she collapsed.

It was horrifying. I awoke, prayed, cried, and asked God why he allowed this to happen. I feel sick. I hate what I have done in the dream, and I hate this day. I feel disgusted. What did I do that deserves this kind of response?

I have given up my life, walked away from addiction and come here. I do the best I can during the day, and this is the torment of the night. I need sustenance, and teaching, while asleep, not abuse and heartache. *Are you listening? I am really upset. I feel betrayed. I am trusting you, but I just got burned.*

Maybe there is a message in the dream, because I was thinking if the girlfriend represents my old life then this dream makes sense. The old life keeps resurrecting itself, and I keep beating it down.

I came to the mainland for recovery, and it hasn't worked. I've been plagued by failure upon failure. Now I am here, and here I waitm, until God and I resolve our conflict. I won't move until he speaks.

What a day. I finally lashed out at someone in anger, and I felt the pain immediately – it was like driving a dagger through my own heart. It hurt so much that I felt the tears rising inside me.

The pastor was at the table when I lashed out, at and witnessed the entire thing. He took me downstairs to talk about it, and I cried with him for half an hour. He walked me through the emotions and did not judge. He helped me see that my pain comes from broken relationships in my life, and that I have had to choose between family and God. A scripture kept entering my mind as we talked.

> "If any man come to me and hate not his
> father and mother… and his own life also,
> he cannot be my disciple."

> Luke 14:26

Seeking God is more important than my family. I have to trust deeply in order to make that statement. I have sacrificed many relationships on the journey that has brought me here. Everything is changed. Partly, it is the separation of one family, and the creation of a new family. Partly, it is the growing distance between us.

In my addiction, I felt ashamed and stayed away, but we still saw each other on a fairly regular basis. Now, I feel ashamed, inadequate, worthless, abandoned, and rejected. I don't think I will ever be a part of their life again. All the mistakes I have made, and my inability to make it right, has condemned me. I can't rewrite the past, or make different choices. My only option is to accept the destruction, and hope God works a miracle.

I destroyed the relationship I had with my father when I was a teenager, and made it even worse in my addiction. Yet that relationship is more valuable to me than all the money you could throw at me. My family was a precious gift given to me by God, but I wasted it with anger and selfishness. I wish I could change the past, go back, and make the right choices in my life.

God, how can I serve you? What use do I have? I have wasted so much of my life. How can good come from all the destruction I have caused, for I am responsible. I have done this. I am not my past, but right now I have a difficult time seeing the future. I choose to focus on each moment as it comes and try to make the right decision each time.

I let the spirit lead me. I listen carefully. I close my mouth, and incline my ears to hear. How can people hear God when their mouths are open all the time? Last night after prayer, I memorized a song. I chose this song because it speaks to God of how I feel inside – so I can sing it honestly with my heart and spirit.

Today it was the first song we sang in worship. I know God is listening and watching over me. I know he sees me. Yet still I feel as though something is wrong, like there is something left undone.

Friday

At least the dreams were not as bad as the night before. I keep waking up an hour before I have to get out of bed, and can't fall back asleep. I start having anxiety about the fact that I have to get out of bed. It's better when I wake up at two in the morning, and fall back asleep, because it feels like I get two nights in one. I pray each night that God extends the night, so that one night will feel like weeks, and I will wake rested.

The clouds are beautiful. I am sitting here, looking out the window, watching them roll across the sky. They give me a sense of freedom and promise. I love the way the sun sends colors streaming over their surface. It reminds me of the greenhouse with all the different types of plants sharing the same space.

Sometimes I need to stop and appreciate the beauty of the creation. It has a tendency of lifting my spirit and changing my perception of the day. I wouldn't trade what I have today for anything. God has given me freedom, and is entering my life again. Him alone will I serve. I will wait for the Lord.

I had a chance to work in the kitchen today, and the opportunity arose for me to pick up the blade once more. It melded to my hand like an extension of my spirit, and I was soon in the rhythm of slicing vegetables. The rocking motion of the blade on the cutting board soothes my soul.

I feel like singing to God. I feel comfortable, secure, and strangely complete. I find myself wanting to pray verbally: to talk to God as I chop away. Some activities just open up doors for me, and this is one of them.

I am tired tonight. I feel fulfilled, in a strictly human sense of the word. The day has been good.

Saturday

It is the last day of the year. I don't know what to expect. I feel as though something important should happen, but I can't say what it is. Maybe it is just because the world makes such a big deal about New Year's Eve. I used to get drunk on this night every year. I haven't for the past few years because I have been in recovery. I know in my heart that I am finished with using. There is no impending sense of doom or failure. The freedom I have today is real and tangible. I experience it every day. I have not forgotten what it is like to be in the grip of a powerful addiction. I was a slave to crack cocaine. I was bled of all will to resist its demands. The frustrating part of this, is that I made the choice to sell myself into slavery.

Now I am breaking all the lies I was told while I was a slave. Now I am transformed through the renewal of my mind. Now my body is crucified with Jesus Christ, and my flesh does not make the decisions for me in life.

I really want to sleep, but have been unable to. I lay in my bed with my eyes closed, but sleep does not come. I pray to God, asking him to release me from this body, and my request is denied.

Earlier in the afternoon, I was moments away from slipping into a dream when suddenly someone started yelling and I lost my concentration. The opportunity to slip into my spirit comes maybe once a day, and I feel frustrated when it is ruined by the other people in the house. Now I can't get my mind back to that place no matter how hard I try – the window has closed.

I worked in the barn this afternoon cleaning out stables and feeding the animals. I love seeing the cats, and playing with the other creatures. Some of them have quite a personality. I think it is good for me to work in this way. It teaches me that God has made a wonderful creation, and that I am a part of it.

I don't understand why we keep the cows in stalls all the time. I think they would like it better in the field, being able to see the world and play with others of their kind. Let the herd roam, grazing in the open field. Maybe it is just that I do not ever want to be confined to a box again. I think the animals are happy to see me. Maybe it's just the grain I carry in my hand.

While I was working in the barn, the radio was tuned into a Christian channel, but it was advertising a male enhancement drug called 'Ageless Man.' I felt disgusted. I can't believe this so-called Christian institution decided to endorse such a product. Are they so hurting for money that they are willing to sell out their values?

It was like watching a late night paid television commercial that praises the wonders of their product. "Buy the lie that we are selling," scream the announcers. It all feels dirty. Am I the only one who notices how wrong this sounds?

Sunday

David Burton

I wake up to crap in both toilets and discover quickly that our water has been turned off. Happy New Year. I can't sleep anymore because of the dream, so I decide to journal. I feel different today. Something inside me knows that everything is going to be alright. I think the feeling is called, **Hope**.

I feel new life rising up in me to face the day. This is when I would naturally pick up my guitar and start playing, but *leadership* confiscated it when I entered The Program. They believe that playing a musical instrument takes our focus off of God, and places it on ourselves. I think they are insane, but I have no power to change the way this place operates. After three months, I become eligible to get my guitar out of lockup – *if they give me permission.*

I've been playing guitar for twenty years, and it is one of the ways I worship God. Strange things happen in my spirit when I combine music with worship. It's like a door opens up within me. To teach people that musical instruments are a hindrance to recovery is just plain stupidity in my eyes. Our addition has stolen so much from us already, and now recovery takes away the few things left in my life that bring me joy?

I feel disgusted by the people around me. As soon as we finish watching a Christian video, they begin to mock God, casting doubt on his work. I can't believe these people call themselves Christians. They bring shame to the name.

They pray, sing, and walk around wearing the mask of religiousity, but their hearts and minds are filled with unbelief. They do all the right actions to fit in, they say all the right words – yet faith is far from them. Jesus 'perceived in their hearts' the unspoken thoughts and intentions of the people. I believe God can do anything, and I believe that with God all things are possible.

It's not a banner verse that I hang above my doorway to garner the praise of other people – I actually believe the scripture. I don't think it's a metaphor, or a quick pick me up when I'm feeling depressed. I believe it is the word of God, and therefore truth.

To many people on this farm, scripture is merely words on a page. They are just words. Why are we here, if not to know God better? You can follow all the rules here, and still be far from God. It is obvious to me, especially in the people who have to *use* again after being here for a period of time.

Please, God, do not allow this to happen to me. Keep me close and teach me your ways. I have not yet resisted unto blood, striving against sin; but if that is what you require of me then so be it. You have given me this place so that I can draw near to you without the interference of the world. I will not waste it. Please grant me the strength to do your will. Reveal your path to me. Guide me in your way.

You are the author and finisher of my faith, Lord; and I wait for your instruction.

Monday

Today passed too quickly. I thought I would have more time, considering it was a day off. At least I got a nap in. Now the day is over except for this study class, and I'm tired.

I think the highlight of my day was working in the barn, although I felt that the people I was working with were rushing. I like to take my time, and enjoy hanging out with the cows, pigs, birds and cats. I just like being in the barn. I feel productive, knowing I have a clear purpose there: clean the stalls and feed the animals. It is straight forward; plus, I like dressing up in coveralls.

My journal keeps falling apart, but I finally got my hands on some duct tape and fixed it. I have now created a seemingly indestructible journal book. Perhaps it will last longer than the last one. I'm pretty hard on my journal. I carry it wherever I go, always having it close by in case I need to vent my fury and frustration in the safety of its pages.

There has been no conflict today, so I don't have much to write about. Most of my journal entries are born out of adversity and suffering, not peace and quiet.

God, please speak to me every day – visit me regularly in dreams and visions. Show me who you are. There is only so much I can learn by reading it. I need to experience your presence and awesome power. This is my prayer, and I will remain until it is answered.

What does the future hold for me? What do you want me to learn? Teach me your ways, Lord; walk with me so that I will know the steps to go in. I feel empty right now. I don't know why. I know your light can change me, so where are you?

Tuesday

My dreams were not amazing, but they were not horrifying either. It was an alright night. I don't have an enthusiasm to face the day, and I have asked for God's help to carry me through. Without him I am nothing.

I discovered an infection in my foot. It is eating away the skin on the sole of my foot. I am very disturbed by the sight of it, and I don't know what to do to make it go away. I have street feet (I think they called it *trench foot* in the war). My feet were soaking wet from the rain penetrating my shoes. I could never take off my shoes, living on the street, so the moisture was continually present. I walked for hours, and hours, every day – never having a place to rest. At night, I slept in the homeless shelter, and that's probably where the infection came from. I'm disgusted, and horrified. What have I done to myself?

I was looking at myself in the mirror the other day, and I noticed a strange tear in my skin. I've never seen a mark like this on my body before, so I asked one of the other residents what it was.

"What the hell is this?" I ask.

"Stretch marks," he replies.

"Stretch marks? Stretch marks!? What the fuck is a stretch mark!?"

I have exchanged my addiction for a new series of problems that I have never before encountered in my life. I remember coming home from college on a weekend, and my father crying because of how much weight I had lost. I hadn't even noticed. The pain in his eyes told me that I was wasting away.

Now I've gained so much weight that I have a tear in my side. What is happening to me? I suppose I will be alright. It's because of all the anti-psychotic medication they put me on that I have gained all this weight, but I have no idea of how to lose it. I've never had to worry about it before. If anything, I've had to remind myself and force myself to eat.

I used so much crack cocaine that I burned the inside of my mouth, had open sores in my mouth, and ruined my digestive system. Eating and drinking caused flames of pain to spread throughout my body. I was a complete mess, and that is how I lived my life on a daily basis. Now I am having difficulty fasting for a single day. The food smells so good when it is cooking that I can't resist, and I get hungry when I haven't eaten on a regular basis.

I can't remember feeling hungry in my addiction. Drugs numbed that particular sensation. When I think about it, I was like the walking dead. I don't know how I survived it. The flu and common cold nearly killed me several times because my immune system was destroyed. Those days are gone, and I pray they never return.

> "Though I have afflicted thee, I will afflict
> thee no more."
>
> Nahum 1:12

Wednesday

I just closed my eyes, and it is morning. I barely slept last night. I had one dream that has quickly faded away. I am very tired, and not in a good mood. I hope this day gets better.

My *partner* is hiding in his room. We are supposed to be reading Proverbs right now. Every morning, the *partnerships* get together to read a chapter of Proverbs, but almost everyone hates doing it. No one wants to be hanging out with sick, twisted, and demented people ten minutes after waking up. This day is going to be a weird one. I can tell already.

The day was difficult. I got into a fight with someone, and had to get help to resolve the situation. I couldn't have done it without the help of the second and third year people. I know this day was going to have problems in it. I could tell from the first fifteen minutes of the day.

I didn't expect it to involve me; however, my foresight is somewhat blurred. I really hope to avoid conflict in the future. Maybe if I talk about what is bothering me rather than losing control and freaking out. I want to think that I am more advanced than this, but I am not.

I have social problems, and my relationships with people aren't good. I don't know how to talk when I need to – I think I can handle it on my own. I don't ask for help most times until the damage is done.

What is God trying to teach me through all of this? I wish I had the answer. I worked hard in the barn all day, and I know it has helped me more than anything else. The simple peace of manual labour. I feel calm and resolved to make the changes I need to in order to survive.

Thursday

There is only one day left before the weekend. I need the extra sleep. I always feel completely exhausted by the end of the week. The schedule here is pretty intense.

It is going to take some time to let go of certain ideas that I have learned in recovery. It is as though I have acquired an evil spirit somehow. I have been hurt, and now sometimes I want to hurt other people, projecting my pain onto them.

I make so many stupid mistakes that I want to sit in a corner and cry. I know so little about living a regular life. I don't understand simple things without guidance or direction. It is similar to my earlier life: my father never taught me how to shave with a blade, because he used an electric razor, so my girlfriend taught me later in life. There are so many things that I don't know how to do, that I could spend a lifetime learning, but who will teach me? I am capable, and I learn quickly, but I constantly look like a fool because I have to be shown basic life concepts.

I am like a man playing hockey with a baseball – I know that I need an object to pass back and forth, but I have no idea what that object is. So I am out there on the ice looking like an idiot.

My knowledge is in different areas. My study has been so focused that I disregarded all else, which has resulted in a genius that can't tie his shoelaces. I struggle with not being good enough. I have self-acceptance, but I am constantly hearing the message that what I am is not enough.

I think it is Satan whispering in my ear, but sometimes it comes from the lips of the people around me. I know that God loves me and that I am enough in his eyes. In fact, in his eyes I am precious and loved beyond comprehension.

It is me that continuously buys into the lie and reinforces the negative message. I know it is not right to seek the glory of men, but sometimes I wish they saw me as God does. I wish that I didn't have to hide. I just want to be who I am without having to justify or explain it.

The class tonight was amazing. I love it when the pastor teaches. He has wisdom, understanding, and the ability to explain concepts clearly. I am reminded of when Jesus explained his parables to his disciples.

Friday

My day has started, but it's already a nightmare. My *senior partner* is having issues, and somehow it is all my fault. He is already threatening me. I am sick of it. I am not his slave, and I won't be intimidated by violence. He rages and expects me to listen. Well, it's not going to happen no matter how many *chores* he hands out.

He told me to pack my bags and leave – go back to the street. He said *leadership* had already discussed it. I know he is lying. What gives him the right to ask me to leave the farm? Is he suddenly staff?

A day ago we got into a conflict, and he came at me with his hands raised, ready to beat me into the ground. Now, I won't go into his room in the morning to read Proverbs, and he is angry about it. A couple of weeks ago, he got drunk while out on a weekend pass. He lied to everyone about it, and hid it from *leadership*. A week ago, he did it again – only this time, he got caught. Of course, the whole story came out, but *leadership* did nothing about it. They preach honesty, confession, and consequence; but when it comes to actually putting these into practice… well, nothing happens.

I don't want to follow his example. He is my *senior partner*, but I have more clean time than him. It's ridiculous. I am supposed to follow his guidance, submit to his authority, and basically do everything he asks of me. That's how it works here. I could die if I drink – that's my reality. It's serious.

Why is my partner raging this morning? It's quite simple. My alarm clock went off, and it woke him up in his room across the hall. As a general rule, we are not allowed to have alarm clocks, but my *house leader* gave me one, so I can wake up early to pray. I've had it for a week, and it hasn't disturbed anyone until today. There is not enough time in the morning to pray, so instead of changing the schedule, I adapted by rising earlier. I don't believe there is anything wrong with my approach.

The time I spend with God alone in the morning and evening is the most important time of day. I sacrifice my sleep because God comes first in my life. He is more important than anything else. I know he will give me what I need to be sustained if I honour him.

I think I am being attacked by Satan through my *senior partner*. I think the devil is using him to destroy the things I am building with God.

So, we sat down with leadership and discussed what was wrong. In fact, I read this journal entry to them. Now everything is out in the light and the infection is gone. I have said everything I need to say for the moment, and I know God is watching over us.

I believe that Satan is indeed working, but not through my *partner*. I think he wants to wreak havoc on our relationship, by attempting to drive a wedge between us. He is trying to do this in several of my relationships, but I am now able to recognize this tactic because of what has transpired this morning.

He is using the pain, hurt, and rejection from my broken relationships to keep me from forming new ones. This will keep me bound, and I will never learn how to love the brethren. Jesus commands us to love one another. That is how we will know we are his disciples. Furthermore, he commands us to love our enemies.

Since this morning, when I identified Satan's tactic, I have found freedom. God has given me the ability to forgive, and cleansed my mind from the lies of the enemy. I am tired. The process was inspiring, but exhausting. I know I have grown today and I hope the growth remains. I have to stay in the light and recognize the shadows when I see them. A verse comes to mind:

> "Butter and honey shall he eat, that he may know to refuse the evil, and choose the good."

> Isaiah 7:15

Saturday

What need do I have of money? Until now I have only used it to hurt myself by fueling my addiction. That will not continue. However, now that I don't get high anymore, what am I supposed to spend money on? Should I just save it?

If I had a lot of money, I know what I would do, but with just a little I can't accomplish it, so the whole thing is pointless. Without some divine intervention I can't achieve what I want to. I dislike thinking about money. In the past it has caused depression, frustration, and anger. In addiction there was never enough of it, and I was jealous of those who had it. I envied them and their life. I wanted what they had, and I fantasized about taking it from them by force.

I used to steal to support my drug habit. I stole from work, banks, and borrowed from people with no intention of paying it back. This has left me with a debt that I may never be able to pay back, especially the student loans which have doubled since I took them out.

God can do anything, so I suppose he could pay my debt, but I won't ask until I believe it entirely in my heart. I am not a follower of the 'prosperity gospel.' I believe God has more to offer than

44

just material wealth, and I think it is an insult to treat him like a 'sugar-daddy.'

Jesus was rejected and despised of his own people. Why would it be different for me? Jesus was God, and made himself a servant. He didn't live in a big house and drive a shiny car – his bank account didn't have a lot of money in it, and what he did have he gave away. He spent three years being homeless, walking from place to place, spreading the message.

How can I honour God if I desire wealth more than his presence in my life?

Sunday

Church service was good. I found the worship very interesting. I have come to the point where I can close my eyes and surrender to God. He provides the words inside my mind and I sing them back to him. I also visualize while doing this. It is a way for me to communicate with the Lord. Now I am going to spend a couple of hours listening. Perhaps he will have something more to say to me today.

*** Insert Dream ***

I laid down, fell asleep and dreamed. When I awoke I didn't know where I was, or who I was. It was pretty intense. What is God saying to me? I laid down this afternoon in meditation, cleared my mind and listened. The dream was the result. Do I need to start reminding myself that God can provide anything he wants and prepare my heart?

> "And he said, hear now my words: if there be a prophet among you, I the LORD will make myself known to him in a vision, and will speak to him in a dream."

Numbers 12:6

Monday

I awake long before my alarm clock is supposed to go off, and I sit at my desk writing. I feel distant from God this morning. I don't understand why he is not answering my call. I suppose this happens to everyone, but I don't like the way it feels. Isn't God supposed to come closer to me now that I am clean?

I don't smoke, drink, or use drugs anymore. I read the word, pray, and worship. I continually seek him. Is there something else required that I am missing? The only thing I can think of is a fast. It is difficult though. I have tried a couple of times and failed. If I do fast, the strength is not going to come from me.

I need your help, God. I need your presence. Please communicate with me every day. Walk beside me at all times. I need this relationship more than anything else in my life. Without it everything else is meaningless.

I started writing my personal history last night. Maybe that is why I feel so messed up this morning. It brought up a lot of emotions, walking through memories like that. Even though it is long past, it starts to feel like it is happening all over again. I made so many mistakes. I want to go back and change what I've done. It's obvious where I went wrong, and I would do it differently, given the chance.

What am I supposed to do now?

I just emptied my second pen since arriving here. Now all I have left is this uniball vision micro. No one is going to be able to read my writing now. It is like giving me a sharp blade: this pen has to fly across the page, because if it doesn't, the ink bleeds into the paper.

I finally got my journal back from the *leader* and read his comment. I was pleased. He had some good experience to share and he spoke honestly. I appreciate the fact that he didn't criticize my writing – he simply took it for what it was.

Today was a really good day for me; it started with a conversation as the sun rose behind the mountains and daylight arrived. I felt blessed; I got the impression that God was watching over me, and speaking to me through the person I was talking with. From this beginning, my day continued to rise upward; it climaxed with me scoring the winning goal in our hockey tournament.

Sometimes I don't feel God's presence as acutely as usual. In these gaps between contact it is important to remain faithful. This was the main point of our conversation this morning. I remained faithful today, and although I couldn't sense it at first, God was with me. I was taught a valuable lesson today, and I will not forget it.

My family called today. They want to come visit me later in the month. I was informed by *leadership* that I can't just accept visitors without their consent. Apparently, I need to fill out a *permission slip*. I don't know how I feel about seeing them. God has healed me, and set me free from the addiction that has consumed twenty years of my life. I don't know how to explain it to them.

I want my parents to see the freedom God has given me, but I don't want to use words. I have said many things in the past that gave them hope, only to have that hope dashed upon the rocks when I relapse. I want them to be free from worry, and have a lasting hope.

God showed me the other day how to ask forgiveness of my dad for all the pain I have caused in his life. It will be a painful experience for both of us, but I hope it brings healing. Timing is crucial, and I don't want to make amends until it is the right moment. I am praying for the Holy Spirit to lead me through this.

I started crying as God showed me this vision. I didn't even realize it until I felt the tears beneath my eyes. I know exactly what I am supposed to say to him.
"Dad, Jesus Christ has set me free. Please forgive me for the years that I have hurt you." I need to do this looking into his eyes, not

staring at the ground in shame. It is a moment of victory and reconciliation.

Tuesday

This day has passed quickly – as fast as the night. I felt awkward in *journal group* today. There were new people in the group, and some have never heard my writing before. I suppose it is about taking a risk, and learning how to trust God with the outcome. He is watching over me.

Several people were having a theological discussion while we were working in the greenhouse this morning. Although I understand the scriptures in a greater depth than they, I decided not to participate in the conversation. Everybody is an expert, and nothing is more dangerous than a little knowledge, and a whole lot of pride. To enter their conversation would have only brought division and conflict.

I don't always need to be teaching. I don't always have to give the answers. My understanding of the scriptures is in direct contradiction to most of the teaching on the farm, and to bring my voice to the table would only bring attention from leadership that I don't want, or need. Their discussion while tending to the plants reminded me of the Sunday School class I attended as a child, each person trying to understand the scriptures in their own way, and wrestling against any sort of guidance.

When these debates about God and scripture arise I usually remember these words: "swift to hear, slow to speak, slow to wrath: for the wrath of man works not the righteousness of God."

People can sometimes become easily offended in these types of conversations and anger will blossom. I think it is because not everyone is able to be objective; they have a personal experience or belief they have embedded into the scripture. They interpret.

It's like the *seven point study* we do each morning. After reading our daily chapter of Proverbs, the entire house gathers for morning devotion. A *leader* shows up to lead the devotion. The devotion consists of reading a random passage of scripture, and then writing out the personal message we received from it.

Sometimes the messages are so bizarre I wonder if we are reading the same book. For example, the text could say: "I give you a paintbrush." One man will write a message saying, "God wants to paint my house." Another will say, "God is asking me to go back to work and support my family." Still another will write, "God wants me to start a union and free my people from corporate oppression."

Each man writes his own opinion, based on personal experience and belief system, sometimes mingled with hopes, desires, and aspirations. Also, each man will defend his position. This makes for a dangerous path to walk. The book of Proverbs has two interesting comments to make. One, "Every way of a man is right in his own eyes; but the Lord ponders the heart." (21:2) And two, "The way of a fool is right in his own eyes, but he that hearkens unto counsel is wise." (12:15)

It sounds scary to be right in my own eyes. Perhaps I will consider the condition of my heart, and speak with a counsellor first, before entering the conversation. Prayer always helps me when I want to open my mouth and scream.

Wednesday

My Dad is building a house. As he is nailing together the pieces of wood, I find a book about Jesus, and I begin to read it.

This is my least favoured day of the week. Why? The farm has made a decree that every week, on this day, *work program* runs all day long. I haven't even started working, and I'm tired already. I don't understand *work program*. There seems to be an attitude here that we will somehow work our way to salvation, and find freedom from addiction in the labour of our hands. It appears to be behavior modification. Cut the rotten fruit off the tree, and hope it doesn't grow back again. Unfortunately, until the roots of the tree are healed, it will always produce the same fruit.

I've also heard *leadership* mention that we didn't work in our addiction, so we need to learn how. This is just a straight lie. I've been working since I was 13 years old. If anything, I worked more than anyone else I knew, because I needed the money to fund my ever growing addiction.

Another common justification *leadership* uses is that many of us have stolen in our addiction. "Let him that stole steal no more: but rather let him labour, working with his hands…" (Ephesians 4:28). They love to use this verse when we question why we have to work five days a week. They paint us all with the same brush, and assume we are all thieves. For the most part, they are correct.

I suppose the real quandary is why they feel it necessary to condemn us all to manual labour, when most of us came here searching for help with our addiction, not looking for work. Many of the organizations that offer recovery include this *work program* crap. Want to hear how twisted this shit is?

We pay to live here. All of us. They won't accept us without funding. No money, no help. That's the way of the world. Especially in the Christian organizations. Once we arrive, the payments begin. While we are here, they fundraise from businesses, churches, and the community – in our names. They claim poverty, but it's an absolute lie. To seal the deal, they ask us to work while we are here, but refuse to pay us. They tell us it is a part of The Program, and if we refuse, we are cast out. Want the final fallacy of all this?

They will send us out to work, invoice the clients, and then keep the income for themselves. They tell us we are working "for God's kingdom," but I think they are just lining their pockets.

Many of us are drug addicts. We've been used and abused by almost everyone out there. A lot of us have done shameful acts in order to acquire our next fix, and as a result, we feel worthless.

Finally, in desperation, we ask for help, and the people that extend their hand, only want to use us for their own gain. Sure, they profess philanthropy all day long, but the reality is that people make their living off our destruction. It serves no purpose for us to get well. They sicker we are, the longer we stay. If everyone was healed, this place would not exist, and everyone who works here would be out of a job.

This farm pulls in almost *2 million dollars a year*, and most of that is in private donations. Operating costs aren't that high, and most of the money goes to the staff. The elite of *leadership*. Over a million dollars raised in our name, but we do not see a penny of it. It's disgusting.

The farm also has some back scratching deals with other high profile Christian ministries. Want to hear one? There is a movement within Christianity, called the Prosperity Gospel. The farm has an established relationship with one of their lead pastors. The Prosperity Gospel pastor donates $100,000 per year to the farm. In exchange, we use his literature. It is his devotional we read every morning, and his magazines that are distributed to all the houses.

This, in itself, isn't really all that surprising. However, this next point might make you question the arrangement. All literature that enters the farm is screened and censored. If it's not approved by *leadership*, it can't be here. I'm not talking about pornography, hate literature, and conspiracy theory – I'm talking about any other doctrinal literature that doesn't match the farm's thinking. We are conditioned and programmed. We are not allowed to question, or think for ourselves...not even other renditions of the Christian faith.

Novels, philosophy, newspapers, academics – all banned.

This censorship extends to the contents of our private mail, personal correspondence, and gifts from our families. Anything that could cause someone to question the farm's doctrine, or authority structure, is confiscated or destroyed.

The *work program* overseer assigns us placement every day after lunch. I hope he decides to send me to the barn. It gets me away from all the insanity of daily life. Besides, the cows are going to slaughter today, and I would like to say goodbye.

Guess what? I was in the barn today.

God is listening, and watching over me. He doesn't have to answer these silent prayers, but he does anyway. I got to wrestle with the cow I like, and then load him up to slaughter. I am going to miss him. He had such an interesting personality. I love the animals. They bring some joy into my life, and build confidence inside me. The time passes swiftly while working with them, and my day seems a little brighter. It hardly seems like work, although I know it is.

I had a counselling session, and it went well. This is the most progress I have made in years. I believe it is because God is working in my life, and people who know him are guiding me. I am trusting.

> "Trust in the Lord with all your heart; and
> lean not on your own understanding."

> Proverbs 3:5

I need to reach out to God with all my heart, and continue learning his ways. The word needs to rest within me as I study it. The power is not mine – it is God's. I need to close my eyes or else I am going to fall asleep at this desk.

I lay on my bed in meditation. I was entering my spirit, just starting to receive, and I was slammed back into my flesh by some idiot yelling, "Praise Him!"

I want to scream. This has happened more than once, and I am becoming very irritated. Consideration of others is a quality that I desire in those I live with. Tonight I am straight to sleep after prayer. I am exhausted.

Thursday

I am playing a video game. I am the character, and the player, simultaneously. Power flows through my hands, and appears as flashes of light, and pulses of energy. These are my weapons, and they destroy the enemy. The objective of the game is to complete the story, and change into another creature – one with wings.

The creature is black. It disturbs my soul. There is corruption here.

The dreams of last night make no sense to me, and I feel frustrated. I am so tired that I can barely open my eyes. My body is sore and weak. I need more sleep. I need that extra hour after dinner. Someone wrecked that for me yesterday and now I am really feeling it.

My heart is starting to open and I am beginning to cry while I pray. This used to happen all the time, but has faded with time. Now it is returning. Anyway, this conversation is not for this journal; it is for prayer. I really want to go back to sleep. I think it is going to happen whether I want it to or not. That is how tired I feel inside today. Now, I have to leave my room, and start this day. There just doesn't seem to be enough time in the morning to do what I need to.

God, I need you to carry me today.

He has given me strength to continue onward, and I am blessed by it. I trusted in his ability, and I am not disappointed. This is a valuable lesson for me, just like the one I learned in the kitchen this morning when I cut my finger – patience and humility.

Friday

As I start praying I hear a strange sound coming from outside my window. It sounds lie an evil laugh, and for a moment I think the devil is laughing at me. It is disturbing. Then I hear the short bark and howl, and realize it must be coyotes. Still the circumstances are odd – it sounds like it is standing right outside my window.

I hope this day passes quickly, and I can sleep in tomorrow. I need rest; my body is acting strangely. Muscles hurt which usually don't hurt, and the pain is irritating.

I am really angry right now. My meditation was destroyed yet again by the ignorance of people living in my house. Anyway, at the end of every week we have a class called *study hall*. This is not so much a class as it is a practical lesson in patience. We sit in silence for a couple of hours, allowed only to read or write in our journals. No one can speak – for any reason.

As I was walking to this class, I lost my pen somewhere along the way. I can't find it anywhere. So I decided to take the only reasonable course of action available to me – *I asked for help*.

"Excuse me," I ask the *leader* watching over our *quiet time*. "Can I please have a pen?"

"Why are you talking?" He replies seriously. "Just be silent."

Are you fucking kidding me!? What am I supposed to do!? Just sit here and stare at the wall for the next two hours? How am I supposed to write without a pen? Sometimes, people get so caught up in the **rules** that they lose their **common sense**.

Saturday

I wake up and pray. I am filled with love, and peace is upon me. I walk out into the living room and find that snow has fallen; it covers the mountain and valley below. I thank God for its beauty and my heart is lifted up. Winter has finally arrived. I told someone yesterday that I could feel the snow coming.

I fell asleep in the afternoon, and someone came to visit me. The memory is clear. I was disturbed by the visit, so I gathered the other people in my house, and held a prayer circle. In the vision, my enemy tried to take my voice, but I've learned how to defend against this particular attack long ago. I finished casting the demon out, and awoke. The rest of the afternoon is lost to me.

This day has been strange. Time passed quickly and not much has happened. I haven't written a lot and I have no idea what to write for a *childhood memory*.

I've been trying to connect with people today, and I'm unsure how I feel about the results. People believe some strange things. They prescribe doctrine that is not biblical. I suppose I have had similar thoughts, but they were based on experience – not because a man has told me it is truth. Men can be deceived and lead astray very easily. I know in my own life I have believed in many lies, until God came and showed me the truth.

My ears are ringing – LOUD.

Sunday

Many dreams last night. I asked God to make one night feel like ten days, and he answered. I'm not going to write these dreams because they were very strange and I don't think there is a meaning to them. Nothing profound. I have been asking God for contact and communication. Instead of contact, I am going on these long journeys.

Snow fell again last night, and when I awoke, the fog was so thick I could barely see the building next door. It was awesome. And that's where the peace of the morning ended. Yesterday, everyone in my house was asked to wake early and attend a meeting. The person who asked us to wake up early, didn't show up this morning. So here we sit, waiting for nothing. Frustrating. Even our *house leader* is sitting here with a confused look on his face, because he knew nothing of this meeting.

At breakfast, I had to break up a fight between two *second year* residents. I stepped between them to keep them from striking each other. One of them hit me by mistake. Afterward, I prayed for them. I was upset. We are supposed to work together and fight our common enemy, not destroy each other in the process.

Every weekend, a different house on the farm prepares breakfast. It is supposed to be a chance for all of us to work together, and strengthen our bonds. It never works out. There is always a power struggle of some sort. It is an especially trying time for me, because I've been cooking in restaurants since the age of thirteen. I watch these men acting prideful in the kitchen, quite pleased with themselves for managing to serve a single meal. They think they have created a masterpiece – when in reality, they've created a culinary disaster. They are man-sized children.

To make it worse, they try to correct me.

Monday

A using dream.

I am completely horrified. I hate myself right now. After everything that has happened, I cooked crack and smoked it. I awake feeling hopeless and disappointed. Where is God? Why does he allow these dreams? I want to scream, and bang my head against the wall. Do you know how difficult it is to continue? I feel like I have relapsed – that is how real the dreams are to me.

Satan is tempting me. I know it. The unfortunate part is that I feel like I have already failed, yet I had no choice – it was automatic. I had no thought of how this drug destroyed my life. How could I forget? Even in a dream! I am angry. I am talking to God and he is not responding in the way that I know he can. How long will it take? Am I doing something wrong? Each time that I pray, and he doesn't talk to me, I feel more and more abandoned. I feel like a child right now – I need my Father.

Everything that has transpired since the events of this morning, has been a response from God. It started in morning prayer, continued into class, and ended with a message from a pastor. All of the content was directed at me. All of it.

At the end of the day, I am alright again. Surprisingly, it has been the human relationships that have brought me out of bitterness, and the animals that have made me laugh. I didn't think anything on this earth could change the way I felt. I have grown used to it being only me and God.

Tuesday

I am a priest, dressed in black, hidden high above the earth in the tower of my church. I look below, and see people entering the doors of the church, but these people do not belong. They should not be there. I am disturbed, so I open a secret passageway and descend.

I see these people meeting in the dark confines of the halls. They are unaware of my presence. I watch these meetings taking place, but I do not become involved. Before I leave, I see a young apprentice [acolyte].

"Have you decided to stay and study?" I ask him.

"No," he replies. "A door has opened elsewhere."

I am within the dream, yet speak out loud inside my room. I am torn between two worlds.

Wednesday

The dreams have faded, and the cold has set in; so cold, in fact, that the farm has changed the schedule, and cancelled class. Instead, we are to clean everything in sight. My room is clean, and our house is clean, so I thought I'd get some writing done.

Last night, the entire farm assembled in the classroom, and we entered into something very strange. It's called *deliverance*. It is not exactly how I fight demons, but it was interesting to watch. Nothing spectacular happened, and I am used to spectacular when it comes to dealing with spiritual evil. Usually, I deal with it directly in the spirit world, but not always.

Fighting demons is nothing new to me personally, and I expected more. I think I held back during the service. I let the minister do his thing, *and I did **not** do mine.*

Thursday

One more day to go until the weekend. I am tired. I went to sleep quickly last night and didn't wake up even once. This is a sign that I am exhausted. My body needs the sleep. My dreams are scattered, with no clear message. I don't like it. Also, they are fading away quickly. This is the strangest feature. I usually have total recall of every single dream.

In prayer this morning, I discovered I have resentments toward two people in my house, and they just happen to be *partners*. They both do stupid and irritating things that make me want to scream, but talking to them doesn't seem to make any difference. I think it will end up in a fight. I would rather not talk to either of them, so I hope God handles this situation, and changes me, if not them.

The fact that one of them is on medication really disturbs me. He makes it out like he is some sort of Super-Christian, yet he pops pills every day and is completely dependent on them. It is a really bad example.

I pray before going to *worship*, asking God to remove anything standing in the way of worship. The first song played is the one I have been studying. I close my eyes, and I am crying quickly. God moves closer. I sing to him alone, and I do not open my eyes for the entire service.

The spirit gave me the words and I sang them. Light appeared behind my closed eyes and I knew that God had showed up. I prayed as I sang and wept. I asked forgiveness. I felt utterly unworthy and completely loved at the same time. All of my experiences with God in the past, came up in my mind, and I examined them closely. I could not stop weeping.

After service I could not speak because the emotion was so powerful. I sat down and read *the word*. I closed my eyes and tears fell on the pages. I can't explain how beautiful *the word* looked to me. I felt it open up inside of me. I surrendered in this process, and he showed me that how I appear to men is meaningless. It is how I appear to him that is important. I am not in *worship* to look good, or impress men with my vocal talent. I am here to meet the Lord.

And, today he spoke to my heart, in spirit.

Friday

My alarm did not go off, and my pen broke. I slept in this morning, and did not have a chance to write. I feel rushed and my eyes are blurry. I am so tired by the end of the week. My body wears down. I like the weekend because I can catch up on my rest and be refreshed for Monday.

The *leadership* here on the farm have told me to stop writing about my dreams, but I refuse. They shape me as much as this waking life, sometimes more so. If I could get access to my dream journal

I could simply record them there. Maybe I will just start a new book. A lot has changed for me lately and that should be reflected in my spirit.

I feel withdrawn right now and all I want to do is pray, read, and sleep. In other words, my day is over and I am shutdown, exhausted from the week.

In *work program*, I seem to have moved into the barn permanently. I am glad because I like being around the animals. There is this one cow that keeps charging at me, and throwing his head at me. I think it is how they show affection. I play with him and wrestle against him; it is funny. The barn isn't the most glorious job on the farm. When it comes down to it, I clean up crap all day long, but it is honest work, and I am content with it.

Now I have to study for a class that I missed so that I can fail another test. I suppose I need to find some joy in the fact that I do not know everything – not as much weight on my shoulders.

Saturday

Compared to the things I have been shown in my dream, my waking life has been mundane, ordinary and completely without excitement. I just about got in a fight over laundry.

Today I watched a resident hurt his family by abandoning them (four children), and walk down the driveway, carrying his suitcase. His children were crying because they didn't understand, and I felt very sad. I didn't know what to do. I wanted to chase after him, but two other people were already following him, so I stayed.

He tried to make his wife take him home. She refused, and asked him to stay here. He didn't get what he wanted so he left. I can't believe how powerful the addiction is. He broke his family's heart. They travel all this way to see him, and he tears his family apart, just because he wants to get high. He might not even know that is what is happening, he could be so far in denial, but to me it is obvious. I hope he stops, turns around, and comes back. I hope I have another chance to show him the love of God and the freedom he has to offer.

I went to a comedy performance at a fine arts school tonight. It was good. I enjoyed myself and laughed. I saw someone a few rows ahead of me solving the cube, so I spoke with him during the break. He could solve it in a couple of minutes. I also saw a redhead girl that looked identical to someone I used to cook with. Same mannerisms and everything. God is amazing in all ways. I am so impressed right now.

Thank you for the night.

Sunday

My day is going well, but church was not good. The pastor decided to turn the Easter story into a comedy, acted out by several residents. I felt that making fun of Jesus, and his miraculous works, is not in my best interest. I wanted to scream, "Stop! What are you doing!? God is here and he is not laughing."

I felt the spirit leave, and the prayers at the end of the service were spoken to an empty room. I put my head down and prayed, asking forgiveness. *Please God, do not hold this against us. There are those here who are not laughing, and for the sake of even one, do not destroy this place.*

I am blind, but I have placed my hope in the scripture. One day Jesus may heal my eyes – he has shown me it is possible. One day while crying I looked up, and through my tears, my sight became clear.

I will not participate in making fun of my God, or his healing power. The gospel is not a story that should be adapted to comedy. It is the truth. It is a record, a witness, of God sending his son to earth, who saved us all by the shedding of his blood. A man who was tortured and crucified because he saw something good within us. He loved us enough (so much) that he went willingly to his death. Is this something to be made light of? I think not, and I am ashamed of the people who think it is okay.

Nowhere that I know of does it say that Jesus laughed; but I do know the scripture says, Jesus wept. People laughed at him, mocked him, scorned him, rejected him, and ultimately killed him. He came to his own people to save and heal them. They treated him with hostility, ridicule, and disbelief.

The subject matter is serious. Jesus never used comedy (that I am aware of) to relay his message. You don't hear his disciples laughing at his amazing stories; in fact, Paul goes as far as saying, "Neither filthiness, nor foolish talking, nor jesting, which are not convenient: but rather giving of thanks." (Ephesians 5:4) He says do not let it be named among you – not even once.

Does this mean that we are not to have a sense of humour? I think not, but making a joke out of the cross (*God forgive me*) is not funny. Some things are to be held in reverence, shown respect, and remembered as the powerful events they were.

Monday

I awake this morning tired and unimpressed with life. I hesitate to get out of bed. I have a feeling that sleeping all day may be a better choice than getting up today. That means trouble is on the way.

Sure enough, as soon as I hear the voice of someone in my house I become angry. I am sick of hearing him talk. He is a complete and utter fake. Every time I hear him pray I want to cut his tongue out. Is this normal?

I am reacting in a negative way to this person in an extreme manner. Something is very wrong here. It is going past simple irritation. I don't want to be around him, talk to him, or confront him. Perhaps my *partner* is right; maybe it is my heart that is at fault here. It could be that the condition of my heart is not right. I do not know how to change it though.

I have lived for a long time seeing certain people as my enemies. Even though I pray for them they still remain my enemies. Also, I am seriously scarred from my experience with fallen angels and their deception. How am I to know who is masquerading?

Sometimes, I don't know who I am really talking to when I speak to a person. The spiritual is not restricted to the spiritual realm. I've crossed over, and so have they. Which reminds me of the prayer I asked of God last night; when will it be answered? Do I need to have patience? What is going to happen to me? I consider my life now as a time of study and waiting. I think of Jacob – I will not let go until you bless me Lord.

Hurt people, hurt people; and, I am a hurt person.

I don't think it is my heart. When this man walks into the room, Satan walks with him.

60 Days

Chapter THREE

I just killed a man. I beat him to death with my fists. He kept wanting to fight with me. I refused and walked away several times. Then he threatened my family, so I hit him, and kept doing it until he lay unmoving on the ground.

I awake.

This is why I avoid confrontation. I have blood on my hands. How can I escape the vision inside my head? I can't. There is nowhere I can run to escape my own mind. I have no choice but to see what I am shown and hear the words that are spoken.

Some days the burden is heavy, as it is today, but I would not trade it for anything in the world. Somehow, I must find a way to live with myself – to accept what I have done.

Today I found inside myself a resource, an ability I didn't even know I had. I think God changed my heart, and it comes as somewhat of a shock. I believe God can do this, but something inside me does not expect it when it happens. It seems so foreign and I don't want to damage what he has fixed, so now I carry this responsibility – stay in the light.

The first thought inside my mind this morning was: this is what unforgiveness can lead to. Not even that, but if I hate someone in my spirit I am murdering them; that is the condition of my heart. I am not sure if I am explaining it right; however, I know I am close. I know that this dream, and day, worked in combination to reveal the change occurring in my heart. It was a painful chastisement, but a wound is healed and a lesson learned.

Wednesday

Last night before slept, I asked God for my wings, and I was given flight. *Thank you, Lord, for answering me, for hearing my prayer. Now I go to face another day. Please walk with me and continue to teach me your ways. Make me as a servant – your servant. Amen.*

Thursday

It has been an interesting day. I am learning to trust God with my life each day as it passes. I have already placed trust in him in some ways, but in the areas which I lack (daily living), he is teaching me.

The more I place my trust in him, the more freedom I experience: mentally, physically, emotionally and spiritually.

In *worship*, I connect with my spirit again, and for the first time since becoming a Christian, I raised my hands in public. I have reached out to God in prayer, but never had the confidence to lift my hands to him while singing. I don't just mean palms up. I mean arms raised, palms out. A verse in 1 Kings helped me come to this place of surrender and acceptance, willing to take the risk.

> "And it was so, that when Solomon had made an end of praying all this prayer and supplication to the LORD, he arose from before the altar of the LORD, from kneeling on his knees with his hands spread up to heaven."

> 1 Kings 8:54

My voice changed and it became easier to sing. I felt my connection strengthen and condemnation slip away. I sang with word, action and heart. I open the doorway of communication. I felt nervous and awkward doing this in a room full of men who could see me, but I felt the call within me and I responded. I got the impression that I am allowed to do this, not acting out of pressure to gain the acceptance of men, but to follow a spiritual lead.

I spoke to a *leader* about the change that occurred in my heart and my responsibility to stay in the light, walking in healing. I spoke to another *leader* about some problems that happened in my house this morning. The situation resolved itself, mainly, (I believe) because I listened to the voice within me that said, "Go lay hands on this man and pray for him. Do it regardless of how you feel about him at this moment, and pray honestly."

I obeyed. I tell it you it surely did not make sense to me at the time, and I could not have done it on my own power; nevertheless, I did it. I felt like crying as soon as I completed the prayer, and a tingling sensation passed through my body.

Class tonight was very interesting. Two people got into a fight, which ended up affecting everyone in the room. We spent the whole night talking about forgiveness. How to ask for it and what it means. We learned that we are to forgive because God has forgiven us.

It is important to examine our heart, being careful not to fall into an attitude of blame, or seek justice for a perceived wrong. We were taught to seek humility and live within it.

At the end of the service the pastor prayed, and during the prayer my nose started bleeding. It was interesting because part of the key part of the lesson about forgiveness, was that Jesus paid for us in blood.

Friday

Dreams slip through my fingertips like dry sand. I suppose God is giving me rest, because today I have had more energy than is normal for the last day of the week. I forgot to set my alarm, so I was late rising and missed devotion with my *partner* because I was sitting on the toilet.

Some change to keep it fresh, and it was a welcome break. My day was good from the start and each time I surrendered to the lead of the spirit, I increased. I don't know how else to say it.

Worship was empty and hard at first, but I desired connection. I didn't know if I could do it every time, so my unbelief caused resistance within me. Half way through I started praying out loud, and realized others were also praying – I spoke the truth to God. Suddenly, the words came to my mind and my spirit opened.

I felt the presence and had an image of a being dressed in white walking through the room amongst the people. I cried and opened my heart to God, communicating with him. I felt acceptance and thankful; awe and respect for the presence I was experiencing.

I continued through my day until something arose within me, a feeling that has found a way to enter me through years of addiction – worthlessness. I confessed to God. I stopped working and started praying. I was alone in the greenhouse. I spoke honestly to God, seeking his help.

Before I realized what was happening, my eyes had closed, tears were falling down my face and the sound of my voice changed. My hearing altered, and even with my eyes closed, the world I saw became light. I was not standing in the greenhouse anymore, and I was not alone.

Although I could not see him visually, I knew he was there.

Saturday

I awake and decide not to write what I have seen, so I have lost some of the details, but the message remains clear.

Last night I was praying, and I heard a voice that was not God. I told it to leave, and the light went out in my room. I was plunged into darkness. It was a strange experience and fear threatened to return, but I fought by quoting scripture and won.

The day has been uneventful. I have an infected hair in the side of my neck which is swollen and causing discomfort. There is nothing I can do about it except wait. After my parents leave I will attack it with scissors and tweezers; it is going to be a bloody mess.

I am nervous about my parents coming and it is causing something to awaken inside me. I had a dream this afternoon that I was back on the Island (although I didn't recognize it at first). People were smoking and I nearly fell in with them.

They were people from *the farm* who told me they do it all the time, like they are living a lie. They hide it from the *leaders*, but have a sin club where it is accepted. I almost fall for the lie because it seems like the right thing to do is to join them. Thankfully, I awake before I light up, but it was close… I had already bought tobacco.

Sunday

Before the dreams began last night, I experienced a strange conscious communication; in the body, yet out of it at the same time, and denied memory of the words spoken. It was powerful.

Church was good. There was a guest speaker. I enjoyed listening to the missionary, and felt comfortable traveling off the farm. My parents came to visit me, and I followed the lead of the spirit. I asked forgiveness of my Mom and Dad. I cried, and they forgave me.

My Mom cried when she explained how she felt about my addiction. God started the healing process right away because we were willing to follow the spirit. We walked and talked. My Dad and I had our first real conversation in years.

I feel blessed by God right now. My trust in him is growing. Family has always been important to me; but God comes first – I hope I honoured him today.

Monday

I dream of returning to school, clean, and in search of a girlfriend. I awake feeling frustrated. There is no girl beside me, no girl in my life, and no relationship in my immediate physical future. Sex. It feels strange to live without it, especially while I am clean.

When I am high and messed up I can understand why no woman would want a relationship with me, but even then I still had sex. When I am clean for any amount of time, I always find a girlfriend. This time there is nothing except celibacy.

When I went to church yesterday I was drawn toward the girls like a magnet. I was fascinated, like I was seeing them through new eyes. I wanted to talk with them and it wasn't just for the sake of conversation. What am I going to do with these desires? They are not evil – God created me with them inside me.

They have moved me out of my room and into the dormitory; also, they have increased my responsibility. I feel strangely at peace with all these changes and I know it is because my trust in God has increased. I have built my foundation in the right place: Jesus.

Several people left the farm today. One I knew was going to leave. A girl pulled him out of the program. I feel horrible about this because the entire situation will ultimately end in failure. It is hard enough to have and raise a family under God's covering, and they are outside of it. Their child is conceived in sin, outside of marriage.

There was a time in my life when I thought that this did not matter, but I see things differently now. With no commitment to each other, they will split when life becomes difficult; and, it is hard already. How is this relationship to succeed?

I watched a man come into The Program, and just barely allowed God to change him, then came the visitor from hell. The man placed his trust in her rather than God, stated to believe that he was healed, and that just the two of them could figure everything out on their own.

Rather than protecting himself, he allowed physical contact to escalate between the two of them. She enticed and he responded. He took on her problems as if they were his own and ended up sacrificing his chance at life and freedom.

I suppose this bothers me more than other people leaving because I became involved with a woman during sobriety, that relationship lead me to crack cocaine, and I lost ten years of my life in absolute suffering. I trusted her more than my counsellors, and in the end, she betrayed me – hurt me. I was outside of God's protection, involved in a sexual relationship outside of marriage. She got pregnant, and the child died before it even had a chance to live.

I look back now and consider it a blessing. God was watching over me and sparing an innocent life the suffering of my addiction. So many problems could be avoided if people only obeyed the commandments God has given. He gave them because he loves us, not because he wants to control our behavior. If only people could understand the destruction that comes from straying from the path.

Another person left because he started returning to the darkness. He allowed sin into his life and thought it was okay to continue, in spite of warnings from people around him. Once a man begins to walk into the shadow, he should not be surprised when evil reaches out and pulls him into the dark.

I have also done this in my past. I tried to justify smoking by saying: other people are doing it, so it must be okay for me. The problem is that I knew it was not okay for me. I know God did not want me doing it, yet I did it anyway. I gave into evil and it became my master.

David Burton

Tobacco smoke does not satisfy and it gives rise to crack cocaine. Then it is over and my destruction is complete. God spoke of a narrow way, and that is the path I must walk – he gives me the power to continue walking in the light.

And, yet another person left last night. Straight up walked out into the darkness. I don't want to comment on this one.

God, please protect me from the deception and lies of my enemy; please keep me from lying to myself. Let your light shine inside my thoughts and your words reside in my heart. You are my strength; you are my shield.

I love you, Lord.

Tuesday

I don't like rising to a room full of people. It is insane. I don't find it comforting or helpful. I feel angry. It is because for the last three years, recovery houses have been taking my money and putting me in a shared room. They claim it is for my good, but I think it is just because they want to make money.

Recovery houses get almost twice as much money from the government than I would get on my own, even though the cost of living on my own is greater. It makes no sense. I feel abused and taken advantage of.

I got my cube back from *lockup*, but no solution, so I can only solve the first two levels. I guess I will play around and hope for the best. If only I had access to a computer.

I worked in the barn this afternoon, and I let a cow escape from his holding cell. It was exciting. He went and visited all the other cows and then went back to where he belonged. Both the other workers were gone and I had the barn to myself. Honestly, I fell asleep for the last fifteen minutes.

I am tired today and I don't know why. Perhaps it is because of the move and becoming used to my new surroundings. I did pretty good with scheduling, arriving on time for classes; however, now I am the one who has to make sure the whole house arrives on time. I don't have anyone to depend on anymore.

This journal entry is not going well. It is hard to concentrate with music playing.

Wednesday

I am incredibly tired this morning, as though I have run a marathon or walked all night. I remember waking up in the middle of the night, swearing at someone. My side of a conversation that I can't remember. I don't know how I am going to make it through this day.

If I hear anything else about people talking in unknown languages, I am going to explode. It is one small chapter in the bible… are we going to make it a big issue? What about the rest of the book?

I don't see how Christians walking around talking nonsense helps anyone, let alone themselves. The more I hear about it, the less I want to be part of it. I feel pressured into faking something just so that I can be accepted, and that I am somehow less of a Christian because I don't speak gibberish. Where is the love in that? I remember Jesus commanding me to love; he never commanded me to speak in tongues.

My day has been difficult, but I believe I have come to a few resolutions. I am giving up on the tongues thing. It is personal and I am unable to explain myself. I don't have the words for it. Ironically, I would have to use tongues to explain how I feel, and probably no man would understand.

Today was very slow which is okay for me, but I think some people feel awkward. Time condensing or expanding is a new concept for me, so I simply observe and accept the pace. I've grown sensitive to it over the years. This probably all sounds science fiction, but it is true.

I have offenses rising within me and I am trying not to allow them to take residence in my mind, but it is still hard to forgive. I don't know why. Shouldn't it get easier each time? Why can't I move immediately into forgiveness?

To err is human; to forgive, divine. I am not God, yet he resides within me. It is his spirit that gives me the power to forgive someone. I suppose I am still bound somewhat by the law; when someone [transgression / disobeys / rejects] the grace they have been given.

God has given us freedom; it is a precious gift. I have waited a long time for it, and it is valuable to me. I yearn for God's presence in my life; my spirit longs for communication with him. I desire to know his ways, and I want to follow his teaching.

The *peer review* tonight blew my mind. God has orchestrated this for healing. Thank you.

Thursday

I am so tired I can barely open my eyes. I need to rest and there is still one more day left in this week before I will get a chance to catch up on my sleep. I used to have a room to myself and after dinner I would try to get an hour of sleep, just to keep me going. There is no chance of that happening down here. Someone plays music all the time and guys are walking around. What am I going to do?

Please help me God; give me the strength to continue. There are some things that my mind is examining right now that I am not going to write in this journal. I am not sure what the result will be, but I hope it is healing. My past is the past and there is nothing I can do to change it. God knows the things I've done, and he has

74

forgiven me. I know the things I've done, and I have forgiven myself.

I still don't understand why my life took the path it did, except this: my choice to live according to sin (or, in the world) led me from one bad situation to an even worse situation. Sometimes I had the appearance of getting better, but I wasn't: it was all an illusion, designed to keep me enslaved.

I have now been set free from my self-induced prison cell, but I am left with the memories of every evil act I have ever committed, every bad choice I made. Perhaps my knowledge and experience will help someone else make a different choice, and keep them off the path of destruction.

I really want to go back to bed, pull the covers over my head and sleep, slipping away into the world where I truly belong.

Friday

I am going to pass out standing up if this continues. I wake up ridiculously tired. I need this weekend to catch up on my sleep. I am going to talk to the *leaders* today about it, that's how tired I am.

People are irritating today. Twice they have come at me with their insanity and I have walked away. I have chosen not to respond. Why? Because I know they are messed up and if they get into their heart they will realize it has nothing to do with me. I am trying very hard to see people as God sees them and it is incredibly difficult. I keep forgetting and returning to my own perception. I need my eyes healed and my vision restored. Please, help me.

My fear of rejection is causing other people to feel rejected by me.

David Burton

Saturday

I stand by the ocean
And the waters inside,
For the dreams that are coming
From the power inside.

I am playing guitar in a high tower that overlooks the ocean. I keep everyone out. This tower is my sanctuary. I warm up with a few chords, and then I sense a calling within me.

I descend from the tower and walk out onto the sand. I am standing on the beach and the waves come crashing toward me. I start playing, singing and writing. I write two verses, which I have forgotten.

Suddenly, the chorus enters my mind and I play it. The ocean responds and becomes raging. I am playing inside of a storm. I feel the presence of God and I know his power. I am truly alive.

I stand by the ocean
Where the waters reside,
For the dreams that are coming
From the water inside.

I awake in the night, excited and completely convinced of God's presence in my life. It is 4:37 in the morning, and I am writing this in the bathroom. God just spoke to me.

Thank you, Lord.

I return to sleep only to continue my instruction.

This time it is an education in faith and flight. I am pursued by my enemies. I climb the side of a building and launch myself from its rooftop into the air. They try to follow, but I turn in flight and strike them to the ground.

"I am angel," I yell back at them in a strange language. I return to a building where I used to reside, but I am transformed – I have risen.

I see things before they occur, I know things other people have no way of knowing, and I fight the demonic forces hidden among the people. It is not on my own that I do these things: it is the power of God within me.

I awake this night with something new within me; I feel it: it is residing. I have experienced the substance of my hope and seen evidence of the unseen. I don't know if I am explaining this right.

Sunday

My night is filled with dreams that make little sense to me. Not every night is a crystal clear contact with God – sometimes it is a mess.

I am going to church today somewhere in the city. I am interested to see what it is like. Each time I leave the farm I wonder what will happen… am I strong enough? I know that God is real and I will stay in his protection, walking with him. I am nervous.

Church went well. The message was about *the word* being planted within us as a seed and watering that seed, so that is becomes what it is supposed to grow into. All the characteristics of the full-grown plant reside within that small seed. All that is required for life is contained within it.

I saw several beautiful women that distracted me, and it was hard to understand a few speakers because it was a Chinese church; nevertheless, I had a good time. It was a growing experience for me. I noticed the change within me, especially during worship.

Monday

I awake tired and angry this morning. I don't like living in the same room as other people. I have been doing this for three years. I want my own room. Some of the people I am living with right now are so completely self-centered, they don't care how their actions affect the other people they live with. All they are concerned about is themselves.

I haven't thought about leaving, not even once, until this morning. That's how living down here in this dormitory is affecting me. They are charging the government a thousand dollars a month so that I can live in a room with eight people? This is worse than any other housing situation I've ever been in, besides being homeless. I only accept these conditions because I like The Program more than any other place I've been.

My mind is not in the right way of thinking. If God wants me down here in the dormitory, it is because he is trying to teach me something. What it is, I don't know at this moment, but it will become clear.

God may ask me to travel the world and live in conditions far worse than these. Will I deny him? No. I will obey, and I will be prepared. There are countries where there is even less privacy and less space – they make it somehow.

I am irritated by having to spend so much time with the same people. I don't think I was designed to live in close quarters with other men.

Today has been a good day. I played ball hockey and found that my lungs are healing. I am able to play longer and run faster. I can begin to enjoy recreation again. It has been long time since I could do this, and I'm happy. The negativity of this morning has passed, but not without several battles throughout the day: lust, cocaine and rage.

My *junior partner* tried to run the show this morning and we got into a fight. I had to go to the *leader* to resolve the conflict. We worked it out, or so I thought. Having learned nothing from this morning, he tried to run the show again tonight – which ended up involving two *houses* and nearly got himself into a physical altercation. That was also resolved by the *leaders*, but I wonder if he understands the common thread.

Is it my place to tell him? What are my responsibilities? These are merely observations, knowledge gained by experience and patience. I suppose time will reveal the matter; truly I can change no man, but I can give him an example to follow.

Lust has continued to challenge me this day: a single memory of a girl who sold and used crack cocaine with me. We had sex one day after a long night of using. She had a heart tattooed on her ass, and her clit pierced. I can see her clearly inside my mind. She arose out of the clouds of my mind to tempt me to sin. It is with her memory that I struggle today, offering me exactly what she gave me that afternoon in her room.

I am resisting, but she is calling me. Why now after so long? I had completely forgotten about her. I have a flood of these kind of experiences in my past, and fighting just one is difficult. Do you understand?

Tuesday

Another night filled with dreams that make no sense to me, but are emotional. I am tired and frustrated with living down here. I think I am going to explode. I feel like screaming. How am I going to make I through this?

I had a dream last night that told me to leave. What do I do? An attack from the enemy? A voice spoke to me while I slept; although it sounded similar to God, it was not: it was a counterfeit. If I did not know the voice of God, if I had not experienced his presence, I would be packing my bags today and leaving.

Which leads me to believe that other people of this farm, and in the world, are indeed hearing the voice of a spirit, but that spirit is deception – and it is being mistaken for the voice of God.

My day has been emotional; up and down, sadness and joy. I faced each challenge to the best of my ability and when it was too much for me to handle, I asked for help. I talked more than usual today and I believe it was because I was processing something.

I was shocked by some of the things my *partner* said and I don't know how to take it. At the end of the day I can say it really doesn't bother me – everyone makes mistakes and is learning how to communicate.

Leader X is going to read my journal today; yes, you – and I am concerned that he may be offended by some of the content. I don't write these pages with the idea that someone else will be reading them. I write them for myself.

Wednesday

I must be very careful who I listen to when it comes to accepting guidance and advice. I can easily be lead astray if not vigilant. I may think it is a great idea at the time, or that I am doing the right thing, but it could end with me being on the street again.

I had *counselling* with someone today and he listened to me without judgement. It is the first time this has happened. I feel embarrassed, as though I have done something wrong. I fear ridicule, disbelief and rejection. When I tell my story to secular counsellors they recommend medication or hospitalization. It was a welcome change to have a Christian hear and accept what I am saying. This experience gives me great hope for the future.

The problem of communication lay within me, and that is where I need to focus my attention. I need to be able to speak without condemning myself. What has happened to me is real, and is continuing.

Thursday

I want to sleep for several more hours, but the clock says I only have half an hour. I keep coughing up black from my lungs. All these years of smoking have left a mark inside of me. I am glad it is healing, but it scares me to think of the damage I may have caused.

I have had a really good day in the area of relationships, conversations and building people up. I don't usually relate well with others, however since I have begun to try lead with love, and see others through the eyes of God, I have had greater success. I must be doing reasonably well because my *partner* decided to volunteer his time to work with me on a *chore*. And this coming from a man who, only day ago, told me he would be happy when he was no longer my *partner*.

I am learning a lot about myself, and social interactions I never thought possible. It originates from my trust in God. The more I trust him, the more I am able to open my heart and life to other people.

Thank you, Lord, for healing the animals in the barn and the people on the farm. Make me a servant, for I am your servant. I don't know what else to say; I am merely rambling on, writing words to fill the page.

Friday

I awake, and while I am still on my knees in prayer, I get into a fight with my *partner*. We spend the morning attempting to resolve the conflict. We resolved the issue and have come closer together as a result.

Class was right on the mark as to what I am going through and it really made sense to me. It was mainly about relationships: with God and other people. I need to lead by example. I follow Jesus Christ and obey his commands – this is my message and in it is freedom. I am still teaching myself to see people through the eyes of God, and I am learning quite a lot.

Today I compared how I see the animals to how God sees us. I love the animals. There is nothing they could to that would make me love them less. I think God feels the same way about us. Now, if only I could see people how I see the animals and extend that same love.

I think I can do it, but it means embracing a part of myself I generally avoid.

Saturday

I awake to a bright light being turned on in the dormitory. I am fairly well rested and my first thoughts turn towards my Hastings Adventure. I am going to Vancouver tonight. I am going to a small church to carry this message of freedom which God has given me.

I asked God last night what he wants me to do and a dream followed, but I don't think I can make it happen tonight. Perhaps it will be the start of something I can't see the end of.

I just had the opportunity to counsel a brother and I am amazed at the words that came out of my mouth. I think God just gave me what I was supposed to say and I shared it. I followed the lead of the spirit and responded to the guidance. I am encouraged by this exchange. I never knew it could happen like this. I have never experienced the spirit if this way before.

And just now I repaired a breach I caused in a relationship by addressing the conflict, asking about the damage I caused, and apologizing for my actions (words).

Sunday

I stayed up late last night. I went downtown Vancouver to minister to the poor and feed the people (burgers and salad). We started the night with worship and a short message from the teacher. I found that worship is the light in the darkness. The people are so broken and weighed down that they do not stand or sing, although they did clap at the end of a couple of songs.

I felt alive and protected down there on Hastings. People were walking around endlessly, a girl was pushing her crack pipe in the church front entrance, and a man the shoes off his feet and tried to sell them to me. Crack cocaine has enslaved these people and continues to torture them daily. I feel sad and overwhelmed, yet entirely comfortable and at peace. I wanted to help, but I knew the only thing I could do is love them.

I had a chance to pray with someone who was drunk. I was not nervous or awkward at all. I felt the change within me: I am free. I was there to be a light in the darkness, and I believe God shined through me.

Today I am back on the farm and I can't help but feel as though it is a waste. Why should I be here while others suffer? I am no better than they. I am angry because the city is full of churches, yet I don't see them on the street ministering to the people. This street would not exist if the people followed God and the Christians did what they were supposed to.

The mission downtown is good and I am encouraged by its existence, but I am discouraged because of what could be and isn't. The truth of a society can be reflected in its poor. In a city filled with wealth and buildings rising into the sky, the streets are filled with the desperate and lost, passed by and ignored by the majority.

So, the city can build sky reaching buildings and water crossing bridges, but it can't give its people a home to live in or food to eat? What good is that city? My worth does not come from my bank account or job; it comes from my love for those who are lost in the darkness. If I can't love the homeless, drug addicted, drunk and swearing man sitting in chapel – then how can I love God?

If I love my own life and I am not concerned for the lives of others, what good is that love?

David Burton

This topic of conversation is dragging me down so I'm not going to write about it anymore today. I feel frustrated because I want to do more, and how will I do that if I am here?

God, please restore me, return my power, unleash my wings. I am drowning, slipping quickly beneath the surface of the water.

And then I lost control and lashed out at those around me, until I finally broke down and cried out to God in front of men. My heart is broken for the lost.

God help me.

Monday

I wake up tired, unhappy and wondering what I am doing here. I am supposed to be getting better, not worse. I am supposed to be healing, not causing new wounds. I made some progress yesterday (or, so I thought), but it was definitely not reflected by the dream last night.

I need spiritual encouragement and I am afraid it can't come from a man. Not in my life. Unless that man is a spirit being. Am I wrong? Men can only help so much; the rest must come from God.

I close my eyes and see things that no man has ever seen: alien and unhuman things that disturb me. How am I supposed to live with it? I trust God, even though I don't entirely understand him, and I suppose that will have to do for now.

Today has been very interesting. I lost my temper in hockey because I got emotionally involved in the game. I really wanted to play and the referee accidently skipped our team in the rotation. I took it personally, as though he intentionally did it just to spite me.

I had to go into the kitchen and unload what was happening inside of me. I talked to the cook until I found some sort of peace. I felt like fighting and I was going to lash out if I didn't calm down. It wouldn't be such a big deal if we played more often, but we only get the chance to play once a week for a couple of hours. That isn't much ice time with four teams and spares on each; oh well, whatever.

So, I went to work with the animals because they always lift up my spirit. They love me; I love them – unconditionally. However, a conversation came up at break time that set off a series of cascading memories: all of my time spent living on the street before coming here. I was in a dark place of depression, hopelessness and rejection. I had given up. I was doing things I've never done before to support the habit, and it was only going to get worse.

I went back to the barn, sat in the office, and raged inside – until someone came and talked to me. I don't discuss the past a lot, but it is a part of me and has shaped how I see myself, as well as influences the choices I make on a daily basis. Anyway, talking about what took me to the street helped me see clearly the destruction *using* causes in my life, and how much I need God to continue walking this path of sobriety.

Finally, to complete the wrongness of this day, I was served a salad that had gone bad. Being a cook by trade, I was very upset and tossed it in the trash. I'm not going to starve, but I was very disappointed in the kitchen preparation. I could never serve someone a salad like that; it goes against everything I've learned. I put love into my work when I cook, and it was very obvious that there was no love in my salad tonight.

It was a finishing touch to a day wrought with anger, frustration and disappointment. I hope that when I close my eyes tonight, I will see beauty, and tomorrow will flow like clear water.

Tuesday

I wake up in the somewhere in the night. My entire bed is shaking for several moments, vibrating against the floor. I don't understand what is happening. Suddenly, it is gone. WTF?

I am slipping. What is happening to me? I knew something would happen, but I didn't expect it like this. I thought there would be a strengthening, not a weakening: I need you now, God. I need to see you and speak with you. The strange part of this is that I don't know what to say or how to feel.

The world of men does not make sense to me. The body I am in is the body I am in. How long ago did I say to you that I no longer need this body to return to? Quite some time, I believe. I meant it at the time and in some sense I still do, but something has changed: I appreciate the chance you have given me to live a life in the world of men.

I need your guidance to continue; I need your voice to inspire me. Last night I awoke to an earthquake. Was that you communicating? It was very strange, and no one else seems to have noticed or awakened in the night.

Please explain.

During the class tonight the teacher started speaking near the end of our time together. The whole time I heard a voice screaming in my mind: STAND. I didn't obey; I questioned. I did not understand, or believe. Then the teacher asked us all to stand, and I finally understood. I need to listen; I need to obey when he calls me.

I feel disappointed with myself that I didn't act. I won't allow this to happen again. I won't live my life in fear or disbelief. I was tested tonight and I failed in a very real sense; however, I heard the voice within me clearly and plainly. And that was the true test: can I hear? Yes. Now I must learn to act on the word.

The Farm

I am learning, Lord; please forgive my mistake.

Wednesday

The first thought in my mind is to leave the farm. I am seriously considering packing my bags and finding a new place to live where I get my own room and a reasonable amount of sleep. These feelings continue throughout the day and do not dissipate no matter who I speak with. It is only once I am in barn and with the animals that I start to relax. I don't know why. I can't explain it.

First, the cat comes to see me, and loves me. Then I go see the cows and play with them. I am suddenly free from the feelings of the morning. They are washed away. People tried to help me today and they couldn't release me from the chains that had somehow fallen on my mind. However, the animals helped me do what humans could not. They are sensitive to the things happening inside of me that people are blind to.

What am I going to do? I need to somehow find in humans what I've found in the animals, or else it is going to be a strange and interesting life.

Peer review was amazing yet again. I love hearing about other people's lives. It touches my heart and opens my understanding. I've built walls to keep people away, but listening to their story tears the walls down. Then our house gathered together to pray, and what started wrong, ended right – all because I refuse to give up or give in.

Thursday

I wake up and pray. The dreams are scattered and carry no message. I am not angry upon awakening, but I am soon irritated by the behavior of some of the people in the house. I end up doing our morning study and prayer in the bathroom, while sitting on the toilet. This is not a good solution. I have to go to the bathroom in the morning. There is nothing wrong with this. My body has adapted to waking up at 5:30 in the morning every day.

Going to the bathroom is a private thing, and I don't want my *partner* in there with me, conversing about Proverbs. The schedule here is so ridiculously filled with activity that there is no time to go to the washroom. When I have to interrupt some function or class to take a crap, people here harass me, give a me condescending look, or outright report it to *leadership*. My bathroom time is that major of an issue and it is starting to piss me off. I don't command my bowel movements; they command me.

Anyway, this adds to the pressure I am experiencing and is so insane that I question why I am subjecting myself to it. I must focus on something good today, or this simple problem will become a landslide. It doesn't take much to incite a riot.

It is difficult to be satisfied with just clothing, food and shelter, as if that was a fulfilled life. I look at the world around me and see in glaring detail what I am lacking. Even here on this farm it is blatantly waved in my face when I see *leaders* living in a house with a wife and family, driving a decent car. I'm not saying that I want these things rather than a connection with God. I am saying that it shows me everything I don't have.

As far as I can tell, this farm has nothing to offer in the way of transitioning back into society: no housing, outside support, or work placement. I will be completely on my own, with nothing – unless God decides to provide something: a pathway for me to follow. And, as far as I can see from those who have gone before me, unless they have a family that provides these opportunities for them, they are screwed.

So, I prayed and prayed, and prayed some more; until I felt balanced. I have to let it go for the moment. I am prepared to face the day, or so I believe.

I can't focus here. Every time I try to meditate: on scripture, God or daily thoughts, I am interrupted by people trying to lay their hands on me. This completely breaks my concentration and brings me back to a conscious level far below what I am trying to attain.

This day completely fell apart. Two of my friends had very bad days and I was involved because I am close to both of them. One had a nephew commit suicide; the other packed his bags and left the farm. I feel responsible for the person who left because we were discussing our problems and I think my negativity may have caused him to leave.

I will be more careful in the future with whom I discuss my problems. It may be better to save it for these pages rather than vocalizing it. I made several mistakes while dealing with this situation today: I didn't take the signs as seriously as I could have, I highlighted problems I see on the farm (which only added fuel to the fire already burning inside him), and I didn't seek the help of another *leader*. I mean, this guy who left was a *leader*. What am I supposed to think? I thought he could handle it. I thought he would voice his apprehension and get through it, not succumb to it.

Enough. I'm done. Tired, overloaded and sad.

Friday

Flames of fire coming out of my hands, palms out.

I wake up and have to take a crap. My body has been programmed. Every morning at the same time I need a bathroom. I am frustrated this morning. I see what is wrong with this place, but I don't know how to change it except to walk away in protest, which will change nothing.

Something very clear came to mind this morning. In spite of what we are being taught, we are not walking in grace: we have slipped into trying to attain it by doing. If we keep the rules, then we will be rewarded. We can lift ourselves up, say "good job," and tell others to follow us. It doesn't work. That isn't the spirit of Christ's message. While we are operating on our own power, we are denying his.

There is a verse that says, let your words be few in prayer, but we think we look better if we pray for a long time with nice words, so we do. There is verse that says, women should keep silent in the church, but we think we have equality and that we know better, so we accept and encourage this. Some people like to get down on their knees during *worship*, but are they doing it when no one is looking and there is no music to emotionally manipulate them?

These are the examples I am being shown here and, in some cases, being forced to follow. Sometimes I feel I am being taught to walk away from Christ rather than toward him. Why do these people follow parts of *the word*, but completely ignore others?

I feel like screaming. I am constantly reminded of a series of books that an author write, which speaks to this problem:

In the past, a group (race) of wizards created a machine to fix the problems of several worlds. They all died before passing on the knowledge of how it worked. Years later, religions began to form among the people, all based on the wrong ideas: each thinking they were right, but all missing the original point (or, idea) of the machine.

After *worship* I felt better. I had a few moments of contact while I was praying, tears streaming down my face.

My *partner* told me his life story as we walked around the track this morning. By lunch time he had packed his bags and was leaving the farm. He told me in graphic detail about the abuse he suffered as a child, the darkness his father taught him, and the murder he committed when he was seventeen. My heart opened up to this man, and hearing his story was exactly what I needed today.

God knows what I need to move forward even when I don't. He arranged the players today and I moved with the process. I did not resist, because even though I felt depressed and miserable inside, I wanted to make it through the pain. I desperately wanted to come out the other side of my suffering. I want to overcome my difficulties, not succumb to them. Sometimes it is only the grace of God that keeps me from drowning. If I hold on, everything is going to be alright. I don't know what else to say. I think I survived this onslaught and the seas will grow calm for a time.

Saturday

I dream with vivid intensity, travelling from place to place, vision to vision – pushing me beyond my limits. I awake, and to the people around me, my day hasn't even started yet. How ridiculously far away from the truth is that statement? Yet, I am restored. God has given me the energy I require to face this day. I am pleased and feel refreshed.

Then people start fighting in my house and the peace which I experienced upon waking is stolen away from me. I try not to get involved, but the person who is having a problem wants to fight and turns his attention on me. I am tempted to respond and unleash a raging tirade upon the man, but I know this situation and have faced it several times before. So, I hold my tongue, keep my calm demeanor, and ignore the commentary stemming from his jailhouse mentality. It is fairly obvious that the core of his problem has nothing to do with me, even if he wants to deflect the focus.

I am angry because I've had a couple of hard days and just when I feel myself returning to balanced state, someone else goes off the deep end and tries to drag me down with them. No way. No chance. I continue about my day still hoping that this day holds something good for me. Due to a miscommunication a few people get left in the dining hall after breakfast. Mr. Angry is one of them and decides to fly off the handle. He starts by calling me 'a little bitch' and finishes by trying to get into a physical altercation. I again decide to ignore the temptation and walk away. I continue walking even though he follows me, still trying to provoke an argument or fight. I don't respond and it makes him even angrier. Why do I have to put up with this crap?

People professing to be Christian, acting like heathens. Once act of love or kindness makes up for a lot of wrong doing, but I don't see much of that here on the farm. People talk love with their lips, and speak hatred with their actions. Only God can see their heart, so I will try not to comment.

I served in the barn today, taking over for a friend who left for the week. I feel confident that I can handle the responsibility, and pleased that I have a purpose here on the farm. A calf is very sick. We prayed over him, and wrapped him in a blanket for the night. I don't want him to die; nor do I want him to suffer, so if death will relieve his suffering how can I stand in the way? I'm not a cruel man and I am making the calf as comfortable as I can.

Life is life; it is not of lesser value just because it is contained in an animal. God created these creatures as well as us. Anyway, it is difficult because I have become emotionally attached to the creatures I care for, and somehow they have become my friends.

Sunday

I awaken in the darkness. "Is anyone awake!?" I cry. "We have to pray." And then it comes and takes hold of me, dragging me through the night and emerging high above the earth, in the black sky. It happens in the blink of an eye. I start screaming the words I know will save me, and trying to wake from this world. I fight with all the strength I have within me, knowing I will be trapped and helpless if I do not. I awake, screaming the words into the night: "In the name of our Lord and Saviour Jesus Christ, I cast out all evil!"

I lay in the darkness of night upon my bed and consider. This is the first time in several months that I've had to use these words. What has happened? I have two thoughts come immediately in response to my question: there are two new people in the house, and what happened before I fell asleep. I was praying on my knees when I began to feel something strange, a change in the atmosphere of the room, a descending of some evil force. I felt it so clearly that I opened my eyes, lifted my head and looked around the room. What did I see? One person standing there like a zombie, staring at me. I felt like driving a sword through his heart, but instead returned to prayer. I wrote it off at the time by just saying: 'he's a freak,' but now I think it is more of what I have thought in the past.

He is allowing evil inside of him and that evil is now working though him. Someone invited this presence in and it sure as hell wasn't me. I set my boundaries the same as I do every night. I think it used someone as a portal and I'm reasonably sure who that person is. I don't care how loud he prays or how high he raises his hands during worship – my enemy is practiced in deception.

I return to sleep and walk straight into the next dream (as usual). *This time it is a girl from my past who gives me a ring. I get the impression that she is returning the ring I gave her, although I can't remember giving her one. We are alone together in a room; at first, she is just a picture on a screen – naked and under water. I respond sexually. She emerges from the screen and becomes flesh. She dances naked around the room, and I react, taking off my clothes and following her. She is whispering inside my head as we dance.*

"It's okay," she says, "We are allowed to do this. You can do anything you want, just don't touch me." I don't touch her, but I can't resist. I get on my knees, stretch out my hands.

I wake up consumed with lust. I can't think. My mind burns with the vision. I walk to the washroom and finish what she started. Then in a moment of clarity I see the night in its entirety and fall on my knees in prayer, asking forgiveness. It becomes obvious that my enemy knows my weakness, and my weakness becomes glaringly obvious to me, as though a curtain has been pulled back.

He couldn't get me in one way, so he came in another. I have left things out and the story continues, but these are the dominant features. Nearly three pages of writing and the day that most people experience hasn't even started yet. This is my life. This is what God has given me. I accept it, and love him for it. I will become what he has created me to be, I will learn what he wants to teach me, and I will pass through these trials and come out refined.

My calf died. I found him cold, stiff, and with his eyes open. I hope he didn't suffer. Another person left today – this one right in the middle of church service. Then while the whole house was sleeping, one person decided to play music. Some people are just idiots, what can I do?

Worship gave me nothing except damaged hearing. It was so loud that no one sang, or if they did I could not hear it. I don't really want to write anymore.

Monday

I awake. Today was an interesting day for developing relationships. It started difficult and ended easily. I had an incredible amount of energy this morning. It poured out of me, and I couldn't remain silent. My *partner* hated me and fought with me until lunch. He just couldn't accept me. Then something changed. I have no idea what, and now yet again another *partner* wants to spend time with me mopping the floors in the morning.

Tonight, we spent time visiting the other houses together and found some commonalities. We have the night off and I am thankful. It has been stressful watching the amount of people leave the farm, and having ball hockey cancelled didn't help the situation. However, we are sitting around the table discussing the day and our lives. So, this journal is ending quickly. Tonight, I will listen and learn.

Tuesday

I am going to fucking kill the people I live with. One guy is snoring so loud that I can't sleep. I have ear plugs in and a pillow over my head. I can still hear him, and I'm pissed right the fuck off. Why the fuck am I here, living like this!? This place can't even provide me a fucking room! I might as well leave and find somewhere that does.

I am sick to death of these fucking recovery places that treat us like shit: double bunking bedrooms for more money and now eight people to a room here. FUCK! Three years of this bullshit. They can all kiss my fucking ass!!! And, I dreamed about going to prison. WHAT THE FUCK! That's twice in the last week.

Something is fucked here. It's straight up 4:30 in the fucking morning and I've been awake since 4 AM. Now I am spending my morning in the bathroom. I am so tired and sleep blind that I knocked over a garbage can on the wat here. Someone from next door came and gave me the what for, and another person asked me what my problem is when I freaked out when I woke up.

WHAT'S MY PROBLEM!? Are you fucking kidding me!? Are you fucking deaf? This is how I start my day; isn't it wonderful? Should I thank God for his mercy that endures forever this morning? How about my mercy in not getting a bucket of water and dumping it on his head?

All I have ever needed from these recovery people is a place to live so that I can get clean and go back to work; but, no – all they want you to do is sit around. We are not allowed to work. Many of them preach: become a productive member of society (which I was before coming here for help), and then they tell me I can't work. More bullshit!

Recovery is a one-way street to destruction; a black hole which is impossible to climb out of. It gets continually worse and no one is offering a way out. I never should have come to the mainland. What was I thinking!? If only I could go back in time and kick my own ass, slap myself across the face and tell myself not to give up. There are no answers waiting for you across the ocean, only heartache, misery, and weight gain.

I've weighed 150 lbs. my whole adult life. Now I weigh 220 lbs. I want to fucking scream when I see my body in the mirror: WHAT ARE YOU DOING TO YOURSELF!?

You know what recovery did for me? Put me on the street; yes, that's right: THE STREET. Homeless, drug addicted and in despair – complete hopelessness with no family and no way out. I am seriously considering burning every recovery house I can think of to the ground and then murdering those who run them.

If I had grown up in the poorest part of Africa, I would be happier than I am now. If I was living in a thatch roof hut in some poor country, I would be more content than I am now. But, I don't live in a poor country, and I grew up in a house. Having my own room is like drinking water out of the tap. If this place can't even afford to provide me a room how are they going to help me transition back into a normal life? If I wanted to share a room I'd have a girlfriend, not several other men who are complete strangers to me.

I was drug addicted, and people who claimed to be Christians offered to help me. I trusted them. They knew I was a drug addict, but when I ended up relapsing they threw me out into the street. Unless you've been on the street you have no idea how hard it is to come back from. No home, no clothes, no shower, no food, no money, no phone – ONLY A CRACK PIPE to keep you company in your despair.

How can you get a job while have no home, or phone to get the message, or sink to shave in to keep the job? How can you get a house without a job? Welfare is a joke. They don't give you enough money to rent a house or apartment, let alone eat – and God forbid that you smoke! People treat you like garbage once they know you are on welfare; human refuse: the scum of society.

Then I came the treatment centers or places like this, where the living conditions suck and welfare gives them twice as much money to house me, but they won't give me the money if I live on my own. And all the treatment centers complain that there is not enough money, so they solicit donations. What the fuck!?

I've gone from supporting myself to becoming a commodity that other people live off of. I want to cry, but I am choking on the bitterness of it all. So, let's take an inventory of what three years of listening to the authorities in the recovery industry has done for me: I'm fat, broke, jobless, homeless, living in a room with eight men; no girlfriend, no friends, no hope of a future, no connection with my family, no prospects, no plans – filled with anger, bitterness, despair, rejection, frustration, vengeance, desperation and loneliness.

It's no wonder that I'm dreaming about prison because I AM IN PRISON! It's no wonder why I return to crack cocaine. At least in her embrace I can forget this misery. I can't believe I cleaned up for this.

I need to move to another country where I can forget that I ever lived in a house with running water, or had food to eat every day. Why did you send me back to this world, Lord? So that I could experience this?

Three and half pages and it's only 5:30 in the morning. Maybe I should start feeding the animals in the morning. I can leave my alarm clock blaring and everyone can experience what I am right now.

Wednesday

The day was hard until a brother pulled me into the office and talked to me. I couldn't handle it. I am overwhelmed and fighting for my life. I broke completely, tears running down my face and a box of Kleenex on the desk. I am hurting and broken, I don't want anyone near me.

Satan screaming and God calling. What can a mere man do? I was born into this war in more ways than one. While I cry a rainbow forms outside the windows and my brother says it is a divine appointment. He is right, more right than he could possibly know. I am in pain, torn open and raw – my wounds are bleeding. I am

David Burton

trusting that God knows what he is doing. Does anyone understand how hard this is for me?

I am a beacon on the mountain. My enemy sees it clearly and is drawn to the light, just as the people will be. I read my journal last night. Everything is unfolding as it should. There is a reason that I write my dreams. I have been instructed. Even if I am the only one who learns from them. Thank you, Lord.

90 Days

Chapter FOUR

I wake up feeling sick. It is starting in the back of my throat and my sinuses are dry. If anyone comes and touches me, saying: "you are healed," I am going to punch them in face. I am asking God to burn the infection out of my body, and he is listening.

I am tired. It is not on my own strength that I continue, it is something far more powerful than my hand. I am meeting with the pastor this afternoon. I hope to find the cause of this disturbance. I have spoken with him in the past and is has gone alright; although, certain things in my life are not for his ears.

I dislocated my knee today in the barn. A cow ran at me and smacked his head into the side of my knee joint. I collapse in agony, screaming and swearing. I was scared. Amidst the cursing, I asked God for help and he guided my hands, reassembling my leg and placing my knee cap back into place. It was an accident. The animal was so scared of me that he ran away. The pain faded and I was able to walk carefully on my leg, until I sat down at the end of the day. It swelled, the pain returned and I could barely walk.

This happened once before in my life. The first time it happened I perceived that is was God teaching me a lesson: never take for granted the fact that I can walk. When I healed, I reminded myself at intervals to be grateful, and remember that it can always get worse. Tonight, the lesson was different, and I was reminded of Jacob: so that I can never walk away from God again.

Just when things are getting hard, God seriously humbles me to the point where I physically can't walk away. I need to depend on God, not on my own strength, because my pride is an illusion: it can be taken away in a single moment.

I could be completely mistaken; maybe it is Satan trying to keep me from ministering to people on Hastings. I don't know. It happened and that's all I need to know right now.

Thank you, Lord, for picking me up off the barn floor, physically and spiritually. Thank you for calling me out of the darkness and sin. I love you. You have my attention. Today was the first time in over a week that I sang in *worship* and opened up. I felt the power flow through me. It was amazing. Coincidence? I don't believe in it. When I was in serious pain tonight I sang to God with an open heart, and believe me – that is truth displayed in an honest cry. He heard. I know he heard. I am burning inside. A fire that is reflected in my eyes.

Friday

I had a dream last night that *I was walking with a preacher, and we were talking about being healed.* Today I can walk on my leg and it does not hurt at all. It is still swollen and sensitive, but not as much as it should be. Last time I dislocated my knee I couldn't walk for three weeks and I used heroin to manage the pain.

I am surprised by the fact that I can walk, shocked that I am not in pain. I kept expecting the pain to return, but it hasn't. Dreams and reality becoming one, and I am only three months clean. It's okay. I'm prepared.

I want to do a reverse lookup on the phone number I was dreaming about a few nights ago, see who it belongs to. Phones and I have a very strange history – very strange. I don't want to talk about it in this journal because I have to read it aloud in *journal group*, and people will be listening. Is that paranoia, caution, or self-preservation? Perhaps a fear of rejection? Things are going so well that I don't feel the need to reveal characteristics of myself that will inevitably push people away from me. I don't understand completely what is happening to me, so how can I explain it to them?

I heard one counsellor refer to my life as: a spiritual being having a human experience. It fits the pieces of the puzzle, but not entirely. I believe that Jesus is fully God, fully man. I have always maintained, however, that in order for God to have a truly human experience he would have to forget that he was God.

In a totally unrelated matter, I just remembered what God told me long ago, "I baptize you to remember what you have forgotten." What did I forget?

Saturday

Before I even awake this morning, I have been tempted by sex, money, and drugs. I refuse to give in to the lust and I rise prepared to face this day. I start as I always do: on my knees. Today I am returning to Hastings to shine the light within me.

As we approach the street I am suddenly assaulted by fear and panic. I know it is a deception of the enemy and I do not allow it a foothold in my mind. We arrive at the small church and begin worship. Not many people are present, so I start praying. Come in, I say. God, fill this place with people. A few seconds later, the doors burst open and people pour inside, filling the chairs (I find out later that they all attend a college on the Island, and are here doing mission work in the East Side).

A man in a wheelchair appears behind me. I turn around just in time to see him cast at me. I acknowledge him, share love, speak a few words, and return to worship. I calling God right now: palms up. I know that now is not a moment for distraction. The man gains no ground with me, so he rolls up the isle and takes on the person teaching. He gets removed from the building.

I watch as the battle unfolds: the man teaching in front of us, sharing God's message, and the man outside, swearing and yelling so loud that it carries through the building. Perseverance takes this one and the message continues. I feel excited.

I talk to a girl and fall in love with her in three minutes. She is so beautiful that I can't believe she is talking to me. I talk to a homeless man beside me, but he rejects me when I offer him help. He doesn't want it, or Satan has bound him so that he can't accept it. Than it is over and we start the process of what we have come here to do: walk the street.

I ask God for a guard; angels in front, angels in back. As it turns out, I walk with two men behind me, two men in front – I walk in the center, and I don't even know if they notice. The first contact I have is three figures wearing hoods, walking in unison. They part ways for me. The second is a girl who meets my eyes; she is fury: I can sense her rage that I am here, but she can't speak. I didn't come here for a fight. The third comes in a back alley. A beautiful young girl whose eyes shine when I meet her gaze. She is immediately filled with hope, as I watch shock and confusion wash over her face. She just saw the light in the darkness. She stares at me as I walk away.

Lastly, the final contact comes as we return to our vehicles. I can sense something, but I can't see it. My senses are on high frequency, ready to spring into action. Then I see it: a man walking down the street suddenly stops dead in his path, turns around and walks back the way he came. I take two steps in pursuit before I become aware of my actions. I have to remind myself why I came, and return to the group. However, the quick eyes of several addicts witnessed the whole thing, even if the people I was with did not.

Returning home my energy was gone. I felt tired, drained. I felt the call to sleep. As soon as we were home, I obeyed the call. I fell into bed, pulled the covers around me, and WHAM – I was in the spirit.

I awaken in the darkness. "Is anyone awake," I cry out. This cry is becoming familiar. "We have to pray." I say these words again, and I become aware of the presence all around me. I am not alone. My voice and hearing are crystal clear, but I can see nothing with my eyes except the waves of a black velvet cloth.

"I am just a man," I begin to say, and with each word I begin to shrivel away from the presence. I can feel myself collapsing. And then I claim something within me, and I snap.

"I am a man," I scream the first part of the sentence into the darkness. I am standing true, in power and faith. I do not have the words to explain the transformation occurring inside of me in a single flash of light. Waking and completely the sentence simultaneously: *"and I will walk in the image of my father!"*

Sunday

The first words out of my mouth go something like this: "Why am I still here? Out of all the places, why did you return me to the earth?"

I walk to the kitchen to help out and it goes well for a while until some idiot decides to correct my cooking technique from his years of experience (I speak sarcastically). I leave, only to return later and put my years of experience (I speak literally) to use by washing dishes and wiping counters. What a waste.

I end up crashing out this afternoon, tired and exhausted. I wake up barely able to move.

Monday

I dream of being homeless, broken and destitute. I wake up thoroughly depressed. I look at my life and realize that I AM HOMELESS, no matter what people tell me here. I can lose this place in the blink of an eye. I get moved from house to house on a whim whenever someone makes the decision. I have no work or source of income, even though *the farm* has us spending hours upon hours in their *work program*. These people could tell me to leave at any moment and I will be on the street.

That is the reality of this life I am living. I have to follow their rules, or I am on the street. I have to believe what they believe, or I am on the street. I am tired of my life being in the hands of other people!

I was denied access to my guitar again, for the second time. I have been here for three months and they still will not allow me to play. I am right fucked up about it. God gave me the ability to play – he did not withhold it from me, so why do men stand in my way? If they think they are doing God's will, they are as mistaken as Saul was while he was murdering Christians.

The longer I am here the more I see people profess love with their lips, and speak hatred with their actions. If you are teaching me forgiveness, Lord, then this surely is the place, because I find their arguments offensive. I am emerging from within, resurfacing. I have been gone for a long time, lost in the darkness, and I do not need resistance from the people around me to hinder my development.

I am afraid that right now I can only use them as stones to walk on as I reach the next level. It sounds callous to myself even as I write the words.

Tuesday

I am in a classroom with a box of white salt in front of me. I move my fingertips across its rough surface until it is spilling over the side. I wake up long before I have to rise from sleep, but I have a difficult time returning to the dream.

This day was a strange one, but I sought help from several people and make it through. I don't know what has changed. I feel so tired and worn out, but it is only the second day of the week. There has been a pattern in my life of *using* until I am broken and willing to accept help from any source. At this point I humble myself because I have been beaten into the ground by my spiritual enemy, and I know without any doubt that I need the power and strength of God to continue for even a moment more.

However, when I have been clean for awhile, I lose this desperation, willingness, and sense of peace. I do not know how to get it back without using. I heard a few answers today but I don't know if they will be able to bring me into the state of mind that I seek. I definitely don't have it right now.

I am in class, watching a video of a preacher talking about the book of Revelation. It sounds like complete insanity. Like I've said before, the problem with Christianity is that everyone is an expert. Scripture can be taken and interpreted in such a way that it can support almost any position. That is why there are so many divisions in the church. If the instructions were clear we would all follow them, wouldn't we?

Add a little verbal skill to the scripture and a preacher can convince the people of just about anything. They've been doing it for thousands of years. Every preacher I've ever listened to thinks that their version of Jesus is the right one. I don't think they ever consider the possibility that they are wrong.

I think about it, quite a lot. I've read the bible a few times and I still question whether or not I have understood what is written, especially prophetic material. I am so tired of people coming to me and trying to convince me to believe what they believe because what they believe is right. I trust my own experience over what people tell me. If I see blue and someone tells me it is white, I trust myself – not them.

People have lied to me my whole life. They have taught me lies, and I have believed a lie. Now that I am standing here alone with this knowledge, trying to find the truth – and my life depends on this search.

The latest teaching in Christianity is this: it's all about having a relationship with Jesus. That's interesting... me having a relationship with Jesus is like a toaster having a relationship with a computer system. He is God; I am man. How is this supposed to work?

Wednesday

I wake up and discard the thoughts of the night. They are not productive. I feel as though it was a waste of time, so I will forget them. I have to go into Langley today to have a beautiful nurse check a skin test I had done on *Monday*. I don't get off this farm very often and doing so reminds me that there is a world laying beyond the boundaries of this property. A world where people function normally, have wives or girlfriends. A world where people get paid for their work and have the freedom to make their own decisions. A world where people are moving forward, not standing still. A world where people don't turn off the bathroom light on you while you're taking a crap.

Today I've failed in several things I am trying to do. I've given into temptation, lost hope, fought with people around me, and refused to pray. I can't handle dealing with other people and their problems, I have enough of my own.

I sought help and 6:30 in the morning, and was told there is not enough time to speak with me. The whole day has passed and I still haven't met with anyone. I spent the day practically alone and I enjoyed most of the time, but something is wrong with me. I am unable to reach the core of my belief.

I saw a picture of myself today. I look like I am in pain, an incredible amount of pain. The strange part is that I can't remember feeling that way, so the hurt inside of me must be entirely interwoven with my being. How depressing.

The nurse was wearing purple lace panties – very exciting.

Thursday

"I don't sleep," I scream. "I can't take this anymore." I am raging and demons are manifesting in the people around me.

I wake. Every single night I dream in vivid detail, and I am completely awake. There is no difference between this world and the world of dreams. I close my eyes on earth and open them in the spiritual realm. I move from one world to the next with no rest. It is endless. And yet, this is the gift I have been given and I would not exchange it for anything.

It is early in the morning and I am filled with anxiety about getting out of bed. I feel the pressure bearing down on me. Somewhere in the night I remove the binding from my hand. I believe it has served its purpose. I pulled my *partner* into a *leader's* office this afternoon and attempted to open a channel of communication. With the help of God and a few friends, I succeeded. I didn't expect it, to be honest. I thought it would cause a larger rift between us but I had to take the chance.

A person who left the farm just over a week ago, and relapsed, has returned. I have been praying for this and hoping against hope. I knew that addiction had him by the throat, but God is stronger, and I really didn't want to lose this one. I suppose I opened my heart to him and the experience left an impression on me. I've heard this man sing during worship and I know his heart is for God.

I don't want the enemy to take what is rightfully God's. Satan is literally trying to kill this man. It is unfolding before my eyes. I feel moved to action. This battle I will join, to the best of my ability and through the grace God has given me.

I entered the pen of the oldest bulls that we have in the barn. One pushed against my knee and it popped out of place again. I screamed in pain, snapped it back in, fell on my knees, and yelled: "Jesus Christ! Give a man a break." I felt hurt, angry, and helpless.

I want to cry, but the tears won't come. I was already crying during class today when the instructor started talking about God's love for me, and how he loves me no matter what I do. He does not condemn me; it is I who condemns myself. It is I who separates myself from God. I do it without even thinking about it. Why? Perhaps I am starting to consider grace my own power. Sometimes the line becomes blurred in my mind. I don't understand completely how this all works. I am still learning, and the process is slow.

In one week, I will have the chance to share my life history in *peer review*. I've been waiting for this. Tonight, I will review the testimony I have written.

Show me what I lack; guide me, Lord.

Friday

"If they can't accept me as I really am, I will reign fire down from the sky and consume them."

I awake tired with no motivation to rise. I consider my messed-up knee and wonder if I will have to fight with people to get permission to sit down during *worship*. I feel frustrated and rejected, with overwhelming sadness just beneath the surface.

I had to fight, I totally called it. I embraced my anger and walked out of the classroom. I can't just stand around because the tissue in my knee begins to swell and causes pain. I talked to a counsellor about some of the problems I am having. He helped me understand this negative perception that I have of my life.

When God communicates with me, I feel complete. When his presence is gone, I feel empty, hopeless, and angry. I live for these God encounters. It is in these precious moments that I am inspired to continue, and I am depending on this contact. I feel frustrated when God does not speak to me in the ways that I know

David Burton

he can. I feel lost, without guidance. I don't know what he wants from me. What is my mission? I feel like a soldier without orders, a captain with no warriors.

I wish I had a clear image of this world and my purpose in it. With the things I've experienced in the spiritual realm, I hardly believe that I am destined to shovel shit in the barn. I want to forget everything I've known and be filled with the knowledge of God. I want to understand the visions I have seen.

I have a desire to share the information I have been given, but I hesitate because I don't want to be lead into a deception. If I give people access to what I know they can twist it and use it for evil. Sometimes I feel like I am undercover, hiding my true self from all those around me, and exposing myself means placing a target on my back.

I'm not comfortable with telling people all the things I know about myself. I despise it when I share something and people can't find the belief within them to grasp what I am saying. I don't know if all the things I have seen and experienced line up with the Christian doctrine. Sometimes I think the entity that has become the church is blind, mistaken, and misguided. I am a new creature; Christ did something to me, and I don't understand why others who profess Jesus aren't changed.

Saturday

After twenty years of being Christian, I am just beginning to understand God. After multiple times of reading the Holy Bible, I am just beginning to comprehend its meaning.

I played guitar for the first time in three months. My fingertips hurt because the callouses are gone. It was difficult to concentrate because I was playing with other people, and I am used to playing alone. I play to worship – to speak to God. The first few minutes of practice felt forced, but I suddenly opened when I embraced the fact the I am designed to lead. The flow comes when I step into that position without reservation.

Near the end, everyone left and I had the chance to focus and sing to my father. My eyes close and my hands speak in chords. My voice increases and something beautiful happens.

Sunday

I fall asleep and within minutes I am attacked by a demon, trapped within the dream.

"This is my room," I say in defense, over and over. I catch a glimpse of its eyes and hear its voice. I start screaming: "Jesus," until I am simply crying his name and awake saying it. I am wrought with fear; I lay in bed waiting for it to pass. I watch the shadows in my room and prepare to return.

I return to a world where people are lined up in order to receive healing. I feel drunk – my balance is off; my vision is different. I am filled with the spirit. I walk toward the people, ready to unleash this power, and it is now that I realize that I can't hear or speak.

FLASH.

I am in a building and one of the people has fallen under some sort of spell, or something: he is catatonic. I go to him, place my hands on his head and say,

"In the name of Jesus Christ, return."

His head snaps up and his eyes open wide. I am pouring power into him as I awake.

I sleep again and return to a classroom; many things are being taught about God, but not the truth. They are words without power – clouds without water. I am very angry and want to destroy the facility; instead, I take over teaching the class. I start teaching.

"How many of you know that you have a spirit?" One person nods his head. "That's it? Just one. When I awake in my spirit I cry out for others. This is my cry: I scream, 'Is anyone awake? We have to pray! Satan is coming.'" One person laughs.

"Get out of my class," I say. "Anyone else who doesn't want to be here, leave." One by one, sometimes several at a time, they all exit the building. I am alone and on fire. One woman comes to me and tries to tell me not to teach what I have, and I reply with,

"Awhile ago God came to me and said, will you still love me even if you are the only student that remains?" I take her outside to the ocean where we stand on a cliff that rises above the sea – the sky is growing dark. I tell her to open her bible and read the first words she sees. I open mine and read the first line. (I have forgotten; lost it). I am teaching her to believe; I close my eyes, raise my hands and call power.

"Wind, Lord," I say. I feel it touch my face, moving across my skin. "More, more, more." The storm unleashes it power as the wind rages and lightning begins flashing in the sky. She is afraid, but I tell her to look. Staring at the lightning moving across the clouds, I say,

"His pain is his beauty."

I awake. I would write about the day, but nothing interesting happened. I attended two church services and had a shower. I did some laundry and had a couple of conversations. Nothing exciting or life changing. I can't believe this is my life.

Monday

I dream about having a life, but wake to this prison camp. I consider it prison. Yesterday I was told that making a phone call to the outside world is a privilege not a right. This coming after someone else in *leadership* had already approved the call. So, they said, yes I can call, then no I can't, and too fucking bad for you. I feel like throwing up all over the floor.

They make it out like being here is equivalent to going to a bible college for three years. That is just a straight out lie that they tell themselves to make what they are doing, and how they are doing it, seem more justified. I guess if you are a complete idiot whose mind has been destroyed by years of drug and alcohol abuse you might believe it. Any sort of good feelings I had toward this place is fading with each moment that I continue to stay here.

I saw a few people at church last night with light in their eyes – more than I see here.

I was in the dormitory today and someone decided to assault me with a table. Yes, that's right – a table. He kicked a table into me from across the room and knocked me right off my chair. This is the kind of shit I live with in this so-called Christian community. If I've ever seen confirmation of something I've written, this is it. In most circumstances, I would just leave, but in two days I share my story with these people, and I know Satan doesn't want them to hear what I have to say.

Or am I just making excuses for myself because I am scared to leave and face the world again?

Tuesday

I wake up to this place that I am beginning to hate, to a room full of men who think they are holy, to pain in my shoulder and knee. I want to scream. These people are fucked. After getting into an argument with someone in the first fifteen minutes of my day, I went outside to have a discussion with someone I've grown close to. I felt compassion as the sun rose to a blue sky.

I got more out of this conversation than three months of the regular morning schedule that we must all adhere to. That's the problem with this place: they care more about the schedule and rules than the person they were designed to help protect and serve.

David Burton

I went about my day and when I finally couldn't hold it any longer, I went to take a crap in the bathroom. What happened? Some asshole came into the washroom and told me I was supposed to be somewhere else, doing something else – not taking a crap. Are you fucking kidding me!? They feed us five times a day and expect what – for it to just evaporate? Complete insanity.

I sought counsel and have been told to ignore the people around me. What they think does not matter. For some reason during prayer this morning, I slapped my arm to expose my veins, and had total recall of an event that happened last night while I was asleep. I've never used needles in my addiction, but last night I stuck a syringe in my arm, pressed the plunger, and found ecstasy. It was an overwhelming feeling of pleasure, peace, contentment and power – followed by a complete obsession to continue using the drug.

I don't even know what I am filling the syringe with, but I am now fighting a compulsion to use something I've never used before. How is any of this even possible? I know the answer: my worlds are combining; the two galaxies are colliding. Waking and dreaming are becoming one.

Wednesday

Today has been an absolute nightmare. I dream of my *partner*. He is evil and mean spirited. I wake up to him acting exactly the same as he was in the dream. He essentially tells me that I am worthless, not good enough, and completely hopeless. In other words, Satan is standing in front of me, trying to project these into my mind and he is using the lips of this man. I feel hurt and rejected.

I leave the house and walk to the barn. I am sick of these people. Not everyone on the farm is like this, but there are more than a few, and I live with three of them in the same room. My attempts at friendship have failed, my attempts at teaching fall on deaf ears, and they all refuse to follow my example.

What can I do? Nothing. The person who apologized to me the other day for threatening me, is doing the exact same thing today with someone else. Another man is encouraging him by approving of his behavior. These people are not only blind to themselves, but also encourage the sin in each other. I knew nothing had changed. Lies and deception – that's what I live with.

My hands are frozen as I write these words. I am writing in the barn and it is cold. Today I share my life history with the people on the farm. I refuse to tell them everything, but I will give them a basic outline of my life and the decisions I've made. My enemies will be present in the room, and I wonder in hesitant expectation as to what will happen.

Thursday

Several times during the night I awake and don't know where I am. It is exciting. I enjoy the mystery of it all. The whole day is spirit lifting. I shared my story last night and something changed inside of me. I found a new love: teaching, sharing my spiritual experience. Specifically, teaching on my favorite subject matter: myself.

I am intrigued by what I've gone through in my life and I am still trying to figure it out. I've studied scripture for several years, and I love to teach it. I have a unique outlook on life and God. I felt powered by the spirit within last night when I was standing in front of the class, wired for sound and fully prepared.

God gave me a twenty page message several weeks ago. I had already reviewed the written material twice. I come from a family of talented speakers and teachers, but I never imagined finding the gift inside of myself. I am surprised, yet at peace, because the entire experience felt so right, as though I was designed for it. I felt satisfaction, complete, excited, and confident.

All of these emotions continued into the next day, and I am still riding the wave that was set in motion last night. Speaking individually and teaching a multitude ignite two completely different impressions within me.

I know have a physical realm context for what I've already experienced in the spiritual realm. The process of combining two worlds is continuing – bring it on.

This is the best day I've had in a long time and I hope the feeling lasts. Even a cow dying in the barn couldn't bring me down. He accidently chocked to death on the grain. How does that even happen? I am still in shock. I've never heard of such a thing.

Two people have already left the farm since hearing my story. How many more will go? Maybe it's entirely unrelated, but I brought some serious occurrences to light… the only way they could be unaffected is by unbelief. Like Jesus said, though a man be raised from the dead – they will not believe.

Friday

I feel her body pressed against mine, and take her breasts in my hands. I feel her nipples hard against the palms of my hands. I am in agonizing pleasure, and wake up – what!? No! I can't believe this.

I fall to my knees in prayer. I have been severely tempted this night and my flesh is screaming at me. I give myself to Jesus and ask for his help to overcome this day.

I had an awesome day, but ultimately fell to the temptation. I couldn't shake the feeling no matter what I tried. It kept returning again and again. Finally, I just gave in. It wasn't intentional, it was natural. I suppose I could have been stronger and resisted, but I didn't. I have woken up twice this week nearly exploding. I am a young man, and living without sex is insane.

I have a physical body and it is working as it was designed to. I can't just suddenly turn off sexual desire by an act of will. The body was created to procreate, understand? It's like saying: I have lungs, but today I will not breathe. Or, today I will walk around with my eyes closed because every time I look at something I sin. Sight is not a sin. God's design and gift is not a curse, or something to be despised. Why do we try to corrupt the creation by attaching our screwed up belief systems to it?

Christians are notorious for messing up people's sex lives by placing guilt and condemnation where there doesn't need to be any. Sex is not evil; nor is it a sin. Why do I dream of these sexual encounters? I think something inside of me is desperately trying to be satisfied, fulfilled, because I am denying my body sexual release. I don't know what to do and I don't know what to think. All I can consider is this.

> "This I say then, walk in the spirit, and ye
> shall not fulfil the lust of the flesh."

> Galatians 5:16

Saturday

Women and crack cocaine all night long. I cram the white rocks into my pipe, fire, and inhale; but I can't get high no matter how hard I try. It is futile. I don't know why I am even doing this. Are these motions so ingrained into my being that I will never be able to escape them, regardless of how long I stay clean?

I wake up, fall on my knees, and give the day to Jesus. I ask for guidance and ability. Today is going to be a long day. I return to Hastings again. I am nearly always tempted the night before I go down to share the message of what Christ has done in my life. I feel disappointed with myself. I want to change, but I don't know how.

I went to the kitchen to cook breakfast for the farm. I enjoyed myself. I was mainly cooking with one other person, and it was the first successful shift I've worked in the kitchen since I arrived here. Until now, I have gotten in a fight with someone every time.

Afterwards, I worked in the barn with another man who has just arrived on the farm. He is facing depression and really doesn't like himself right now. He has been teased and rejected his whole life, but today I showed him acceptance and tried to build him up.

Perhaps the next segment of my stay here will focus less on myself and more on helping other people. Sometimes I forget how wounded the people are that come here. Many do not make it through the first week. Please give me your heart for your people, Lord, and the power to help.

Sunday

In the first hour of the night, I am trapped in the darkness, caught inside a dream within a dream. It is incredibly difficult to wake. At one point, I give and say: "Fine. Speak then." I can't see anything, but I sense the presence. I lash out with my fists and connect with something. As usual, I continue to fight until I awake, screaming: "In the name of our Lord and Saviour Jesus Christ, I cast thee out!"

I am so captivated by the darkness that I turn on my light and lay awake for awhile, but my eyes are so tired that I can't hold them open. I turn off my light, close my eyes and fall asleep again. I dream of many things before waking again in the morning. Too many to write about here.

I returned late last night and lost an hour of sleep because we set our clocks ahead an hour. I am really tired and I have to feed the cows because the regular person is working a shift in the kitchen.

Breakfast wasn't very good: cold toast, runny eggs, and the wrong kind of sausage. What a disaster. Did I mention that I am really tired this morning? All I want to do is sleep. Yesterday I expended more energy than I expected to. I played guitar during worship at the church on Hastings. I felt completely at peace on stage, but slightly frustrated because the lead player didn't communicate his chording before we started, and the sheet music had all the wrong chords. He kept switching keys and it was driving me crazy. And yet, I felt excited at the same time. Weird, eh?

I fell asleep in church this morning and saw a bright white light. I can remember nothing else, and people here have been making fun of me for falling asleep. Maybe they are jealous, or maybe they derive some sort of pleasure from tormenting me.

Sometimes I think no one listened when I told my story on Wednesday, or don't believe – I can't decide. I don't know what you are trying to say God, but here it is:

I fall asleep this afternoon, and I am transported to a house. It is suddenly filled with people, and they continue flooding in. I walk toward the nearest and cast him out of the house, saying,

"I bind you, and command you to leave." He turns, and I follow until he steps out of the threshold. Then I turn to the others and scream: "Take authority! Don't you understand what is happening!?"

I walk through the house until I find a woman; she is walking slowly, upset about what is happening. I stop her, and I find out that this is her house.

I start praying for her and telling her about Jesus. Her eyes are faded color, glossed over with white, and I know she is blind. As I am praying, her eyes begin to restore; the white leaves her eyes. I can see the iris but there is still no light.

I leave her for a moment to end the fight in the house, but when I return to her, she is once again in the darkness, whimpering the name of Jesus. I take her in my arms and heal her in the name of Jesus Christ. This time her eyes are restored completely with light burning deep inside the hazel.

I tell her that Jesus has done this for her and that he loves her.

FLASH.

We are at the farm in the driving hail; I stand and start yelling,

"What are we doing!? I just healed a blind woman." As I describe what has happened I become filled with the spirit and I look around for someone to unleash the power on.

The woman stands up and comes toward me, eyes blazing; the healing is permanent. She gives me her first born daughter. I am stunned, shocked and in awe. I don't know how to process what is happening.

"Were you blind?" I ask her.

"Yes," she says.

Several people approach me, place money on the table and say, pray for me. I stand, refuse and walk away saying aloud, "You think I do this for money, but it can't be bought, it is the grace of God, and I am merely his servant."

I awake in utter ruin. God has a way of demonstrating things so that no opposition remains. Before I slept this afternoon, I said to him,

If you want to communicate with me, let the vision be clear inside my mind so that I cannot forget it, otherwise let the dream fade so quickly that I can't capture it.

In response, he sends what I have just written and it is etched into my mind. He has taught me and it is so real to me that I have a hard time trying to convince myself it was a dream. I awake saying, "I just healed a blind woman." Just now, before I returned to this physical body. Do you understand?

God, if this is your kingdom that I am experiencing then let it come. Let this world you show me become manifest in the earth. God, if this is already manifest then give me understanding. I am yours; teach me, raise me, fill me with your spirit. As I have been shown, so will I do.

Amen.

Monday

I slip in and out of consciousness, surrounded by strange music. I awake to a knock at my door. I am not pleased to be awake, but I can't say why. Right away I realize that I need to feed to cows. I ask the *house leader* for permission and he refuses. Welcome back to the house. I've moved out of the dormitory and back into the rooming house. The *leader* is the same as when I left: a raging freak, obsessed with the rules, and not at all concerned about the people. He hasn't changed and it is obvious.

Things like this increase my hopelessness, especially after having lived with my last *house leader* who is a caring, compassionate, and understanding person. He is more concerned about how I am doing rather than the rules, and is always available to discuss my problems. He helps my find a solution.

One cares about me, the other cares about rules, authority, and looking good in the eyes of other people – which one reminds you of Jesus? I could say more, but I won't. What is the point? I can't change him and he won't even acknowledge me. He reminds me of many people I have met in the church: deceived. I feel sad that his is living his life in a prison cell, unable to relate to – or love – another person. One day he will wake up and realize that he missed it. I hope this day comes sooner rather than later, for his sake.

The really depressing fact of all this is that he is not alone, there are many people like him here on the farm. It is easier for me to love the people suffering and dying on the street than the people I live with. I think it is because I think they should know better. They've been taught, but refuse to put it into practice. They attend the same classes and lectures as I do, most of them pray, some read *the word* – why are they not learning?

I think Jesus said it: "seeing, they will see but not perceive; hearing, they will hear but not understand." Sometimes I have a hard time living the teaching of Christ, but I desire the power to live it, and understand what he has said. I want to teach others what he has taught me. I want to give others what he has given me. The problem is that many people do not want it.

Anyway, my day went on and I continued to overcome the trials that appeared in the day – and there were many. One person wanted to fight it out after ball hockey. I had to resist, overcome, and walk away. I felt angry, but didn't give in to violence. I wanted to though. I thought it would satisfy me and finally get this person to leave me alone. I know different. Rage never satisfies and it always leaves damage: broken doors, walls, and people. In the end, everyone walks away hurt, whether they throw the punch or receive it. How long will it take for these people to realize this?

The work in the barn is where I found solace. The animals yet again have changed how I feel about the day. They are all growing older and developing personalities. It is amazing to watch and be a part of. I influence these creatures, and by taking care of them I shape in small way who they become. Am I having the same influence on the people around me? Why can't I see it? I spend more time with the people than I do the animals, but they are far more resistant and won't listen.

I preached Jesus to the cats the other day and I think it has had more of an impact on them than some of the people on the farm. Am I losing my mind!?

Tuesday

I have a very long and disturbing night filled with images I would rather forget, expressing desires I sometimes wish I didn't have. The only image I want to retain is the scene where I take my guitar, walk out onto the sand near the ocean and play a song to God. Even that was interrupted. I don't understand why I dream about some of the things I do. It seems to come out of nowhere, and makes little sense.

I awake long before my alarm is supposed to go off and within a couple of minutes I am filled with anger. Why do I have to sacrifice even more of my sleep to feed the animals? The rules say to feed them at five thirty in the morning. Why should I wake up earlier? The cows need to be fed and watered (that's just the way it is), but somehow a few *leaders* here on the farm figure that not only should I subject myself to a brutal schedule, and work five days a week for free, but now I should wake up even earlier to do even more work for nothing. This is complete insanity. I love the animals and have no problem taking care of them, but the schedule is going to have to become flexible in order to incorporate this activity into my day.

I am adapting; so must they.

I had to spend time in prayer before starting this day. I didn't get off my knees until the rage inside of me subsided, but I don't think it is gone. It will probably resurface later in this day, most likely this morning when someone decides to take issue with me feeding the animals.

My *house leader* said yesterday that he thinks his kindness is mistaken for weakness. He is completely deluded. I don't see any kindness in him at all, and many other people don't either. It's not just me. How can someone know so little about themselves, and have such a warped perception, even though they haven't used drugs or alcohol for several years? I suppose delusion and denial are not dependent upon addiction. They are free standing characteristics of any human being.

Class was amazing today. God showed up and started to play with the lights. While the teacher was speaking, a light flickered and went out. When he approached the light it would come back on. Finally, it went dark and stayed that way until he said: "There is something special here for you," and the light suddenly lit up and stayed on.

A few of us noticed the lights because the class was about the Holy Spirit. I started to pray quietly and the light went out again, this time I watched carefully. When I reached the part of my prayer where I said, "And we think all he can do is turn the lights on and off." The light suddenly came back on and stayed on for the remainder of the class.

During this class the teacher mentioned something that had me crying and emotions swirling around inside of me like a hurricane. I knew the spirit had shown up. At the end of class, in a prayer of repentance, tears fell from my eyes again. My heart had been touched, opened by the presence of God. How is he doing this? I keep thinking that I should understand this whole thing better, but God is speaking on an emotional level, not intellectual.

Wednesday

Nightmares so terrible that I slept with my light on. Twice I tried to go back into the darkness, and twice they came. I gave up and left my light on all night. I had one horrible vision of the cows in the barn, slaughtered, skinned – laying in a pool of blood and feces. It wasn't so much what I saw last night that scared me. It was what I felt: a pissed off presence wandering around, trying to invade my mind and dreams. I have not slept with my light on in years. I can't remember the last time, that's how long it's been.

Last night, the people on the farm decided to have everyone cast out demons from their houses. The people in my house attempted to do this, but ended up fighting with each other right after. Any demons that were evicted were invited right back in – only now they were choked with anger. There is a story in Acts that tells of people trying to take on a spirit, without knowledge or power. What happens? Not only do they lose, they are also wounded in the process. Teaching people that have nearly no faith at all to take on spirits that are millennia old is ridiculous. And guess who the demons come to visit and express their gratitude?

ME.

One of the female cows didn't come down to eat, so I went in search of her, expecting to find a new born calf and healthy mother. Instead, I found her dead, and the calf as well. She died during birth, in the throes of agony and pain. The ground was torn up from where she had been thrashing her head and legs. Blood trickled out of her eyes. The calf was only half born, eyes closed and blood pouring from his mouth.

I think the birds had already started to eat the dead flesh. I slammed my pitchfork into the mud, removed my hat, and spoke with God. I wasn't pleased. I accused him of wronging me and these creatures. I asked why. The calf came into this world long enough to breathe, opened its eyes to the sky and field – then died before it even had a chance to truly live.

I feel responsible, as though I could have done something. I hate myself for going to the doctor yesterday, rather than staying on the farm and possibly saving this calf. It is in times like this that I wish my mind didn't operate in such a visual way. I can see the entire scene crystal clear inside of me, every detail. I can't forget or run from it. Why, God? I don't understand why this happens. Aren't you watching over us? Do you care about the animals as I do, or am I completely insane?

The world lies to us and says it doesn't matter. I know it does. All life has value. The oldest female of the herd was standing watch over the dead. She wouldn't leave the field. The others came down to feed, but she refused to eat. Since when do cows refuse to eat grain? They sensed the death and tragedy of it just as I did, probably more so because she was of their own kind. Unlike pigs, who will drink the blood of their own slaughtered, cows seem to have a perception of death.

I can't help but cry inside of me. I am sad, for their loss, and mine. I see these creatures every day. I feed and care for them. Some of the people in my house could care less how I feel or what I am going through. They are more concerned with the rules than me as a person. Fairly typical of *the farm*.

David Burton

Thursday

I wake up before my alarm goes off and immediately my mind starts thinking about how *authority* works here on the farm, and the problems with it. I just want to sleep, but apparently, God has other plans. He shows me scriptures in my mind. A few things are laid out clearly for me to say to *leadership*, but I hesitate because more than likely they won't want to hear it. One *leader* in particular. I know I wouldn't if I were him, but I know that what God saying is true. The message is for me primarily, however, when I speak to *leadership* they will probably take it as an attack.

I find that some people want to hear from God, but only when it is convenient, and only when it delivers nice warm feelings; not when it is challenging what I believe. Especially when it is something that I believe about God.

What an amazing day. God showed up and revealed his presence in a powerful way. It started this morning during prayer. We were asked to do something called scripture prayer, where we read scripture back to God and communicate with him about it. I had opened the blinds and was watching the sunrise crest over the mountains. I opened my bible to a random page and read the first passage my eyes caught:

> "My soul waiteth for the Lord more than they that watch for the morning; I say, more than they that watch for the morning."

> Psalm 130:6

I thought that was fairly spectacular, but God wasn't finished with me yet. During the next class the teacher began to speak about 'waiting' on the Lord. How the Hebrew word for 'waiting' means to bind two objects together; entwining. He used the example of dental floss becoming interwoven with the anchor of a ship; we are the floss, God is the rope, and waiting is the process of becoming one.

The day continued into *worship*, where we gather together and sing to God. I felt his presence and tears fell from my eyes. In shock I pulled back, severing the connection. I realized what I had done and reached out for him again. He was there in a moment. There is give and take in this, an opening and closing, moving closer and drawing away – communication. It reminds me of the way the ocean moves.

I also tried something new: memorizing scripture while singing. It was amazing. I didn't even know I could do this, never mind the fact that I found it easier than forcing myself to remember. By now I was really impressed by what was happening to me, but God still wasn't finished speaking.

I went to work in the barn and I just kept singing. I was off key and I forgot the words, but the point is that I want to communicate. There is a quiet desperation inside of me that I am just now learning about. The sun shone brightly and I thanked him for the day. I have been missing the weather on the Island where I grew up: the bright sunny days, intense rain, and ocean storms. I guess God read my mind because as work was ending it began to rain and lightning flashed across the sky.

I ran outside. I have had two dreams about God showing up with the lightning since I've been here. I instantly knew deep inside of me that now was a chance to speak with him. I stood in the pouring rain and rather than calling, I tried waiting in worship. Hands spread to heaven, I begin singing. The wind swirled around me as the sky darkened. Flashes of lighting and the sound of thunder graced the sky above me. I felt relaxed, calm, at peace, and loved. No more world – for a moment it is just him and I.

Thankful, that's how I feel. He doesn't have to respond to me. The gift he has given is already precious to me, but he is God, and his ways are not my ways. As I sit down to break bread at supper, a rainbow appears outside of the dining hall windows. I walk outside. I am lifted to a new level of understanding and love for my saviour. A full arc rainbow shines brightly in the sky, both ends touching the land I live on. As if that wasn't enough, he adds a second faint bow above the first. I am truly captivated.

> "And the bow shall be in the cloud; and I will look upon it, that I may remember the everlasting covenant between God and every living creature of all flesh that is upon the earth."

Genesis 9:16

Friday

I just had sex; crystal clear. I couldn't stop. I didn't want to stop. Forgive me, Lord. I am incredibly weak in this area. I have a really difficult time seeing this as wrong, even though a part of me says it is. Am I doing evil with my sexual desire? Is my desire evil of itself? When I smoke crack in my dreams I wake up feeling guilty, but when I have sex in my dreams I don't feel the same conviction. I feel aroused and physically unsatisfied.

Please help bring clarity to this area of my life. Please teach me your ways, and keep the traditions of men far away from me. If it was a temptation sent by Satan, I have failed. Not only failed, but embraced the evil as good – which in my mind is far worse. Do you see why I need clarity in this situation?

Anyway, I am going to continue with my day, acknowledging that I have made a mistake, but not allowing it to drag me down or pull me under. I woke at five in the morning and thought that I needed to pray. Instead of praying I went back to sleep, and that's when I had the dream. So, I am seeing that I resisted God and fell into temptation.

I have hurt people by speaking against them, and being critical of their actions. I have been saying that God has made a mistake. I have been slicing up with my sword the people that God has chosen to place in my life. I repent, Lord, of character assassination. Please forgive me. It is heartbreaking for me to discover that my words and wounding the innocent, those that have laid their lives aside in order to help me, and carry the message of Jesus Christ.

It has been a day of revelation marked by emotional pain that has inspired me to change, and assured me that I won't forget the lesson. My eyes were closed for nearly the entire worship service and I've been crying since early this morning. I am tired; rest is coming. Thank you, Lord.

Saturday

My day starts well. My *house leader* sleeps in and doesn't wake us up. I show him love and grace. It's not even worth mentioning. He knows he has made a mistake. He has to leave and serve in another area of the farm, so I take over for him. I run our weekly group and soon find out that he has taken out his frustration on another member of the house. I am not impressed. I reassure the wounded man that he has done nothing wrong, and tell him that it is the *house leader's* problem, not his.

At breakfast, I talk to a friend. I usually come to him with my problems, but today I tell him that I have come through a hard couple of weeks, and I have risen to a new level. I have a sense of victory. Thirty seconds later, the *overseer* informs me that I have been *chored*, and must spend the next four hours working in the greenhouse. I tell him that the *chore* police can kiss my ass, and I'm not doing it.

Every weekend I spend a couple of hours in the barn. No one else works on the weekend. I am choked and livid, anger rages inside me. I got these *chores* for feeding the animals in the morning. One responsibility interfered with another and someone in *leadership* decided that I needed to be punished for it. I show this man grace and forgiveness over and over, but he continues to live by law and punishment. He has appointed himself as the rule sheriff and has handed out *chores* to several people in the house. Instead of extending love, grace, and forgiveness – he brings out the judge's gavel, expending justice as he sees fit from his bench.

He has completely missed the message of Jesus Christ: forgive, love, and show kindness. I have had many conflicts with the man and I am nearing the breaking point of my patience. I am constantly rising up to overlook their transgressions while they continuously hold mine against me.

So, I worked in the barn and then walked up to the greenhouse to work for several more hours. I wanted to murder the man who had *chored* me when I started. I considered slaughtering a cow (blood sacrifice to appease the rage within me) to cover his sin. I thought about breaking down his door and destroying his room. I planned all day in my mind how to verbally annihilate him tonight.

I'm not thinking about this anymore. I'm exhausted. I going to bed.

Sunday

Attacked by a demon again. I fall asleep, and walk down a sidewalk. I see something suspended in the air. I've seen this before, and I know it means that a spirit is there. I run toward it and kick beneath into the empty air. Too late I see someone to my left already captured. It's a trap. The second I make contact, I am spun around, hands bound behind my back, and taken captive. "I cast you out in the name of Jesus Christ," I scream. I am raging and scared at the same time. I say it again and wake up yelling the words into the darkness of my room.

I turn my light on and leave it on. I can't understand why this is happening. Even more disturbing is the fact that I got caught by it. This is not supposed to happen. I haven't spent years learning how to fight only to be taken prisoner by a simple confrontation such as this. What the hell is going on!?

I have been tired all day and lost the inspiration I once had. I need rest and time to meditate. That was taken from me this weekend, and I'm still upset.

This afternoon I fall asleep and dream about going to war. We load up a vehicle with soldiers and head into enemy territory. We are forced to stop for a moment, and when I turn around, everyone is taking a coffee break. I freak out and ask them what the hell they are doing. We are on our way to destroy an enemy refueling station, not going on a field trip.

Sometimes, my perspective of the farm is the same as the dream. For me it is war, for others it appears to be summer camp.

Monday

Struggle after struggle, trial upon trial, with temptation scattered throughout. I am so tired that I pass out on the cold concrete of the barn floor. I couldn't get up because my muscles are ridiculously sore from playing ball hockey this morning. I woke up exhausted and I am no less so now that I've worked all day.

Months of this with no end in sight unless I find somewhere else to live, and where is there for me to go? Nowhere, that's where. I may be sober but I'm still stuck. My options are very limited. I live in a room that can be taken away from me at any moment. If I don't follow the rules here on the farm they kick me out. My life is dependent upon obedience, but this place doesn't inspire obedience in me. I feel frustrated and full of bitterness. Honestly, I would probably feel better if I could sleep until I felt rested, prepared with the energy to face the day. I will probably just fall over and leave my body if I get over tired, or I will start acting like I am on speed: those are my options.

I don't have anything profound to say tonight.

Tuesday

I am falling apart. I don't think I can survive this. I wake up exhausted and my body aches. The first thought in my mind is that I don't have to do this. I just have to leave, but I am trapped. They won't let me use the phone to find somewhere else to go. They will force me to walk miles into town and I will end up in a homeless shelter.

I was tossing and turning all night long. I am unsatisfied, unhappy, and unimpressed. The first thing I hear upon waking is one person criticizing another – in the first five minutes of the day. This kind of attitude makes me sick. I have enough problems in my life, I don't want to hear that crap as soon as I wake up.

God, where are you in my daily life? I am losing my prayer time in the morning because of this schedule, and the fact that I can't rise earlier than I already am to pray because I'm so tired.

I need to write my sister, telling her about the shame I feel for the way I've treated her, and ask forgiveness – although I don't deserve it.

Interesting day. At the end of it I have come to the conclusion that I am being trained, this is my training ground, so don't leave when it gets difficult. Reach out to God, because he will provide what I need to continue, and I will rely on him.

Today I took the pigs to the slaughter house on the side of a mountain. They didn't want to leave their pen. I had to chase them out with a shovel. It ain't no easy thing fighting a pig when he doesn't want to go. They pack a lot of weight and they are low to the ground. After persuading them out of the pen, we boarded them into the trailer and unloaded them into the holding pen at the killing place. There were hundreds of pigs. I've never seen so many before in my life.

Apparently, this place receives all the animals for the grocery stores. They are killed and then shipped to a meat cutter for processing. In some senses, it was sad to see all these creatures in a cold, dark building, waiting for their death in the morning; but I've never really had a heart for pigs. You can kill one and the other will rush in to drink the blood of its fallen friend. They literally rush to the slaughter.

Anyway, it was good to get off the farm and see a part of the world I haven't seen before. It's nice to know there is a world outside of this place even though it doesn't appeal to me. I speak of the society. The natural landscape I love, but not the civilization that has destroyed the land. The snow covered mountains encased in cloud were spectacular to see. I am constantly captivated and amazed by the beauty of God's creation. He truly is an artist with heart – emotion and spirit imbued in each brush stroke.

Wednesday

I open a blue door and enter a house. I see that the house is clean, yet barren. There are several reading chairs in the front room and a fireplace, but the house is cold: there is no fire, neither has there been for quite some time. I brush dust off the seat of one of the chairs and place my book, open to a page, on the seat. I begin to clean the house.

I awake, and the day starts in an amazing way. I am filled with energy; prayer comes easily and swiftly. I am surprised, almost shocked at the sudden change in my perception, knowing that I had nothing to do with it. Later in the day I am tempted to sin and fall quickly. I can't seem to retain the dream in my mind and I embrace the sin of this world. After a false sense of security, I feel sick and quickly repent. I start thinking about scripture and come to rest on this:

> "The fear of the Lord is to hate evil: pride
> and arrogancy, and the evil way, and the
> forward mouth do I hate."

Proverbs 8:13

The illusion and deception that Satan has placed in my life is stripped away by the word of God; however, I have discovered that Satan's lies are still within me, waiting to be unearthed. When tempted to sin again in the same way, I find that it no longer holds any power over me. I am free, but I need to be vigilant.

I thank God that he can use all things to teach me, but I need to be careful not to return to the sin he has freed me from: it holds nothing but emptiness, sickness, and loneliness – it truly is separation from God.

I left the farm again today. This time to bring the cows to slaughter. I will miss them because they had such interesting personalities. In some sense, I feel guilty because they trust me and I loaded them up into a trailer destined for death. However, with death comes new life, so we went to pick up a new calf for the barn. Our new addition to the barn is healthy and strong.

I need to find someone who is willing to take on the responsibility of feeding the animals in the morning. I don't know if I can rise an hour early each day and maintain my studies. I barely have enough time and endurance to accomplish what I am already assigned, let alone adding more to it.

Thursday

Last night before I fell asleep I looked at the clock, it was ten to ten. I fell asleep, had a dream, awoke and went to the washroom. As I returned to my room, I casually glanced and the clock. It hadn't moved – it was the exact same time. I was very confused.

134

I fall asleep and dream of relapse all night long. I smoke crack and can't get high, I drink and can't get drunk. I wake up to my alarm going off at five in the morning. These people need to find someone else to feed the cows in the morning. Getting to leave the farm every four months to go to a slaughterhouse doesn't make up for losing the sleep every day, and losing my free time on the weekend. The weekends are precious; it's when I catch up on my sleep.

The more I sense the attitude of this place, the more I figure it is not for me. I am not a slave, and I didn't come here to work. I came here to learn about myself and God. I came to find sobriety and a place away from the world I hate. Although God has freed me, they use it as an opportunity to enslave me to the farm. I am pissed off. I am not about to replace one cruel taskmaster for another.

I also found out yesterday that they are going to remove another day of classes and replace it with a full day of *work program* (which is essentially unpaid forced labour). I won't let these people turn me into a slave in the name of God, all the while making it seem like they are doing me a favour. Have they lost their mind and all common sense, or do they think I don't have any?

Friday

I am sleep blind and exhausted. I can't believe I have to feed the cows. It's turning out to be a really good day. The sun is shining and there are no clouds in the sky. I had an awesome message to give in study this morning. God is speaking to me and I am listening. I am so incredibly happy that a few storm clouds that I have experienced lately are passing. The wind has started to blow in my life. If I can only ride this freedom like a wave heading for shore.

Sometimes I wake up angry and I want to take it out on the people around me, although it is no fault of theirs. I cry out to God and he gives me grace so that I can rise above my sinful nature, putting

David Burton

to death the old man and stepping out in faith. Jesus has given me this ability to live in the spirit, and when I am tempted to condemn the people for their actions or behaviours, I remember that God sent his son not to condemn the world, but to save it. I need to meet the people where they are rather than where I want them to be. The light that is in me is Christ, not myself: it is a precious gift, like that of eternal life given to me with salvation.

I need to set my mind and affections on the things above, stop getting caught in the small situations of life, and believe. Even though God loved me, I was the man who loved darkness rather than light. And though God has translated and forgiven me, I do not forget where I came from. Compassion, understanding, knowledge, wisdom, love, patience, kindness, acceptance, restoration, and forgiveness: these are the things I seek now, a few of the heavenly things Jesus speaks of. Thank you, God, that you care enough about me to teach me your ways.

This day has been amazing and the sun continues to shine. I feel blessed. Last night I was in prayer when the spirit started speaking to me, and I was a part of something that hasn't happened in years. I listened and wrote, interacting with a presence within me. I have been waiting for this, but did not expect it to occur this soon.

My entire perception of this place has changed. God has once again reached inside of me and done something I don't understand. I also heard the history of the farm from the resident pastor last night, and gained some insight into its spiritual development over the years. They have chosen to follow God ad refuse the evil of the world to enter its boundaries. Through prayer, fasting, and worship, the program has been designed; and it appears to have been led by the spirit.

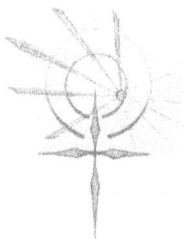

4 Months

Chapter FIVE

I wake up extremely tired, not enough sleep, but what I have will have to do because I have no time to spare. I have to get ready and prepare myself for Hastings. Lord, please guide me, I put my trust in you. Before I am even dressed, my *house leader* attacks me. I swear the man works for Satan. He just pretends that he is one of us. I feel sad that he has decided to play this game because he has lost the battle before it even begins. I attempt to rise above the conflict, but he pulls me down; so I give up, take all of my money and shove it in my pocket.

Screw these people, I'm out of here. I don't need this attitude on the morning when I am about to enter into battle with the enemy on the streets of a major city. God's spirit doesn't do this to people, Satan does. Enough said. Time will expose this man for what he is, so I don't need to.

Before I even leave the farm, Satan has reached out and tried to prevent me, or convert me, and I have acquiesced to his request. I take my contact lens container and a hoody – I'm not coming back. I empty my mind of everything I have ever known and place my trust in God. Either I will end this day with a crack pipe in my mouth, or he will intervene. I pray for divine intervention because I know I don't have the strength to make it through this.

When we arrive, we immediately hit the street in the beautiful sunshine. Hookers, needles, glass pipes, and insanity assault my eyes. Everywhere I turn I see the instruments of my own destruction. The first person I lay eyes on takes a pipe from his pocket, pushes it, and fires away. I avert my eyes. I can't watch this.

I start to walk down the street. A woman approaches us right away, taking each of our hands and bowing. She doesn't say a word. I don't understand what is happening. Does she see Christ inside of us?

The church opens, we walk inside, and I pick up a guitar. The world fades away and all is right between God and I. With the sound of the first chord, I am carried away to a place that I can't describe to you. I flow with the spirit and my fingertips sign words to God. Before I understand any of this, a microphone is placed in front of me, and for the first time in fifteen years, I amplify my voice to sing. I learn quickly the things that I have forgotten. I follow the lead player and learn songs on the fly. Soon, I am singing and chording songs that I've never heard before, and I know I am in the spirit. It just isn't possible without the presence of God.

I am grateful, but tinged with confusion. We just keep playing and there is nothing that I want more. I have lost myself in worship. I feel complete, at peace, at rest, comfortable, wanted, accepted, satisfied, fulfilled, loved, accomplished, teachable, new, and changed. Twenty years of love for the guitar poured out to God, and there is no end to the wellspring from which this living water flows. I am thirsty, and I drink deeply.

When it ends, I feel awkward, and as I sever the connection I begin to understand what Rand Al'Thor experienced when he released his hold on *Saidin*. Yet, unlike the source, I am left changed and lifted: a lasting effect. The peace remains within me and darkness does not return. I am standing in the truth and I am free.

Service has ended and I walk outside into the sun. I am ready to face myself. I start walking up the street and begin praying quietly. I don't know what God wants from me, so I continue walking and talking to him about what I see. I ask him to reveal a person that I need to speak with. Nothing arises and I soon understand that today the walk is about myself, and I am the one I need to speak with.

When we are about to leave, the thought crosses my mind that I could run from the people I am with, disappear into an alley, and hide until they are gone. I resist, and without even knowing it, I have made a decision. God has answered my prayer and intervened. The last thing I see as we turn off of Hastings is the same thing I see every time we come down here: the word 'Messiah' spray painted on a concrete retaining wall. I am the only one who sees it. Thank you, God.

I return to the farm and it all seems like an illusion, unreal. It is quiet and abandoned. No one walks the property and the silence is deafening. I watch two eagles soar in the air above me. I just stand and stare, exhausted and captivated by the grace of my saviour.

Sunday

I had the chance to cook breakfast for the farm today. My *house leader* tried to attack me again, but nothing is going to bring me down. Now I know who he is working for. One dream last assured me that he will be stripped of authority and revealed for what he truly is. I will stand in that assurance. I don't care how long it takes.

Meanwhile, after rising above the enemy I created a beautiful breakfast with the help of several others: buttered waffles topped with whipping cream and fruit salsa, scrambled eggs with cheddar and mozzarella cheese topped with diced tomato, and sausages. It truly was a masterpiece. The salsa had apple, orange, and pineapple with brown and white sugar mixed together. I am pleased. I love to cook, but it has been awhile since I could lead the kitchen and create something amazing. It is called culinary art for a reason. Creativity and imagination with a touch of love. And the *leaders* on *the farm* can't understand why I have a problem with submitting to the *authority* of someone who wants to serve rock hard waffles, burnt sausage, and destroyed eggs?

Just because this farm places someone in a position to lead, or a position of *authority*, it doesn't mean that they have an ounce of talent, ability, or concern for the people they are to lead. How am I supposed to accept or respect that? How am I supposed to acknowledge that system? To make it even worse they throw scripture around to support this corruption. They say we must submit to *authority* and all **authority** is established by God, so trust it. I'm sorry?

Authority is God given, and you don't have any. You can't make a cow the leader of this farm and expect people to obey. This seems like a far-fetched example, but it is exactly what these people are asking of me. They are setting up something they see as authority, but it is a man-made concept, not a God-ordained construct.

What a day. Someone wants to leave, and they are trying to blame me. Guess who? The person I dreamed about last night. It's the same as the dream. I don't even know what to say.

Monday

I awake to the light being turned on. I'm back in the dormitory again.

In ball hockey this morning, I became frustrated and lashed out. I hooked someone with my foot and tripped them deliberately. I was raging and walked out of the game. I wanted to break something, but God wanted to break me. In a single flash of light, he stripped the rage from my mind, showed me what I had done, and broke my heart. I collapsed crying, completely out of control. I could see the man I hurt falling to the ground: a friend, someone I like and care about.

These words might not make sense to you: I hurt the very person I came to save. I was overwhelmed with sorrow. I haven't acted this way since I was a child. It is exactly the way I treated my younger sister, and something I swore I would never do again. I can't believe I did this. It is malice, causing deliberate harm. It happened in a single moment. I didn't even think, I just acted.

It goes against everything I believe in and everything I've been taught. I switched into automatic mode on the ball hockey court today, and I am horrified. I didn't have a chance to intervene my decision making process. It is the same thing that used to happen when I smoked crack. I didn't want to use, but I would snap into automatic mode and something else took control. It sounds terrible, doesn't it? Fighters do it while training. They go through a series of moves so often that when the key happens in a fight, they don't think, they just react.

However, the weapon turned on the people it was designed to protect. Not good. I could not stop weeping. God tore me wide open and pulled something out of me. I have not cried so hard in my life. I couldn't hold on, or keep composure, or reign it in, or shut if off – it just came with force, power, and authority. I hated myself, and when someone suddenly spoke to me I was in shock, because I didn't even know they were there.

We talked for awhile, and then I apologized to the man I had tripped. He had no idea what was happening inside of me, and forgave me. The wound was in me, and the pain was great when I understood what I had done. My mind feels numb now. I don't think I can feel anything else today – I'm burned out.

I don't think anything else I write today is going to make any sense.

Tuesday

I see a wall of flames in front of me and several dragons beyond it. A man stands beside me with weapons in both hands. The master dragon stands in the center of the flames with the others surrounding it. There is a pathway that leads directly to the creature.

The man looks at me, and I see resolution in his eyes. I ask him not to go, but he says it must be done. As I scream for him to stay, he walks straight into the fire, and approaches to the master dragon. He stands beneath its head and raises his weapons upward.

The flames begin to consume him and I watch him collapse; as he falls, the weapon in his hands goes nuclear and burns the head of the creature into non-existence.

I awake. I am frustrated this morning. The powers that be have decided to move me to another room and my life is in complete disarray.

Wednesday

Something is coming, full force from the sky, an ancient evil presence. I am working in a space launch facility where the people have been deceived by Satan. A shuttle is being launched to meet this coming entity, but people start freaking out because the launch isn't authorized.

A meeting is called to discuss what is happening; I attend. Someone who is deceived stands at the front and tries to give an explanation.

"Stop," I cry out from the back of the room. I walk to the front of the room and continue speaking. "An angel, from Revelation; this is what is coming." The lights go out and the auditorium plunges into darkness.

"Pray!" I scream. "Everyone must pray." I can hear people who professed to be Christian mocking me at the back of the room and many people are fleeing.

"You pretend to be something you're not; and when the time comes, you are nothing – you are the enemy."

I awake exhausted, and nothing is making sense to me. I've finished moving and my new *house leader* does things completely different than the last one. I am so tired of all this: what is acceptable in one house is unacceptable in another. Every person in this so-called *authority* is unique and I am supposed to submit to them all, without question. If I do I will ultimately be drawn into a confrontation, and when that conflict is brought to *leadership*, I will be told that I am in the wrong. They all tow the company line.

This nonsensical authority, where each person makes their own rules and runs the house like a dictatorship, has brought me to a place of losing all control. I can't take it anymore. If someone freaks out on me, I will send it right back at them (multiplied and amplified). If I am slighted, I will attack. I've held back my whole life, now I go from zero to freakshow in three seconds.

All I want to go is go back to bed, but every time I turn around there is something else that I have forgotten to do. There is no time here to do anything I enjoy, for example: drawing. I've managed to acquire some blank loose leaf paper, and a couple of pencils. I know the image I want to create – the vision from last night. I don't know how it will render on paper, but I am excited to find out.

Thursday

I am walking down a very dark path with a girl, through a university. I am not scared, but she is afraid. We pass through the darkness and emerge into the light, standing in front of a bookstore. We enter and she asks for directions; as we come out I turn on my flashlight to light the path.

Around the first bend of the path the moonlight is so bright that we don't need the flashlight anymore. There is a large house in the distance, and I assume that is where we are going. There are flowers on both sides of us.

"What's that smell?" she asks.

"Honeysuckles," I reply. We arrive and go to sleep, waking to someone cooking us breakfast.

I wake up to someone knocking on my door, and I am disappointed. I can't believe the night is over so soon. It's just not enough sleep. I am going to fall asleep wherever I can today: class, group, breakfast – I don't care. I need rest.

It is amusing to note that I was not tired enough to fall asleep. I am receiving from the spirit what I need to carry me through the day. A *leader* asked me to explain my dreams, and I will do it just this once.

The dark path is my life, the girl is my spirit (soul), the light is a beacon (Jesus), the bookstore is the bible, and the flashlight is *the word*. Have I lost you yet? The *word* leads me to the moonlight, which is God, and the house is a place in heaven.

I never write the interpretation because it changes. My written dreams are prophecy and can be understood on various levels. Most of the dreams I have are self-explanatory, and I don't want to corrupt the image I am given with a human explanation. This particular dream gives me hope and a sense of love. There is only one thing that disturbs me, and I left it out for a reason: it is not the focus of the dream, only a warning, and personal.

A man followed us nearly the whole way, hovering near us. I could feel his presence, but I don't know if she could. I ignored him, refusing to acknowledge his existence, and eventually he was gone. The man represents Satan, and he plagues my every move.

These dreams are usually specifically coded for me, made up of parables, metaphors, and symbolism – at other times, straight truth, and direct communication. Sometimes, I am tempted and fail; sometimes, I overcome in ways that are not humanly possible. I don't hand out interpretations or explanations because I don't think the information is common knowledge, nor is it supposed to be. I don't think people are prepared for the message I carry within me. They can barely deal with a physical world, let alone the possibility of existing in a spiritual one. I am extremely grateful for these dreams. I have paid, and would pay, almost anything for them. In them I find understanding, strength, and hope.

This week has been intense. When I made an offhand comment to someone about something I had seen in a dream, the person listening started speaking with, "I don't believe – ," and that is the problem. I don't even know if they have the ability to believe. God is teaching me and I don't think I am supposed to tell other people about it yet. That's why I feel alone. Sometimes, in spite of this, I have tried to communicate, but even if they want to understand – they can't.

One author has an interesting opinion that I am beginning to understand: only a prophet can read the writing of a prophet; the words speak images.

Friday

Today has been difficult. I felt angry at God because of the dream, and I found it hard to pray among other people. I felt ashamed of myself and couldn't even look at a *leader* in the eye. I had just relapsed in the dream. I tried to explain it to him. He kind of understood, but not really. He prayed for me and it helped because I had the impression that he cared. He didn't judge me.

Would he see me the same way if I had done it in the physical rather than the spiritual? There is no difference between the two except that I woke up in my bed rather than the street. People who say *it was just a dream* can't relate, even though I appreciate their kindness. To make matters worse, a person on the farm came to talk to me about using crack cocaine. He shares his history and past experiences with the drug. There is always a strange look in his eye when he speaks of it, and we have had these conversations for several days now. I think he wants to *use*, and by the end of the day, so did I.

Every day he comes to visit me, we start conversing, and I have to run to the bathroom to take a crap. Just mentioning it triggers off a physical response in my body. I have welcomed these conversations because I want to overcome the urge. I don't want to be enslaved to something I don't do anymore. I can't go through my life running for the closest washroom every time the drug is mentioned, referenced, or thought of.

However, I believe this is extremely dangerous, and I started crying while praying to God after he left. I told God how I felt about the loss I am experiencing. I poured out my heart to him: the emptiness and aloneness I feel now that crack cocaine is gone from my life. He may not have been pleased to hear such honesty, but he knows everything about me so it couldn't have been a surprise. It may not have been to him, but it was for me. I didn't know how I felt about it until today.

I thought I was past this, over this, and beyond temptation. I was shocked and bewildered to have this venomous poison rise up out of my heart. How much damage have I done to myself?

Crack had become my lover.

She was always there for me. When in pain I ran to her for relief, when in sorrow I came to her for comfort, when hurt she consoled me. She aroused me, removed the anger from inside me, and whispered words to my spirit. I desperately needed her. I would be sick without her. We were bonded together. I have stolen for her, abandoned my family, forsaken my life, lost my hope – all to pursue her.

Now, I have walked away from her, and whether or not I want to acknowledge it, the truth is that I am heartbroken and grieving for the loss of our relationship. She was my companion, friend, and lover. The part of me that she resided in is empty and barren.

I told God that I love him, but sometimes want to smoke crack cocaine. I asked how this is possible. He told me that I don't understand love. Sounds true to me because I don't know how I could love someone so much and still want to get high. Isn't it a contradiction? Why are they in such opposition to each other, and how have I become caught between these two?

The day is over and I believe I have come through the storm by the grace of God. He gives me the power to continue, and although Satan attempts to hinder me, I will not allow him access to my life.

Saturday

Our house prepared breakfast for the farm this morning and it was beautiful, a stunning success that expresses our love for the people, and beyond this – for God. Just before we finish I find out that I have been *chored* again, and I am the only one. Out of thirty men, I stand in alone. I suppose I could rejoice that God has singled me out, but *leadership's* expression of love feels like rejection to me.

I freak out, losing control of my anger, and try to figure out what the hell is going on. I search for a *leader* to explain, and he starts rambling on about 'laying everything down' (whatever that means). I can't handle it anymore, lock myself in the washroom, fall to my knees, and cry. I cry until my eyes catch fire and light pours out of them. For the life of me I can't understand why people can't see **ME**. I am completely heartbroken.

"Rejoice evermore," is what I read last night before falling asleep, written by a man who was beaten, stoned, and rejected for preaching about Jesus Christ. How, Lord? How do I love someone who hates me? Please, God, teach me to turn the sword white.

Sunday

I am dreaming on the female cat in the barn. She comes to greet me in the morning, but she is smaller, and I know she has given birth. I turn to my side and see several small kittens bouncing toward me.

I awake.

I walk to the barn, and she is waiting for me, just like the dream. She has given birth and hidden the kittens somewhere in the hay. I am touched by the quiet accuracy of the vision. I know what I am, and I know the gift I have been given.

I read my journal last night, and it wasn't as exciting as I thought it would be. The dreams come whether I am *using* or not, so what is the point of all this discipline? As if I could earn salvation by somehow making myself good. I can't – I know it. What am I doing here? What difference will it make in my life? Is something supposed to happen? Some dreams become reality as soon as I wake, others take time to manifest. I suppose the world is calling to me again, and I am losing what I once saw in this place.

I accept some things, and reject others. My patience for people is fading, and to bring the situation to a head, I have finally caught a sickness. My breathing was raspy all night, as though something is inside my lungs. It's probably fluid. Either God is, or he isn't; either we are healed, or we aren't. I don't understand this mixed philosophy of being somewhere in between. Have I completely blinded myself with religion? Am I trying to make sense of something completely beyond the realm of my intellect?

Monday

I am sick. I have an infection in my lungs, sinuses, and throat. I spent the whole night tossing and turning, having difficulty breathing and sleeping. I want to sleep, and if this gets worse, go to a doctor for antibiotics.

The farm doesn't believe in sickness. It goes against their doctrine. We are not supposed to get sick. If we do, it is because of our lack of belief. They claim that we speak our sickness into existence by agreeing with the enemy's lie. So when anyone has a physical injury, they speak healing over them. I think they are all living in denial.

If someone says, 'you are healed,' I'm going to punch them in the face. I am even sicker now then this morning. I am sitting her with a blanket wrapped around me in front of the fire. My lungs are worse. I have been coughing all day and now I have a fever. I feel like I am going to pass out, working all day was a mistake. I feel like I've gone on a crack binge. I need to recover.

I am glad I have a place to rest rather than being on the street. I am thankful that I have a room to sleep in, and people who care about me in my life. I know have conflict on the farm, but show me a family that doesn't fight with each other. We must continue to press forward, moving toward our common goal. In ball hockey this morning I tried to make this point. For the sake of unity during the game all differences are set aside. Our small conflicts with each other must not interfere with what we are attempting. We must move together, as a unit, in order to fight this war.

Where has this understanding come from, and how am I able to bring the power of it? Not from myself. God did this. He showed me. He powered me. It feels awkward and uncomfortable to exist in this new state of unresolved conflict. I love you, Lord. Please be patient with me because I have been slow to learn many things.

Tuesday

I wake up very sick. I dream of a girl I loved all throughout my school life. She returns to my life and loves me even though I am a drug addict. When I wake up I feel empty, knowing the dream is past and I have returned to a life where I am alone. I don't want to be here anymore. Nothing is happening, and now I am sick.

All this talk of God's healing power and I am burning up with fever, lungs aching, lost voice, infected sinuses, and sore throat. Sure, God has healing power, but it is not being displayed in my life right now. I asked *leadership* if I could go back to sleep for one hour, and just when I fell asleep, they woke me up and dragged me out of bed. I ask for medication and plead with them to allow me sleep for another hour. They acquiesce, I return to sleep, and just when I fall asleep – they wake me up and drag me out of bed. I want to fight and scream, but I am exhausted, my body is drained, and I can't find the energy to resist.

I could he healing in my bed, but instead I am in class listening to how God is my healer. Great! God is my healer, so, I SHOULD

GO TO BED SO HE CAN DO HIS WORK. This infection that I have in my lungs killed a calf in the barn last night. His lungs filled with fluid, he couldn't breathe, and he died. The second calf in just as many days. I am starting to think that this placed is cursed in some ways. We interfere in the natural ways of life and expect everything to be okay. Well, it's not.

The calf was so happy and full of life less than a week ago. Now he is a corpse. What the fuck happened? Why is God not helping us? He was a strong calf, well built, and full of fire for life. He had a good spirit. Now he is dead only a few days later. I feel angry and disappointed, and I get the impression that no one really cares. It's just a cow, so, whatever. Well, that calf was entrusted into my care and he did not survive. I can't help but feel miserable, and that his death is a reflection of my character or actions. In my eyes, I have failed yet again, and my failure has cost an innocent creature its life.

Wednesday

I started praying while I was asleep (what I consider being in the spirit). I transitioned into half consciousness and continued praying aloud. It was a very strange experience. I am participating in something I don't understand. My spirit began praying, and I entered into it. Has this been happening for awhile?

I am still sick, but I think I am getting better. The fever has left, all that remains is fluid filled sinuses, infected lungs, and I've lost my voice. I don't even think this writing is making sense. My mind and body are exhausted. Hopefully, class this evening will fly by and I will be back under the covers of my bed before I know it. It's almost over. Another half an hour and I am free.

I sent away for replacement identification today. I have been delaying the process because I don't know how having access to my bank account will affect me. It's only a few hundred dollars, not even the equivalent of a single paycheque, but to me it screams crack cocaine: a single day where nothing matters except pursuing the high, and the silence that comes with it – peace at the expense of my freedom.

It seems natural to use drugs, and unnatural to abstain. Pornography seems right and pleasurable, abstinence and celibacy is a perversion. What's right is wrong, and what's wrong is right. I dream about getting high all the time. What's the difference if I act it out? Jesus said, to lust after a woman is to have sex with her, so really I've already committed the sin. Some people may say that I am creating justifications and excuses for a relapse, but I am going insane trying to wrap my mind around this Christian philosophy. By just thinking about the sin, I have committed it? So, the thought police are going to be breaking down my door any day now, and dragging me off to prison for all the sins I haven't done?

I feel normal when I am high, I feel crazy when I am sober. I even considered taking up smoking again, to see if it will alleviate this weirdness inside of me. Why would I walk back into slavery willingly? Why would I pick up a cigarette after being free from it for the first time in my life? What the hell is wrong with me? Sometimes I think, what is wrong with just one or two days of *using*? I'll *use* until I am satisfied, and then get sober again. I think about these things, even though acting on them means staying on the street to get high, and eventually ending up right back in the exact same situation I am in now, because I can't do this alone.

Perhaps it is true that I have become the student of two masters, and I think one of them is laughing at me.

Thursday

The whole day has gone downhill, a never-ending stream of problems, which end with me sitting in the counsellor's office. I don't want to talk about it. I have lost so much in my life that I want to cry for hours.

I don't want to be in class. I am sick, and I need to be in my bed resting so that I can heal. How am I supposed to heal with my eyes open? I feel more and more misunderstood as time goes on. I thought I might have a chance here, but I don't think it's going to happen. I could be wrong. I have been before. I am kind of screwed up right now. It's Easter, and when I wake up in the morning it will be the symbolic anniversary of the death of Jesus Christ.

I usually get high to deal with these special occasions. I don't take any pleasure in remembering the pain and agony of his crucifixion. As he was tortured, I torture myself. He suffered, so I suffer. Did I ever tell you about the dream I had? The one where I was kneeling in the sand while darkness fell in the height of the day? The gospel speaks of such a day, but how many have seen it, or felt the power of that darkness descending? How do I say this without saying it? I am not going to explain. I know what happened, and I don't think I will ever forget – how could I?

Friday

My daughter and I are standing on a bridge that we have just crossed over, and a creature is pursuing. I am a creature changed, *something I will not explain here.*

"I don't know if the power has passed to you," she screams as I turn and run toward the oncoming evil. I meet it head on in battle, and I am assured of victory. It will not touch the one I love, even if it means sacrificing my life.

I awake with these images playing across my eyes, and feelings risen within me that have no place in this mundane world. My spirit cries out against the return. It is unnatural to return to this body of death. Once again, I have been imprisoned in my flesh until I can close my eyes once more and take flight.

This morning I went to Fort Langley to walk around the town, in the honour of Jesus; they called it the stations of the cross. At each station, a different church group spoke about Jesus and sang a song of worship. For the crucifixion, we stood in a graveyard. Some people cried, but many sang. We ended the procession in a church where a pastor spoke, and then we gathered for coffee and socializing.

I talked with a woman who sat beside me, and even though I was encouraged by the conversation, I felt embarrassed when I told her where I live, and how I have struggled with addiction for many years. She didn't judge or condemn me, as I thought she would. I was tempted to lie se asked about my life, but I spoke the truth, and it set me free.

The sun was shining brightly in the sky, and felt complete. The world doesn't affect me as it once did because something inside of me has changed. Thank you, God.

Returning to the farm, the kitchen served up steak and omelets. Fantastic. I am so impressed. This is surely one of the best days I have had in months, especially after the painful days of negative, pessimistic, and oppressive lines of thought that have consumed me for several weeks. Perhaps the tide is changing, the seas shifting. I can't see, or say what it is, but I feel the power of something coming. It excites and terrifies me at the same time, a paradox.

During the walk, I saw a girl that I love and dream about all the time. It wasn't her exactly, but she looked so similar that I almost wrapped my arms around her when she came to stand beside me. I felt like I knew her – completely. It was strange to me that we didn't come together in mind, body, and spirit.

Saturday

I have awakened changed. I have had what they call a paradigm shift, and it has altered how I see people. These people that I live with have become my family. I have grown closer to them than my family of origin. They know more about me than the family I grew up with. I have found acceptance and understanding here. I share my emotions (good and bad) without rejection, we work together, pray together, and share in each other's pain or triumph, depending on the day. Sometimes I even see the spirit awaken in their eyes. I suppose the shift was inevitable if you look at the situation. It is, however, still a shock to actually have it happen.

At the end of the day, I am undecided as to whether this is a good thing or not. God gave me my family, and I don't know if he intended for me to abandon it.

Last night I was dreaming of a house. An alien presence came in and attacked me, trying to hold me down. I fought, and awoke screaming, "Go back to hell you piece of shit!" I shook the whole house with my voice. I knew it was loud the moment I finished screaming the words. I felt at peace though. I stood against evil, and felt the assurance of God.

I returned to sleep, and many other dreams came. Satan came, speaking to me with many voices, all whispering, evil things that I have blocked out and forgotten.

Sunday

I come to, wandering the streets of a distant city. The landscape is barren; buildings rise out of the dry ground. I don't know where I am supposed to go, or what I am supposed to do. I am lost. I see several people that are familiar to me, but I don't know where from. I walk with them toward a restaurant where many are meeting for dinner. When we draw closer several men from a foreign country pass by us; their conversation is strange and my attention is fixed on them.

They are talking about our clothes, how they do not fit properly [are not right for us, are lacking: poor]. I want to talk to them, but I don't know how to begin. I have the impression that these are important people where they come from. Finally, one man turns and addresses me. His purple shirt has what appears to be a dancing flame on it and the colors change as I watch it, the material is shimmering. I don't know if I can translate this:

"[Who are you? / What are you? / Where are you from?]"

David Burton

I reply with,

"[I am a Christian / one who knows Christ / of God / harmless / lost in this world / waiting for directions.]"

It is not speech vocally as a human would understand it; impression, projection, thoughts and verbal sound are all wrapped into a single sentence. He seems pleased, almost indifferent, and he is not threatened by my presence.

"[Where are you from? What race are you? Sudan, the Middle East, Egyptian?]" I ask quickly as I turn away. He has a look of shock and surprise as he quietly turns his head without replying.

As soon as the contact is broken I am standing in front of a large gate that opens to either side, doors sliding. Guards stand beside it and several people emerge from expensive vehicles. I see the main figure climb [crawl] out of a white transport, but he is veiled in a black darkness. My mind refuses to see this figure, but he is aware of my gaze. I think he is shielding. I don't know why.

"He must be a prince," I say as I wake. "Of this world," I finish quietly in my mind.

I awake, and walk through this earth, wondering what the hell is happening to me.

I've just written a song, the first in many years. It came unexpectedly, appearing in my fingertips as though they were guided by an unseen force. I don't know how this happens: it is spiritual. Today could only end in this way. It's Easter (the symbolic anniversary of Jesus Christ rising from the grave, overcoming death). Writing this song is a sign to me that I am rising. It has been a very long time sing I put pen to paper, words to chords, in order to create music. It can't be forced. I felt like I was composing with someone, and the lights in my room kept flashing as we wrote.

Monday

The sun is shining brightly outside of my window, and I think today is going to be a good day. It is a day off for us here on the farm, the first in a very long time.

The day was slow and uneventful. It is hard to find anything to write about. I was awake early, and went for a walk up the mountain in the morning sun. I felt rested and peaceful, until my mind turned to the politics of this place. For a moment this morning, I had my monastery, but it was shattered by the reality of my situation. I am losing part of my time with God, and I am getting caught up in the ways of this place. It is funny how something that is supposed to be all about Jesus, can be so far away from him. He said it himself: they honour me with their lips, but their hearts are far from me. Most people here don't even know they are doing it, but they mock the miracles Jesus did, expressing and confirming their ignorance.

Tuesday

I am so angry right now that my anger has erased the dreams. I hate this. A couple of people in my house decided to get up early and have a shower, banging around in the washroom, and waking me up. Fucking inconsiderate assholes. I want to scream. My room is right beside the washroom. I was wearing earplugs, but the people were so loud that they still woke me.

This day has been terrible so far. The class material was borderline propaganda, and the discussion afterwards was one sided. I don't want this for my life. I don't want to be a slave that must do as he is told, and not think for oneself.

The new people on the farm are driving me crazy. I can't believe the crap they are pulling, and it's only their second day. One guy goes to the river for a swim yesterday, and today he is so sick that he sleeps the day away? Give me a break! Another guy seems to think that he knows a lot, and is trying to bless others with his knowledge and opinions. Are you kidding me!? You've been here two days and you think you have something to offer? How about this – shut up and listen. I just love watching guys come in so full of themselves, arms raised, screaming Hallelujah, saying all the right words, learning the lingo of Christian slang, thinking they're something – then they are gone, walking down the driveway or getting a ride to the shelter, so that they can return to their addiction. Yet these are the people that love to try correct, convert, or guide me – as if they could.

If it wasn't such a sad and pathetic attempt at control, I might be laughing. What wisdom do they have to offer me? None. What example do they set for me? None. I have been through so much in the last four months that it makes my head spin when I think about it. God has given me several gifts in that time: freedom from tobacco, alcohol, and cocaine; restoration with my family; the ability to sing and worship, visions (prophecy, dreams); relationship with other Christian men; and, strange encounters with some sort of manifestation of his presence.

Most of these came through prayer discipline, reading *the word*, continuing when I felt like walking away, conflict, anger, hours of conversation, reaching out to God and man in desperation, hours of teaching and counselling, perseverance, patience, attempting love, and repeated failure. Not to mention the literal and metaphorical battles with demonic forces that stand against me in opposition to what I am trying to accomplish.

And what do I know? Nothing. Sometimes I tell God: I think I am ready to start now, but I'm still not completely sure. God exists whether I believe in him or not. I am transforming, whether or not you believe is of no importance to me. My belief is not in question here; my belief in the church is.

Wednesday

I live with a couple of inconsiderate jerks, who consistently wake me up by banging around in the washroom, as though they lived by themselves. I confronted them yesterday, and they both basically responded with: Fuck you, I will do what I want, and I don't care how it affects you.

As I said, I am awakened to a crashing sound in the washroom, but at first I think it is the washer and dryer. When I get out of bed to turn of the machines, I instead find the same two assholes from yesterday.

We begin our morning study, but I'm told to be silent when I begin to share, as though my opinion is valid. Everyone else throws in their two cents, but I am censored. I leave the study, walk to our *morning prayer* group. We gather at six in the morning, every morning, to spend time in prayer. It is corporate prayer, guided by certain topics, and we are free to pray as we feel lead as long as we pray out loud. As I am walking around the room, prayer aloud, a new resident tells me to stop praying because it is offensive to him. I am shocked and confused. If he was praying, as he should be right now, he wouldn't hear my prayer at all. Besides, I am talking to God, not him.

Before prayer ends, I am pulled into the office by *leadership* and yelled at. It is a strange because I've done nothing to have this vocal tired thrown in my face. I try to console the man, but he is really losing it, and I am the focus of his rage for some reason. I am the counsellor and he is the client, as I try to get to core issue of his problem. I won't repeat what he said, but it was very critical, condemning, and judgmental.

In spite of everything, there is a peace that is residing inside of me, and it can't be broken, overwhelmed, or stolen from me.

Thursday

David Burton

I see stars in space, and then several figures walking out of the fires of hell. I quickly realize that this is demonic, and close my mind.

I awake early in the morning, and can't return to sleep. A voice within me asks, "Why didn't you rise when I called you, and record the first vision I gave you?" I wanted to sleep. It was so vivid that I thought I could retain it, even if I went back to sleep. This is not acceptable. If I have to get up and write, then I HAVE TO GET UP AND WRITE.

I lift my hands to God, and call the lightning. A storm appears out of nowhere, and the rain falls in a fury. I enter into a conversation with God that other people really don't understand. Near the end of the storm, I am standing outside, praying. A *leader* sees me through the window, and decides to come outside and confront me on my blatant violation of the rules – being alone. No one is allowed to go anywhere alone, not even to step outside. I ignore his speech, turn my back on him, and face the sky. He walks away, returning to the shelter of the dining hall. I stand alone in the rain.

"Only here would someone say this to me," I yell in frustration and disappointment. The sky responds with fork lightning, and the sound of thunder crashing all around me. These people know nothing about me. I am a complete stranger to them. They profess to have the same faith as I, but I am an outcast among them. They want me to be like the rest of them, lose my independent ways, forget what I know, and embrace their teaching. Not going to happen.

Whether they choose to acknowledge it or not, I have been taught by God, and he is still teaching me. Why would I turn away from the source to embrace a misconception? I will accept help from men, but I will never choose man's ways over God's.

> "It is better to trust in the Lord than to put
> confidence in man."

> Psalm 118:8

I have not yet wrapped my head around what has happened today. I have witnessed the awesome power of God unleased, and I know this is his love for me. I listen to people here on the farm mock the power of God. I used to feel angry, but now all I feel is sadness for them.

An elder taught the class tonight. It is the class that appeals to me the most because he is willing to share with me what he has learned in a lifetime. His experience and knowledge is a storehouse of wealth. When people show disrespect or boredom in his class, I am offended. I value this man and the time that he sacrifices in order to be with us is of great worth. Why can't other people see this simple truth?

Tonight he spoke about his personal history, and his childhood growing up on a farm. This specifically is an intriguing and important topic of conversation. People today have no concept of how much this world we live in has changed in a single lifespan. In one generation, a way of life lived for thousands of years is gone. It is significant, and I don't think anyone is paying attention. Society as we know it today can be quickly and easily destroyed. Many will die because we no longer know how to provide for ourselves. We purchase everything we need. Is anyone paying attention? The knowledge that we need to survive will die with this man, standing at the front of the class. Understand?

Many people in the classroom just don't care. They can't sit still, there is a steady stream of people getting up, walking around, and talking at the back of the room. Some of them are outright mocking him from their seats. I am embarrassed by these people, and ashamed to be counted among them. More than anything, it is a sadness at what could be, but isn't.

Friday

God has a sense of humour, and today he showed it to me. The torrential downpour of yesterday's storm created a flash flood that washed out the gravel along the sides of the driveway. It deposited the sand and gravel on the road further down the hill. Two of us were given the privilege of cleaning up the mess. We shoveled two truckloads of gravel, and put it back where it belongs.

Water is a powerful force. It completely rearranged the hillside, carving out a bank, and undermining the asphalt of the driveway. We finished by sweeping the sand off the road. The sun was shining brightly and I couldn't help but be amused. A furious love was unleashed in the sky yesterday, and its message is still resounding.

While we were working, I talked to my companion about my life on the Island – where I grew up. I miss the ocean, forest, and mountains in the distance. I am yearning for my home. The only home I have ever truly known. The Island in ingrained within me, and without it I feel incomplete. It is beautiful here in its own way, but nothing compares to the sanctuary of my home.

Saturday

I am with a girl. We sit across from each other, a table between us; I notice that she has a dark figure beside her, but he is obscured from direct view. It could only be one, the dark one.

"We need to pray," I say. "He is the answer; he can help us; he can provide. He is God." I close my eyes and pray. I feel filled, complete, at peace, secure and protected. I open my eyes and motion for her to pray.

She starts to pray, but she twists her words into a mockery of God and I catch on to the fact that she is making fun of the Lord. She glances at the person beside her, smiles and laughs. They conspire.

"You don't believe in God?" I ask, shocked and confused. "How is this possible? You need to turn to him and pray; otherwise your life is going to get worse." I project to her what is coming in her life, but she does not receive it.

I awake.

I return to Hastings. I am standing on the street outside of the church. I am surrounded by people buying, selling, and smoking crack cocaine. I glance to my left in time to see a man inhaling deeply from a pipe. Ahead of me police lights flash red, white, and blue. People line the street, standing against the walls, sitting on cardboard wrapped in blankets, and wandering in a hopeless enslavement. Can't sense joy, peace, faith, or hope in anyone. The darkness has consumed the people. I start praying quietly because I don't know what else to do. Lord, I need guidance. Show me what your will is for this place.

I walk down the street, past the sickness, and enter the church. I help setup the stage, and tune the guitar I will be playing. The only way through this is worship. It will transform me. I reach for the spirit. I sing to God, for God, about God, and I pray the people hear. Let the sound spill out the doors of the church and be heard in the street. The church doors remain open as we play. People come, and before I realize it, the church is full.

Some come and go, walking in and out, unsure if this is the place for them. I can only pray that God will reach them. The message that is spoken talks about deception. I don't completely understand until I am standing outside after the service, watching a man sell crack cocaine in front of the church doors. He is deceived by the enemy, and enslaved to the drug.

I was enslaved, the same as he; now I am free. Jesus Christ has rescued me, and the evil I once embraced now looks like a lie. It is nothing compared to the awesome power of God.

Sunday

I couldn't turn off the music when I arrived home last night. It was playing inside my head, words floating around endlessly. I prayed, wrote, read scripture, and asked God to stop the merry-go-round. I spoke to the fear I had last night and told it to leave. I cast out the shadows that were dancing in my room, and told them they have no place in my life. I invited the spirit of love, peace, and

David Burton

sound mind to come and rest within me. I turned off my light and walked into the darkness.

I found it difficult to sleep. I don't understand it. My body refused to enter into rest. I had a really hard time sleeping in past five in the morning. I have done something to myself unawares. I'm not sure exactly what it is. Perhaps being on the street yesterday set something off inside me.

Now I am awake, showered, dressed, and ready to go to the next performance: the homeless shelter from which I came. Although the farm sends people there every week, I have refused to go because it carries with it many memories of failure, depression, and hopelessness. The place itself represents failure to me, because every time I relapsed and was kicked out of a recovery house or treatment center, I ended up there. At the end of a binge, after not eating or sleeping for several days, I would finally arrive and seek shelter: broke, alone, and hurting from the drug use.

Today, we are the worship band for the morning church service. Yesterday, three of us got together and practiced our song set, but to my frustration, two of the other musicians decided to change keys without informing me, right before we began. Although I am sitting right beside them on the stage, they don't tell me of the changes, as though I don't even exist. What was the point of practicing one way, and then changing it at the last moment? And what's with not telling me? I feel like a fool. I am rejected. Some cruel joke has just been played on me, and it stings.

Twice they change keys without telling me, and I am left on stage, just holding my guitar and looking like an idiot. All they had to do was take a moment and tell me the chord sequence for the alternate key, but they don't. Yesterday, we all practiced without a capo. Today, they both bring one. Of course, they fail to mention it, and I don't have one.

One of the players thinks he's a superstar, alters his strumming pattern, and messes up the timing. Yes, it's all great when you are playing alone, but not in a group. It is distracting and confusing for everyone else. He is making it quite clear that he would rather be alone, and center stage.

What's the point of practicing plays, if come game day, you run plays that no one else knows? I am left behind, and I feel the exact same way as I did in high school, always trying to gain acceptance, but never fitting in. I eventually turned to the drug addicts for acceptance and companionship because the never rejected or excluded me.

All these musicians had to do was acknowledge my existence, and give me a few simple directions. Instead, they overlook me, and I feel the sting of their willful act. It's not like they just forgot I was there. It shows me where I stand in their eyes, and it's just another example that I am not good enough for them. They talk a good game of love, but their actions speak the truth.

Monday

I awake and face the day. "Humans can't comprehend, understand, or fathom the unconditional love of God, because everything in their life is conditional." This epiphany is the result of a conversation I had with God in prayer the other night. I confessed how I have seen him as a punishing God, among other misconceptions. I thought in times past that he walked away from me, or turned away his eyes, and closed his ears to my cry. I come in repentance, and I have received his answer.

Today has been alright. Ball hockey was exciting, and the only tragedy is that one person raged on a leader (and was sent back to the intake house as a punishment). He was demoted. Another person lost his wife, and is facing deportation, which will result in his murder by gang members. Not that bad of a day, I suppose. Is it difficult to understand why I don't write about the problems facing men who live on this farm? From depression to depression, failure to failure, and tragedy to tragedy. Where are the success stories? Oh. How about the people who return here over and over again?

I saw the cats today. The male and female together. They have become one. It's obvious that they love each other. God has created something beautiful here in this world. It's too bad that humanity would rather pave it and build a shopping center, high-rise, or housing complex. People spread like cancer. Technology has just allowed them to accomplish their destruction a little faster.

Whatever. Enough of this. Let's talk about something else for awhile. The trees have green leaves of them, and the flowers are beginning to blossom. Beautiful.

Tuesday

Because of the ridiculous schedule here I have not written this morning, and have forgotten the dreams of last night. I am exhausted, with no rest in sight. So tired that I am making spelling mistakes in the first sentence of the day. I am growing weary of this place. I never should have thrown away my identification. I hated myself, and decided I no longer wanted to be who I am, so I tossed my wallet into a ditch. Sheer stupidity. As if that single action could change a lifetime of behaviour patterns. It was a futile gesture.

I am tired of the teaching here that was created by a man. Clearly a human interpretation of scripture, projected onto my life, as though they knew what they were talking about. It's like these people think I can't read or reason for myself, as though my ears are deaf to the voice of God. There are some things here that I am starting to hate. It's getting difficult to turn a blind eye, and act like everything is alright. I don't know what to do. Whenever I speak up, my voice is ignored and unheard.

I have been waiting to go for an x-ray for six weeks. Every day I watch car loads of people go to the doctor, while I wait. For the past couple of weeks, I have seen people who have been who have been here for less time than I, get priority and sent into the clinic. I dislocated my knee. Nothing is even wrong with these guys. What the hell!? I didn't see a doctor for the first two months of my stay, so I don't see why these guys need to go.

I feel slighted, abused, and taken advantage of. If I waited this long to see a doctor in any other treatment program, the program would be over before I got there. Patience is one thing, stupidity another, and this situation has moved from patient to plain ridiculous. Why do I care? It seems like the farm is designed to take my focus off God, not bring me closer. I think this people work for my enemy, not my Saviour.

My friend left today. He freaked out yesterday, and left this morning. I watched his eyes change, grow dark, and something left him. Within a day, everything he worked for is lost. I had hoped that he would come through the anger, but it overwhelmed him instead. I am sad, but a part of me is growing numb to these outcomes. I invested a lot of time into creating a friendship with him. All for nothing. This continues to happen over and over again, but I still press onward: dismayed, but not distraught.

Wednesday

I worked all day, and talked to someone about all the drug experiences I've had. This has been going on for several days. I'm tired of it. I don't like using, or reminiscing about it. It always ends in destruction, and it isn't very appealing. I think that the person initiating these conversations wants to get high, and will leave the farm soon. I could be wrong. He has wanted to leave many times before, but somehow stays.

I lost my room today, and moved back into the dormitory. I was furious. I've packed my suitcase for the last time. It will remain packed until I walk out of here. I am frustrated with the constant moving around, from room to room, house to house, and place to place. I keep having to alter my daily routine, and adapt to different people. It's the same as living in a homeless shelter. What are they thinking? It's complete madness to move people around almost every week, on a whim, for no reason at all.

I want something more for my life. I can't keep living this way. I want stability and continuity. I don't know what direction my life is taking right now, or what will happen next, and I don't know what I am supposed to do. I will wait until it becomes clear, but I think the coming summer season is already starting to affect me. I always go hard in the summer.

Thursday

Dreams filled with war. I don't know why certain parts are blocked from memory. I am so disturbed upon waking that I start crying. I am hurt and torn up inside. This war will never end, and the battle will follow me wherever I go. I don't need the added conflict and pain of being here among people who don't accept me, and can't help me. I thought this place would be different, but I am learning that beneath the surface it is the same as all the others.

I am the last of my kind. There is no one left to teach me except God. I go to war for these people, but they want nothing from me except for me to be more like them. They have created a society within a society, with its own rules and traditions. They even have their own form of punishment and humiliation, when someone breaks their man-made commandments. The part that cause revulsion to rise within me is that they do it in the name of God. I have seen this before.

Friday

The theme of the dreams is the same all night long. I search for a girl. I need a girl in my life. I yearn for her. I can't live like this anymore. It's unnatural. No women anywhere to be seen or heard. This farm consists of only men. I've seen how the cows handle this situation. They turn gay. No fucking way. I wouldn't believe it if I hadn't seen it with my own eyes. God did not create us to live like this. He created us male and female, and designed us to come together.

I have been living with men in these kind of housing situations for three years, or longer. Have I gone long enough without sex? No offense, but an ongoing all boys summer camp is not what I am looking for. I mean - really!? Is this the abundant life God was speaking of? I think not. Does this sound like a complaint? Let me assure you, it is an accurate examination of the facts.

My birth certificate came yesterday, and I am one step closer to claiming my existence as a person in this world. I will not allow people to condemn, criticize, or complain about who I am. Nor do I feel compelled to become like the people that surround me. Most of them are so completely lost, or deceived, that I have little hope for them.

Saturday

I almost left today. I packed everything I own, put my money in my pocket, and was ready to walk. Why? I spent my weekend working in the greenhouse, as punishment for breaking one of their stupid rules. I was so upset about having my free time stolen from me that I was ready to throw it all away. I knew this would happen.

I feel like a prisoner here, being held hostage. I can't go anywhere by myself, not even with another resident. I can only leave the property in the presence of a leader, or someone who has been here for several years. I can't believe how restricted my life has become. This is basically a jail without the fence. What holds me here? I don't know how to leave, and the farm won't help me transition out. They want me to stay.

There are some things here that I enjoy, but not enough for me to lay aside the fact that I am a man. God did not design me to live like this. Of course I am experiencing resistance. I am fighting a war that started a long time ago, and there are days that I do not feel like picking up the sword.

I want peace to reign in my heart, and in the world. I want the promise of the word. I want to ask, and receive. I want to heal the sick, and walk with power. I need faith to rise within me with such absolute assurance that it lifts me from the ground with wings, and pulses light from the palm of my hand.

Anyway, I'm still here, and I'm thankful I didn't leave because I have nowhere to go except the street, and that path ends with me smoking crack cocaine.

Sunday

I want to return to sleep, but can't because my body his finally adapted to rising early. Someone asked me to leave the farm with them today, but I refused. They packed their bags and left. And that is all I have to say about that. It is true insanity. I watched this person break into a sweat, pace back and forth across the room, until he finally slipped into the delusional plans he has for life. It doesn't matter what he is telling himself in the moment, I know he is going to get high.

I have a hard time here somedays, but I don't want to leave only to return to the street. I want success, not failure. This person decided to leave with no money, no plan, and no hope. Even as I write this sentence, I can see him walking back up the driveway. Looks like he changed his mind. His future seems uncertain. Perhaps he should remain at the intake house until he is stabilized and is sure he wants to stay. What's the point of allowing him to enter the program and disrupt the other residents with his behaviour? He has come and gone several times. It's clear he can't handle the pressure.

I have found that my guitar acts as a telephone to God. I know it's a strange metaphor, but it's true. The purpose of playing guitar and singing is to speak with God. It is for no other reason. I raise my voice to heaven, sending sound within. I am learning how to use this technique for worship. I'm not sure how it all exactly works, but I trust he will teach me. I need to left my heart and voice, with spirit and truth. I am standing at the beginning of something amazing, and I can't completely grasp it.

> "For ye have need of patience, that after ye
> have done the will of God, ye might receive
> the promise."

> Hebrews 10:36

5 Months

Chapter SIX

U seless dreams. I awake to a new day, ready to face what is coming (I hope). My ears are ringing and my muscles ache. I can't believe they let yesterday's runaway enter right back into the program as if nothing happened. He is delusional. Apparently, God told him to stay. I don't think God has anything to do with the voices in his head, or the hallucinations he is having. He is mentally unstable, and it frustrates me to no end that leadership ignores it, acting like everything is fine. Are they blind?

Somehow, I have ended up with another *chore*. This time I am being punished for walking away from a confrontation. This better not interfere with my visit to Hastings on the weekend, or I am outta here. I've come to the end of my personal restraint. People are trying to take away the few things that actually keep me here. Some of the leaders abuse their power, and I'm not having it anyone. I have weapons, same as they.

At least now I understand how people go to jail for theft, and end up staying for murder. I don't need this conflict and irritation in my life. Several people here have started mocking and ridiculing me for my speech patterns. I have a tendency of vocalizing why I am upset, how I got that way, and what I want to do about it. I also share the inspiring moments, but they are reject just as quickly as my complaints.

They tell me not to complain, and some go as far as to call it a sin. Ridiculous. I am being corrected and condemned by people who haven't even read the scripture, let alone studied it – so let's take a walk in the word.

"Therefore I will refrain my mouth; I will speak in the anguish of spirit; I will complain in the bitterness of my soul."

Job 7:11

I have written about this verse in the past, but I think I need to refresh the memory of people who have forgotten. It appears to me that this man had no restraint when it came to speaking about his agony. Why then should I refrain?

"I remembered God, and was troubled: I complained, and my spirit was overwhelmed. Selah."

Psalm 77:3

It is interesting to consider that these men had no desire to withold their tongue. The Hebrew word used in these two verses (complain) is defined as this: to ponder, by implication: converse with oneself, and hence, aloud. It seems that these men go to God with their sorrow and affliction. They speak openly and honestly, holding nothing back.

I will follow their example, because truth is more important than looking good in the eyes of others. I speak to God, not them. They just happen to be standing there when I do so. Now, moving right along to my next complaint: we have been taught a lot of strange things about grace, so I decided to look it up. The word is defined as: the divine influence upon the heart, and its reflection in the life.

Not even close to what they teach here. In this day and age, words only mean what we want them to. If enough people believe and teach one meaning, it must be true, right? Nope. I am tired of listening to carefully crafted teaching which confuses and condemns the listener. Jesus warned us of this very thing:

> "And Jesus answering them began to say, Take heed lest any man deceive you: for many shall come in my name, saying, I am Christ; and shall deceive many."

> Mark 13:5-6

It is spoken of again in the new testament. Another fairly clear warning, and although different than the one Jesus gave, it follows the same line of thought – if you pay attention.

> "For the time will come when they will not endure sound doctrine; but after their own lusts shall they heap to themselves teachers, having itching ears; and they shall turn away their ears from the truth, and shall be turned to fables."

> 2 Timothy 4:3-4

Do these so-called Christians of today's world think they are immune? Does anyone understand how easy it is to lead people astray? Satan has been doing it for thousands of years. Do I really need to continue offering more evidence from scripture?

> "But I fear, lest by any means, as the serpent beguiled Eve through his subtilty, so your minds should be corrupted from the simplicity that is in Christ."

> 2 Corinthians 11:3

Interesting. A subtle and cunning angel that has fallen to earth who is well practiced in deception. How is this possible? Surely we would know if Satan decided to appear in our lives and lead us down a pathway of hellfire, wouldn't we?

> "For such are false apostles, deceitful workers, transforming themselves into the apostles of Christ."
>
> 2 Corinthians 11:13

What!? How can someone follow Christ without following Christ? Because they look like the real thing. The outward appearance, the words, the teachings, the eloquent sermons: truth mixed in with lies, so that the lies become undetectable.

> "And no marvel; for Satan himself is transformed into an angel of light."
>
> 2 Corinthians 11:14

The author doesn't even seem surprised. Why? Because he knows something of the nature of his adversary - more than he writes, I am sure. Keep in mind, this man was once deceived himself, imprisoning and consenting to the death of those professing the very religion he later established and spread to the world. So how does Satan do it? The answer, I believe, lay within the author's final thought.

> "Therefore it is no great thing if his ministers also be transformed as the ministers of righteousness; whose end shall be according to their works."
>
> 2 Corinthians 11:15

He doesn't even think it is difficult, and people here on the farm wonder why I have a hard time just accepting whatever doctrine they like at the moment, or why I don't just follow a man because he has a self-proclaimed title of pastor or minister? Hello!? Is anyone listening!? The more people believe it, the more suspicious I become, because Jesus said <u>many</u> will be deceived.

> "Because strait is the gate, and narrow is the way, which leadeth unto life, and few there be that find it."

> Matthew 7:14

Tuesday

I follow someone into a building. It looks similar to the dormitory I live in. I close my eyes. The lights go out, and I can feel evil surround me. It grabs hold, smothering me in a blanket of darkness. I turn my head from side to side, trying to break free, but I can't. So I call on God. "In the name of our Lord and Saviour Jesus Christ, I cast thee out!"

I awake screaming the words into the darkness. I catch my breath, close my eyes, and return. This time I am walking down a forest path toward a building in the distance. A girl walks at my side, and we are talking quietly. As we approach the final curve, she starts freaking out. I launch myself into the air, taking flight. She is yelling at me about an evil presence near the trees, and there is desperation in her voice. "Can't you see it!?" She screams. It is a blood curdling scream. "In the name of our Lord and Saviour Jesus Christ, I cast thee out!"

I awake yelling the words, and I'm nervous. Two sequential attacks, and I am wings spread, descending in a final embankment.

David Burton

It is the girl's scream that echoes in my head. I can't even see the demon. I quickly discover that it is three thirty in the morning, so I return to sleep, and continue dreaming.

I dream of a girlfriend I once had, or will have. We have been separated for a long time, but we have come together once more. When I see her, I draw her close. I look into her eyes. They blaze with crystal blue light, clear and powerful: it is the most beautiful color of blue I've ever seen, and her eyes are intense.

More visions come, until I finally wake to the dawning light.

Due to my sunny disposition, people here have started calling me 'Sunshine.' They mock, and try to hurt me, as though it were amusing. I assure you it isn't. After a few days of wondering why it bothered me so much, I finally remembered the truth.

My mother used to call me Sunshine because she loved me, and I was the light of her life. I can see her smiling face inside my mind, and her words echo inside my head. I can hear the tone of her voice, and the love it contains. I am crying because through this God has just revealed the truth of the people around me. The same words, spoken either in love or hatred. Had I not known the light, I would not have recognized the darkness. God just stripped the illusion from my eyes, and restored my vision.

Not everyone here rejects me, but most of them. There is a theory that I have rejected myself. Not sure how it is possible, but sounds interesting. A counsellor told me that people can help me, if I let them. How are they going to help me if they don't experience what I do?

The girl I met last night has eyes like mine. I can still see them blazing blue fire light inside my mind. My eyes catch fire through tears of agonizing and cleansing pain. I've seen my eyes change color, and pulsate with the amount of crack cocaine coursing through my blood. Why did I think about that?

I guess it goes back to the original question: how can people relate to what I am going through? I feel alone, even though I am surrounded by people at every moment of the day. If someone tried to relate I probably wouldn't believe them, and that's how far down the path I've travelled. I know there are others like me (there must be), but where? Who is going to teach me? Is there something I need to know?

In all the novels I've read, the teacher appears almost immediately after the student manifests the gift. What am I supposed to do? I need help. I need guidance.

Tonight we had a discussion in class about temptation, although many didn't realize it. The question was this: If I gave you a million dollars, who would stay on the farm? A fight nearly broke out while we discussed the question. Crazy. It demonstrates the power money has over people. Negative, or positive, it controls their thinking. I been tested by this in my dreams, and seen the consequence so often, that I doubt I would fall. I know the emptiness that lay at the end of this deception.

> "For what shall it profit a man, if he shall gain the whole world, and lose his own soul?"

> Mark 8:36

What's the problem? It appears that people don't understand the value of soul or spirit. Perhaps everyone has fallen into the misconception that they are entitled to the world, and their soul. If I gain the world, do I forfeit my soul? Can't I have the lust of the flesh, and the power of the spirit - simultaneously? Honestly, I haven't thought about it in these terms before tonight. I thought I would eventually have everything and anything I've ever wanted.

I need to examine myself, carefully. What does God say about all this, because that's all that really matters.

Wednesday

It's been a messed-up day. Borderline psychotic. I felt the psychosis coming. It moved quickly, and how I avoided falling into a break I will never fully understand. The pressure I am experiencing internally and externally is so great that my mind will literally snap, and I will become a raving lunatic. No one here knows anything about my history of psychosis, except one man, and I doubt he will say anything. I feel rejected by several people, and condemned by all the others. I am struggling to remove their voice from my mind.

This is why I don't like letting people into my life. They will never understand. If I expose my history of psychosis, and then speak of something spiritual beyond their comprehension - they will say I am insane. What am I supposed to do? When will my ears stop ringing? Psychosis would almost be welcome at this point in my life. At least I wouldn't have to try anymore, nor would I be concerned about social norms and fitting in among the men.

The problem is this: the psychosis is the real me trying to surface, and I am holding it back with all the strength I have. I refuse to let go and scream the words echoing inside my mind. I am still trying to gain acceptance in the eyes of men. I will never truly be free until their opinion means nothing to me.

Perhaps a manifestation of the power will convince them? I do not need confirmation or conversion, but the people around me are living in darkness. Perhaps not an expression of power, but the divine influence on my heart. Maybe that will finally awaken them. I know that God is able to do this in my life, so that all can see. The problem has been trying to convince myself that the tactic is the most useful in this situation.

I am at war. I will never forget, back down, or surrender. Nothing will turn me away from this path. Today, I made a choice to alter the coming result of something set in motion against me. I was shown something which I thought was inevitable and unchangeable. However, when the moment came, I found that it could be grasped and molded. When I found the intersecting pathways of time lines, I folded space: compressing one and expanding the other - simultaneously. Without hesitation, I abandoned myself and trusted the unexplainable action I had just taken. All is not complete, but something has changed. I don't know if it will be enough.

I am dealing with things I can't accurately explain with these words. The result, however, became crystal clear in a conversation I had with a counsellor this afternoon.

"If this continues, I will have to ask you to leave," he says, with all seriousness.

"You already have," I whisper. I don't think he heard, or understood, but I know the truth and I have done what I can to change the outcome. Without prophetic vision, I would not have identified the moment today, or understood the seriousness of it. More than likely, I would have become offended and hastened my own destruction.

After writing all of this, I feel I have explained it no better than if I had not explained it at all. Understand? Why would I have hidden the truth of myself from myself?

Thursday

Demons. Girls. Demons. Girls. I can still see her naked, inside my mind. I want her so much it infuriates me. The people here have told me to stop masturbating because it is a sin, and something to be ashamed of. How convoluted is that? I stop masturbating and start having wet dreams, so what's the difference? This whole thing is screwed up. The very fact of me being here goes against nature. I am made for sexual intercourse, especially at my age.

I am a young and healthy male. Not some old man whose sex drive is gone. Personally. I am sick and tired of people talking, and making rules, about masturbation. Besides, these assholes are married. What they have to say about the issue is meaningless to me.

In the last week, I've been told that I have a bad attitude, black heart, don't know God, and that I am in the darkness. I've been told that my personality will spread like cancer in the community, I am arrogant, prideful, negative, have nothing to offer, nothing to impart, nothing to teach, no message to carry, and that I've set myself up for people to abuse me. Apparently, I am also wrong, deceived, and dangerous.

I've been told to leave the farm if I want to 'do my own thing' (whatever that means). I couldn't find the strength, ability, or desire to participate in singing as a group, mainly because I have been excluded, and criticized for being who I am. I just stood there the whole time staring at the blinds, wondering why they were closed, and how I am supposed to be okay with the whole situation. Having the blinds closed is distracting. I can't help but hear the voice within, saying, "men loved the darkness because their deeds were evil." These people have rejected me, and now I am rejecting them. They are ashamed of me, so I have become ashamed of them.

Is there a way around this? I guess that I have finally seen through the glitter, and all that glitters is not gold.

Friday

Another day that doesn't appeal to me, and it hasn't even started yet. Inside I feel corrupted by anger and overwhelmed by bitterness. As I told someone this week, I have been poisoned by the farm, its rules, and the many people who themselves leaders. Their venom courses through my veins, and I am desperately trying to draw it out before it reaches my heart.

Worship seems to be my saving grace, but the second it ends, some asshole comes over and tries to steal the joy in my heart. This is why I want to leave all the time. My peace is constantly threatened by the people who claim to want to help me. During worship, God breaks through, and speaks to me. His voice rings clear in my mind: "UTTER ABANDONMENT, OR COMPLETE DESTRUCTION." I am singing, with arms raised, until I hear all I hear is his voice, and I collapse internally, tears falling from my eyes and soul screaming in silent surrender.

What am I supposed to do? I want to stay, but I don't know if I can resist the temptation to medicate the pain I feel inside. It is the first true doubt I have had in a long time. The change that has rocked my heart is still continuing to echo inside me. I feel something in the center of my being, growing outwards and consuming the darkness.

I just watched a video about authority, and it was complete shit. I can't stand listening to this garbage. It isn't the content so much as the message. Let me try to explain. Using the word of God to force submission, cause shame, demand obedience, and exalt a man - all of this is straight from hell. The anger I feel right now is surpassing my decision making process. I am ten seconds from absolute rage.

Why? I have been denied my Hastings adventure. One leader has decided to shut down my outreach excursion. I have to go on my own, or forget it entirely. God has warned me of this man, and shown me how he will stand in my way. I knew it was coming, but the reality is always painful. He can't see me, or hear me, and his desire is to control and punish me. I am engaged in battle. He is actively deceiving others while working against me. I want to expose him, but I don't know how. Underneath the forgery is a hurting man that refuses to accept the very salvation he preaches.

Anger within me gives way to sadness and sorrow, at what could be but isn't. Sound familiar. I've said it before. How can I respect someone who is so insecure about themselves? Do I want the man to heal? Or, should I walk away from the whole travesty?

Saturday

I had disturbing dreams that I would rather forget, and my day was crazy. I felt hurt and rejected because I couldn't go to Hastings. Why am I still here? What's the point? Someone left the farm last week, returned, and then received a sum of money. He asked me to leave with him. Not just in a passing conversation, but active pursuit: tempting and trying to convince me to leave. All the lies I have heard Satan use before came through this man's lips. A demon spoke through him - understand?

"It will be fun. It will be an adventure. You have already relapsed in your mind, might as well make it a reality. I have money. We can get high and pick up a girl. I'll pay for a hotel. We'll go to

Vancouver." Lie. Lie. Lie.

I tried to reason with the man, explaining that I've been down this round many times before, and I know how it ends: broke, depressed, homeless, hopeless, and on the street surrounded by people who want to use and abuse me. Then he offered me a ride out of here. Feeling frustrated and hurt, misunderstood and alone, I gave in and packed everything I own.

I felt trapped, like my only option, the only way to make people listen, was to hurt myself with a crack pipe. Fuck That! I had a shower, prayed, asked God to intervene, and went to bed. I ignored the tempter and temptation. I didn't rise until he left the farm. I started crying, overwhelmed by my emotions and mental anguish. Satan engineered the entire thing, and it was obvious. He has been using this man, and trying to take me out.

I went to leadership earlier this week and explained the situation. I spoke to several leaders, not just one. They failed to act. I need warriors, not paper pushers. I need people to walk beside me, not fight against me. I need others who are willing to see the world as I do, or trust that I CAN SEE.

I'm sorry that God hasn't gifted everyone with the ability I have, but I can't change it. I know things other don't because God reveals it. Why? Ask him. People feel threatened by me, rather than embracing who I am. I was attacked today more subtly, harshly, and abruptly, than walking Hastings in the daylight. My enemies are those of my own household. I quoted the verse to a leader who obviously missed the significance or implication - DO SOMETHING.

God intervened. He was my defense. He stepped in between my spirit and flesh. Today my defense came from a Higher Power. Twenty years of addiction and experiences dictates that I should be high right now, not sitting here writing this journal. I have never been able to resist as I have today. This is God in my life. This is grace.

I don't think anyone understands the true power that has been displayed in my life today. I failed, but Jesus is stronger than my failure: his power and spirit carried me, answering a prayer that I have spoken for years without a response. Why would he bless me even though I have sinned? Why does he show mercy when I manifest rebellion? I feel so inadequate and unworthy of his love, but in his presence I am whole, complete, fully loved, and at peace.

Sunday

I am grateful to awake in my own bed this morning, knowing where I am, and surround by people I know. I have a certain level of peace, and I hope it remains. Guarding my heart is important; ruling my spirit is imperative: I will not allow other people to control me, nor will I give away the power. Other people are now denied access to the core of my being. The decision is made.

At breakfast, a leader tried to place conditions on my life. I have nothing to prove to this man. He has no control over, or say in, my life. He has only hindered me in the past. I suspect that he has an agenda, but guess what? I'm not falling for it. I've been rejected from the association of men here. Certain cliques have formed, but I just don't care. This isn't highschool. I don't base my self-worth and self-image on the opinions and acceptance of others. Whether they frown at my behaviour, or smile, it has no bearing on me.

So, in some senses, I have now done with recovery what I did with addiction. I will not be oppressed, and I have decided not to allow people near my heart. I must protect the spirit. A gift is given, now I must watch over it. It has immense value, and worth beyond this world.

People talking about the workforce, but they are drug dealers. People talking about godly change, but leave offerings for native gods. Hello!? Does anyone piece this together except me? Class discussion rarely go well for me, and I don't give much weight their opinions.

Monday

I am running across a grass covered plain, carrying two swords in my belt. I come to a wall made of stone bricks. I remove a stone, and hide my weapons behind the brick. A tidal wave comes, and washes away the world. A woman stands in the distance. I run to her, and as the wave spreads across the land, we hold each other tightly. We are in distress, but are together in the storm.

I awake so extremely tired that I want to pull the blankets over my head and return to sleep. I had a difficult time falling asleep last night. It could be the coffee, but more likely it was the thoughts in my head. Satan standing, accuses me of my life.

By lunch time, I am making plans to leave, and I end up in the office telling leadership exactly how I feel. I admit that I trust no one, and in order to stay here I must trust someone. I need to trust that at least a few of the people who are in authority are dedicated to God, and will not lead me astray.

In the end, I decide to trust the man in front of me, not because of any rational thought, but because I must. When I told him I wanted to leave, he did the exact opposite of what I expected. I thought he would abandon me, but instead he showed compassion, asking what we can do to get through this troubling time. He didn't reject me. Strange. He displayed humility and honest concern. Unbelievable.

I feel childish. Being in relationship with people is not my strong point. I would say I know nothing about it. I've decided to trust, hoping against hope, and in direct contradiction to my emotions. It is the first time in my life that I've made this decision with a sober mind. I feel uncomfortable, and unsure of what to expect. I don't know what is coming.

I am a blind man, Lord, and right now someone else needs to be my eyes. This is the truth. Unfortunately, my tongue is quick and sharp. The clearer my mind gets, the more I want to mess with people. What is a few years here, compared to the rest of my life? I need to get real, and change. This crap has gone on for too long. Seriously. I've been measuring myself by an external standard, and coming up as a failure every time.

Failure? How many people can call a lightning storm?

I want to know the depths of God's power. I am distracted by what Satan has offered, and tormented by the visions I have every night. I never sleep. I move from one world to the next, without end. The only rest I receive is in God's presence. I continue to press onward, even though escape and release can easily be found in a crack pipe (temporarily).

I am an alien and stranger to this world. I am starting to feel somewhat human, which I hate with a seething passion. I am binding my spirit to this earth by eating, drinking, and living as a man. I want to self-destruct, and free myself from the host. I want the twisted visions to stop, and freedom to start reigning. I want to soar and sing, rise and not fall, live clean and sober. I don't want to return to a life of addiction.

I don't want black wings, if they mean what I think they do. I need to see the unseen, hear the silence, and start fasting.

The English language has changed, and the dictionary now defines words differently than when the KJV was written. This causes me great distress. I understand the text in a way others do not because the words mean something else to me. I wonder if people know about this. Does it ever occur to them? Language is always changing, and is a constant state of flux (ebb and flow). The waves are moving the words around like rocks on the beach. The scenery is being arranged by the passage of time.

Tuesday

God comes to have a conversation with me. Of course, he removes the memory of it. As usual.

Wednesday

There is no escape from the Lord. I wrote one journal today, tore it up, and tossed it into the garbage where it belongs. I won't write the evil inside me anymore. I won't give it a voice. I have made a decision, and although not easy, it is done. I can't help but speak it out over and over again. Each time it gains strength.

God spoke to my spirit last night while I slept, and denied memory of the conversation. He has done this before, but this time I can't remember anything. I just KNOW he spoke.

When I awoke last night, I rose from my bed, and walked to the washroom. As I was returning to my room, a flash a light coursed around me like lightning. I turned around, searching for the source of the light. I saw something in front of the door at the end of the hall. It looked like a whirlwind. I can't even draw it properly because it defies the rational explanation. I can see it in my mind, but can't articulate it.

David Burton

"That shouldn't be there," I thought. Then I walked away. I didn't stop to investigate because subconsciously I was afraid, and it didn't make sense to me. Is this the beginning? I wasn't asleep.

Thursday

Maybe it was nothing but shadows playing with my mind while I am half asleep, but I saw it again last night. Maybe it's nothing at all, and my life on the farm with be nothing but a cruel less-than-normal existence, with no appearance of God, or manifestation of the spiritual realm.

Every morning I wake up with the same thoughts, reasons, and conclusions. I don't write them here, and I am starting to wonder if they will lead anywhere at all.

I went to the women's facility this morning to help deliver some plants. It is the equivalent of our farm, except it is located in a different valley. Both farms have industrial greenhouses, although ours is larger because we have existed for longer.

Every time I leave the farm, to visit a restaurant, city, or facility, I have a new hope that a normal life is just around the corner – then I return here. Enough said? I've been up and down, spun around, tossed on an ocean wave. I don't know what I am doing anymore. I am afraid to talk to people about the real issues because of what has transpired in the past few days. I am extremely paranoid. I don't know who to trust because my words have a way of getting back to *leadership*, even words I don't say. I was accused of telling people that I want to get high. I never spoke those words, not once. I was confronted, and the accusation was placed on me. I thought they were going to drag me into the office and pummel me with their rhetoric until I conceded defeat. I thought they would threaten me with eviction unless I obey their man-made doctrine.

I'm considering ripping this page out of my journal before some leader reads it.

This journal is for God, and I – no one else. *Leadership* needs to get over themselves. My thoughts will not be censored. How am I going to heal if all I write here are lies and niceties? Should I fear punishment by the establishment for speaking the truth? How can I come before God, and say: I stopped writing because I feared man?

He will turn his gaze to my heart. Will he see that I betrayed him because I feared man? Will I sacrifice my eternal spirit? NEVER. I will never betray God, not even for a moment. My heart stands, and will continue to stand, regardless of what people say about me. I can do nothing else. I am a new creature. There is no returning to what I was before the change.

I am so sick of the situation I find myself in here. I am tired of the insanity. And that's what it is – insanity. Religion is living by principles and traditions, without the power of God. Empty. That's what I see here. A whole lot of people professing to be something they are not, all pretending that God is moving in their life. It's a travesty.

All day long, they tell us that the sky is green, and the blind believe it. They present us with all kinds of instruction, documentation, and quotation, that supports their belief that the sky is green. Some people become so convinced that they begin to tell others the sky is green. They teach classes on how the sky was created green, and so forth. "The sky is green!" They yell. If you don't believe the sky is green, you become an outcast.

It won't change anything, because I <u>know</u> it's blue.

Friday

I went world hopping last night, from dream to dream, walking through portals, and watching the landscape shift around me. I would walk through the portal, the world would darken: thunder and lightning flashing all around me. Then the world would shift.

I awake utterly exhausted, and aching in my body. This day has been strange and disturbing. I have conflicting emotions, and I am destroyed inside. I have cried four times, and I'm not sure that it is over yet. I am wrecked. I nearly left this week, but at the last moment I changed my mind and stayed. As a way of saying, 'thanks for staying,' leadership *chored* me twice, and I get to spend four hours in the greenhouse, wasting the only free time I have each week. What the hell are they thinking!? I am barely hanging on, and the leaders are poking sticks into the fire. I am burning, and will soon become an all-consuming fire. I went straight to a leader, and confronted him.

"Are you trying to help me? Do you even care? What are you thinking? I am telling you right now, this is not the way to reach me." I don't play politics, and I'm not interested in making people happy. That's why I end up in these situations. Sure, it hurts when I'm rejected, but it only strengthens my resolve to continue speaking truth.

The people here lead you to the edge, push you over, and throw rocks at you on the way down. With friends like these who needs enemies? I am beyond the point of caring. God is within me, and I ain't in this to put on a performance. No sign for these people, even though I want to explode.

Saturday

Two of us are working in a store. The girl is leaning over a glass display case, cleaning off the streaks. She is singing: "Be my life-long passion, Jesus." Her voice is angelic, and her appearance is beautiful. I want to wrap my arms around her, but instead I walk away. As soon as I am out of sight, I raise my hands and start singing. As I walk out of the store, I see that the world is in literal darkness. I run, spread my wings, and fly, screaming out scripture, piercing the darkness. I stay in the air until I awake.

I am depressed, angry, and irritable. I can't believe they've stolen my one day off. I want to scream and put heads through walls. Violence is becoming a viable option. I wonder how my mind has reached this point. I am right screwed up in my head. Everything I am experiencing tells me to run away from here as fast as I can, but here I am, allowing them to treat me like a two-year-old child.

Even writing these thoughts down will result in being punished by the farm thought police. I won't be surprised if we start burning books soon. Do you want me to say it? Fine. I am in a cult. This place has nothing to do with God. It is run by a fanatic, who has a lot of charisma, same as all other cult followings and organizations. He has all the power, and people follow him out of fear, intimidation, and demonic holds on their spirit. I've seen it before, but this is worse than most. The conditioning is twenty-four hours a day, seven days a week.

I am thoroughly disgusted by their use of God and his precepts as a method of control. Many people here believe the lies they are being taught because they know nothing else. They have no frame of reference, and they refuse to read the word.

This week I was asked to give my life to 'the program,' and betray God. Forgive me, Lord, I am an idiot. I walked right into it. They used scripture to justify the request, saying: "servants obey your masters." Satan is the master of this place, that much has become painfully obvious. How much damage am I doing to myself by staying here? My spirit is crying out against me being here - it's screaming bloody murder.

When I am out of here, I am writing the newspaper. This place is fucking evil. They are using the broken, destitute, and vulnerable – those most susceptible to their conditioning and sleep-depravation technique. Someone must stop these people. I wonder how many people have committed suicide after coming here? Try get that statistic from the office.

I am planning my escape. I have acquired a backpack, and saved some money. I have my birth certificate and tax return, so I can replace my license. Now, I need to decide where I am going. I have no access to a telephone, internet, or mail – until I am off this farm. No one here will help me get out. They refuse to give me a ride to town, so my only option is to hike out of here. As soon as they know I am gone, they will send someone after me, so I need to plan this carefully. They will fight against me every step of the way. I've seen them do it to other people, and now I know what it is like. How could I have been so blind?

I need a destination. I can't end up wandering aimlessly, and becoming frustrated. I'll end up getting high. I think my psychosis is returning. The shadows I saw the other night were just that – SHADOWS. The flashing light was the fire suppression system. How embarrassing.

Sunday

I am at the academy, and we are attacked by witchcraft. I walk quickly down the hall to the children's class, and speak to them about Jesus. I try to explain who he is, and why we need to pray to him. I don't know how successful I am, but my voice is filled with passion.

As I turn to leave, I discover that a demon has entered the building. Two of us isolate him in a room and, kill him. As he dies his body turns into insects that scurry out from beneath his corpse, climbing the walls. I've seen this before, but usually they just disappear. Instead, these insects go on the attack.

I awake. I am crying while talking to the children, explaining that we are being attacked by witchcraft. It is at our very gate.

Monday

Nothing but nightmares, horrible imagery that leaves a sick feeling in the pit of my stomach. I asked God to show me a way out of here, and last night he did. A man approached me about leaving the farm, and starting a new life. He has the help of a pastor, money saved, and a general plan. The plan is escape from the farm. Is this an answer to prayer, or just another temptation?

I am screwed up in my mind. I don't know what the right thing to do is, and I don't trust anyone. I told a leader last night that I have schizophrenia, and he told me I don't have it - I've believed a lie. He's an idiot, and he's in charge of the farm. Maybe God has healed my mind, who knows? Who am I to say he can't?

I lost another Hastings outreach because a *leader* here thinks I have an attitude problem. I spend every weekend working in the greenhouse because I break the rules I don't believe in. This week they decided to add another day to the work program (unpaid labour, of course). Why did I come here? I'm off drugs, but I'm all fucked up with cult programming, and now I'm scared to leave. Why? In order to leave here, I must trust wholly and completely in God for a pathway.

I'm officially institutionalized. Oh, and guess what? The person who offered to leave with me decided to leave in the middle of the night. He couldn't even wait until morning. WTF!?

My house exploded in conflict this evening, and many were betrayed. Some things were exposed because one person felt guilty. He decided to confess some things, and dragged in everyone who participated. The spirit of confession isn't to examine another man's motives or behaviour, it is to examine your own. Apparently, the attitude here is if I can't do it, then no one can. However, the word speaks of something entirely different.

> "I know, and am persuaded by the Lord
> Jesus, that there is nothing unclean of itself:
> but to him that esteemeth any thing to be
> unclean, to him it is unclean."

> Romans 14:14

If I do something that someone else is offended by, it doesn't mean that I have committed an evil act. I like the modern saying: "One man's garbage is another man's treasure." Not the same meaning, of course, but similar. The whole situation tonight was about dragging as many people down as possible. However, we are to judge and confess our own sin, not the man standing beside me.

> "Let not him that eateth despise him that
> eateath not; and let not him which eateth
> not judge him that eateth: for God has
> received him."

> Romans 14:3

It almost sounds like this writer knows something about our nature, how we judge each other constantly. I really like what he

says next.   Come on, people! Live in freedom.   Cast off the
shackles.

> "Are ye so foolish?   having begun in the
> spirit, are you now made perfect by the
> flesh?"

Galatians 3:3

It find it sad, and amusing, that so many people seem to think that
they can somehow make themselves more appealing to God by
works of the flesh. It's a common misconception that plagues the
people. Even more of a tragedy is when people think they have
attained a certain level of righteousness, and then use it to
condemn others. I am a master; you are simply a slave. I've
completed my checklist; you haven't even begun.

Confession is supposed to lead to freedom, not condemnation, and
if your confession has condemned others, I question your motives.
Did you try throw someone under the bus in order to save
yourself? What's the point? We have all sinned, and fallen short of
the glory of God. We are justified by his grace, and that is in Christ
Jesus. Guess what? I can't justify myself, no matter what I do. No
work will every purify me enough to grant me entrance to God's
presence. Jesus is the only way. Grace. What a beautiful concept,
and I'm still trying to wrap my head around it. Anyway, carrying
on...

> "Who are you that judgest another man's
> servant? to his own master he standeth or
> falleth."

Romans 14:4

I need to stop being concerned about what God should or

shouldn't be doing in the lives of others, and start focusing on what he is doing in mine. I need to stop playing network administrator, and start examining my own computer to find the problem. We all do stupid things. It's par for the course, but we all came here to build our own relationship with God, not change the people around us.

If I have a problem, I can talk to God. I trust God with my spirit. He is my healer, my priest, my all in all. Sure, we can confess our faults to each other, but that is so we can help the person, not judge them. Examine yourself. There is a psalm that captures it eloquently.

> "Wash me thouroughly from mine iniquity, and cleanse me from my sin. For I acknowledge my transgression: and my sin is ever before me. Against thee, thee only, have I sinned, and done this evil in thy sight: that you might be justified when thou speakest, and be clear when thou judgest."

> Psalm 51:2-4

Does this sound like a man who is concerned about the sin of other people? No. It is a man pouring out his heart to God in complete abandonment. He knows who his sin has truly affected, and it wasn't other people. This man is examining himself. He isn't deflecting or shifting the attention away. He is facing the agony of a godly confession. There is no standing in front of other people to make a performance. This is standing in the presence of God, and crying out:

> "Create in me a clean heart, O God; and renew a right spirit within me."

> Psalm 51:10

Followed by a heart rendering plea of anguish:

> "Cast me not away from thy presence; and
> take not thy holy spirit from me."

Psalm 51:11

This is true confession and repentance. Understand?

Tuesday

I dream of kittens, coming out for the first time.

I wake up early and start packing. Is every day going to be like this? How often does this have to happen before I actually listen? I've never experienced anything like this before in my life. The things I once loved are become the things I hate. My mind is turned upside down. My desire to leave isn't disappearing because God doesn't want it to. He has impressed it upon me for a reason, probably a warning.

Watching the conflict, chaos, and condemnation, among the people here over a few cigarettes was almost too much for me. We had an emergency meeting because someone confessed to smoking. We were hauled into the classroom, and held hostage while they crammed rhetoric down our throats. Then came the shaming. Apparently, we are all going to hell for having a cigarette. Has everyone lost their fucking mind!? If this is their response to someone smoking a cigarette (which is completely legal, and still socially acceptable in most of the world), imagine what would happen if someone actually relapsed. Suicide? Murder?

This program's belief system sets people up for self-destruct. It is the same as the first treatment center I ever went to. They indoctrinated us with one concept: "To use is to die." They set the psychology up really well. They programmed us. When someone in my group eventually relapsed, as we all do, he shot himself in the head. Good job, psychology. No one saw it coming except me (as usual). Messing with people's mind is not a game. Exhaustion, conditioning, repetition, sound exposure, and the destruction of all things 'world.' Then rewrite the person. In a computer system it is called: formatting, and installation (with whatever operating system you want).

All is not lost. I went to the barn, and the kittens came out for the first time. They're so cute.

Wednesday

I awake empty and destroyed. It is absolutely hopeless. Where is the freedom? For the first time in several weeks, I don't want to throw my clothes in my bag, and walk away. I've started working in the kitchen, and today I was overwhelmed with gratitude. I haven't been able to work in the kitchen because it reminds me of when I was using. The drug dealer used to deliver to the back door of the restaurant, every day. My mind associates restaurant work with drug use.

Today, I was set free from that association. God is restoring me. Where else can I play with a sword and fire all day long? In my addiction, I asked myself a question: "When was the last time I was happy?" The answer revealed something interesting, and changed the course of my life. The answer was, when I was working in a restaurant as an apprentice: unofficial, of course. I went back to the employer that I had left in a rage several years earlier, and asked if I could wash dishes for them. I knew that walking away was wrong. I had allowed the anger inside to consume me and dictate my choices. Returning to this employer showed me what humility really meant. I hope it did. It was painful and embarrassing, stepping on my pride.

Here on the farm, they tell me I am prideful. I disagree. They can't see inside of me. My heart is hidden, and has been for years. I remember placing it safely behind a door, and then burning the pathway. I am misunderstood most of the time, but I am learning a lot about myself, and that's all that really matters.

I was free to work in the kitchen, without the inevitable use of crack cocaine at the end of the day. My emotions overwhelm me, and I fall to my knees in tears. Words fail me. My heart is crying out to God in thanksgiving. No one knows what goes on inside my spirit, and I'm thankful for that privacy.

Tonight, I heard something that changed my perception. I've been searching for a purpose, and a reason to remain here. I think I found one. Sometimes, I think I know everything. This causes me to stop searching, learning, and reaching. Instead, I start judging, criticizing, and condemning. Satan has set a trap for me, and I walked right into it.

I listened to someone give their testimony tonight in *peer review*, and it was inspiring. I think I just found another reason to stay. It means leaving my life behind for the sake of another person. How can I do this? God understands this concept, but I don't. Perhaps he will teach me. I heard hope in this man's voice, and suddenly realized that I've lost my hope. Did I ever really have it?

The fight is not in vain. I must continue. THIS IS WAR.

Thursday

Why would I expect to dream of something peaceful? I close my eyes, only to have the truth revealed: this place is a cult. A nurse walks into my room, and tells me to leave the farm. She says it will end in violence if I remain.

I awake, and examine the dream. Everything says LEAVE, don't stay here, don't associate with these people. I thought something was changing. I thought I'd found a reason to stay. What a disaster.

I have attempted to define the problem. Instead of accepting that God has set me free from a life of addiction, suffering, and slavery – I see myself as having failed God. I think I just broke through an invisible barrier. I still think I need to leave. Does this make sense?

Listen carefully. I pray for years, asking God to provide a place for me away from the world. I finally arrive, he starts working in my life, and six months, I want to walk away? Why would I ask for something, only to run away from it when it arrives? Does this sound like a man in possession of all his faculties? I have fought hard for several weeks just to remain here. No one knows the extent to which I have battled, not even I.

How did this happen? That is the question I need answered. How did my train of thought get derailed? What triggered this slide into complete destruction? These are important questions, because if I don't identify the primary cause, it will happen again.

I spoke to a *leader* today about psychosis, and gave him a brief outline of my history. He was receptive, and willing to discuss it. I appreciate this conversation immensely, and I feel like a weight has been lifted from my shoulders. The true purpose of authority is to protect the people. I don't like asking people for help. A friend, perhaps; a stranger, no thanks.

I love you, Lord. Please don't give up on me. I want this life of peace and power – desperately. Show me the way.

Friday

I spend the day setting up the stage and sound equipment for a Christian band from the United States. I've done it before, so this time I am relaxed. I am fascinated by how the crew sets up and tears down so quickly. The same crew is working as before. They must know each other intimately from being on road together for so long. The guitars these guys have are impressive, all custom work. I'd love to play one of them.

A recovery house is also volunteering as a road crew, and I recognize four people from years ago. All of them relapsed, and have returned in search of recovery. My first instinct is to run away screaming, leave the farm, and start a new life. I will go as far away as I can. I don't want my life to continue like this. I am sick of seeing the same people spinning their wheels and getting nowhere. Failure upon failure. I can't take this, God, get me out of here. I don't want to relapse ever again to the point where I have to live in a recovery house. Is this whole thing pointless and hopeless?

No. I will rise above. I don't know how, but I will.

Saturday

I am going to Vancouver today. The sun is shining brightly in the sky, and I know that this day is going to be awesome. I'm wearing a white shirt, and loose fitting pants, because I can't see a single cloud in the sky. Summer has arrived – finally. I take two hundred dollars with me. Money isn't a trigger anymore and I like to be prepared. Never know what could happen.

We get a ride to Langley, catch a bus through Surrey, and jump on the SkyTrain. I watch the city beneath me out the window. I miss this feeling of freedom and adventure. I need it in my life. I am complete the moment I step out onto the street. I breathe in the air, and walk into a world I once knew. I'm at home walking the city streets, surrounded by strangers. I can't explain it.

We walk through the West End to Stanley Park, and follow the seawall. The sun is high in the sky, and many people are roller blading, running, and cycling. The ocean is right in front of me, and it brings a peace to my soul. This is the life I want. This is where I want to be. The only thing I desire more is to catch a ferry and return home, feeling the ocean breeze on my face and watching the water race beneath the bow of the ship. Oh God, set me free.

When I started to realize that I would have to return to the farm, I lost it. I couldn't face the thought of returning to an institution. My mind refused to accept the thought of returning to the farm, and internal stress triggered my coping mechanism – use drugs. It took everything I had, and some help from a friend, not to run terrified, and frustrated. At this point, I just about caught a bus and jumped on the ferry.

Instead, we walked to "The Gathering Place," a community center for the broke, lowly, and homeless. As soon as I walked in I felt relief, and a peace descended on my heart. I sat there for a half an hour, and the insanity began to subside. By the time one of the *leaders* reached out to me on the phone, I was calm again. So, what happened?

Why would I sacrifice six months clean because of fear and frustration? I must be fairly messed up about living on the farm, if this is the reaction of getting away from it for a few hours. I want to walk in freedom, not live in a bubble. I remember being clean and living in society. I did it by choice, not force. I always had the freedom to fail if I chose to, but I didn't. I chose to stand, because I believed in what I was doing. Do I believe now?

I can't believe I'm even asking the question. I used to think nothing could destroy my faith, but the church itself inspires me to abandon it. I can't stand the people that call themselves Christians. They are forgeries. I'm sure there are a few true believers scattered amongst the counterfeit, but I have a hard time finding them. I believe in Jesus Christ, I read the word every day, I pray without ceasing, I've experienced the power of God, I have dreams and visions, and I'm in love with my Saviour. However, I can't stand the church.

Sunday

I wake up to people entering the dormitory at six in the morning. The last two days have taxed my strength. I'm exhausted, once again. I just found out that a leader is missing. The second one in a couple of weeks. They just vanish into the night without a trace. Their phone is off, all contact is broken, and no one knows anything. Relapse. I don't judge the man, but the truth is he is out *using*, and it's obvious.

I spend most of the day playing the guitar, and writing music. My friend who left last week has returned. He looks destroyed, as though he has been *using* non-stop for the entire week. So, I guess his plan was a lie after all, and he was just looking for someone to come *use* with him.

The church service this morning was ridiculous. A self-proclaimed prophet was invited to speak to us, and give a message. He was full of crap. I ignored him, and spent the time catching up on my journal, which brought a reprimand from *leadership*. This place is crazy. I mean, really.

Monday

I dream of sex all night. It appears obvious to me that I need a woman in my life. My spirit is calling out for one. I've said it before: it's unnatural to live celibate. I think God said it best, "It is not good that man should be alone." (Genesis 2:18). I agree with the Lord. He kind of knew what he was doing. Why do we think we know better? We can justify our position, and support it with scripture, but it all comes back to the beginning.

I am exhausted, and my writing is starting to reflect it. I hate feeling this way, because in the past I've always used drugs to cope. A drug that keeps me awake until I collapse after days of nervous anxiety and paranoia.

The farm has increased their *work program* again, adding another day. I can't believe it. Did I come here to learn how to labour? No. I am one of those addicts that has worked for years to support my drug habit, and only stopped because my use was literally killing me. I think I am ready to return to the world I left behind, with a new perspective, and a different plan. I've stopped circling the drain. The amusing part of this is that no one seems to recognize this except me. My confidence is returning.

Tuesday

Expect the unexpected. It was a long day in the kitchen, and not a moment to spare. I get spun out of control, hyped up, and in the zone, but nothing to release the energy on. This kitchen is too slow. I thrive on the challenge of multiple orders, stretching across every section of the line: pans, grill, fryers, and salads. That is where I find peace in the rhythm. I ride the wave of power coursing within me.

Wednesday

In my dream, I am playing with the kittens. I am protective, and watch over them as a guardian.

I can't tell the difference between being awake or asleep. Some things happened this morning, and after consulting someone else, I discovered they didn't happen while I was awake. My dreams are beyond vivid. They are as real as the waking hours, but usually I can distinguish between one world and the other. Not this morning.

The farm has a way of turning positive things into negative. Working in the kitchen has turned out to be the equivalent of a full time job. This is in addition to the vicious daily schedule, classes in the morning and evening, as well as choir. Wow. This is insane. To complete the picture, I pay to live here, and work for free. As if this wasn't enough, they demand even more of me, and expect me to form a relationship with God. When!? That's my question. When?

I don't even have five minutes to myself from the moment I wake and fall on my knees, until the moment I collapse to knees at the end of the day. I am learning how to cook for an institution, which is a new challenge, and exciting. I am used to cooking to order, not preparing meals for large groups of people. I am quickly adapting my style, learning new techniques, and moving forward. Always something new to learn.

I received another piece of identification in the mail. I am now ready to have my driver's license replaced.

The stress is going to be the thing that causes me to snap. I just about walked into a full blown psychotic episode tonight. My body is exhausted, my mind is drained, and my spirit is starving. The pressure of the schedule here, and the unrelenting works based doctrine, is triggering psychosis. I felt it coming on. A couple of more minutes and I would have been *koo koo krazy.* I recognized the symptoms, and immediately removed myself from the situation. Who needs crack cocaine!? I get psychosis from just living on the farm.

It is not confidence inspiring to have my sanity slip through my fingers. It's embarrassing. In a single moment of intense stress, I can change into a raving madman, and I have almost no control over it. I must reduce the stress in my life. Why can't these people figure it out? I'm not your average crackhead. I've been this way my whole life; drugs only highlighted what was already present.

I couldn't tell the difference between waking and sleeping the morning – NOT AT ALL. There was nothing for me to go on. No thread, no comparison, no reference point. One day I am going to wake up, not knowing who I am or where I am. It's already happened, but next time will be worse.

Who am I? The man whose mind is broken? The man who is awake while he sleeps? The man who walks the earth? The fallen? The risen? The addict? The psychotic? The lost? The found? Whatever.

Thursday

God, please forgive me. Thank you for the day. Teach me your ways, how to handle the daily struggle, and allow me to continue with hindrance. I am tired, but pleased with my performance today. Does my work make any difference? I can never earn the gift you have given me. There is nothing I can give in exchange for it. It appears that our relationship is very one sided. You give me everything, and I have nothing to offer.

It's strange that I've never considered what I could do for you in the world. I have no idea what that would look like, and I've failed to ask for instructions. Will you give me a clear path to follow? Will you guide me? How will I recognize the guide when he appears? So many questions, a not a lot of answers.

I don't think the farm can offer much in the way of guidance. They are lost and confused, even more so than I. Not to mention, they can't understand what I'm going through. I've tried to explain, but I've been unsuccessful. No one gets it. How can they? One must live it in order to understand it. Everyone I know is only interested in the sparkles, glitter, and magic of the makeup.

I am trying to find a reason to stay here, and a way I can accept it. Partially, I found a place for me in the kitchen. It gives me purpose. I come alive inside, and I want to share this joy with people around me. The crew I am working with are well suited to my personality. I had to overcome something within me, and accept them the way they are, not as I want them to be.

I am also learning to have faith in other people. I don't have to control them; I need to trust them. So, what's next? Honestly, I've just been waiting for my identification, so that I can access the cash in my bank and get away from here. There's nothing stopping me in that area, so why do I remain? I must have found some reserve inside of me that I never knew existed.

I feel frustrated at times, but there is something fundamentally different within me. Maybe it was the visit to Vancouver, and returning clean. I've never done that before. I had to make a choice on that day, and my choice brought me back here. I don't understand it, but there it is. I have accomplished was I came here to do, so everything beyond this is unchartered waters, with a different motivation, inspiration, and intention. Now I just need to find it.

Something is happening. A cry gone far too long from my life.

Friday

And, back to normal. I hate this fucking place. Every time I move forward, they pull me back. Rules, rules, and more stupid rules. All designed to keep the image of a relationship, but in fact destroy it. All these people want from me is to be a working slave, and conform to their gospel of no power. Why should I wait any longer? To torture myself a little more? To have the sword of rejection driven through my heart one more time? To have one more person say something with their lips that is in direct opposition to their heart? Or, how about psychosis - let's not forget that?

No one understands. The Lord looks from heaven to see if any man has turned his heart toward him. I'm exhausted. I fell asleep on the floor at lunch. I don't think I can hold it together, maintain this schedule, work through conflict, and remain unaffected by the people around me.

I'm out; game over.

Saturday

It has been another retarded day here on the farm. I was crying so hard I couldn't speak. What was the cause of this pain? A cigarette, or should I say, the lack of one. Someone smuggled a pack of smokes into the farm. They offered me one, and I declined, but I said nothing while they decided to partake. When it all came to light, and leadership discovered the transgression, I was confronted. I received no word of encouragement for my abstinence, only condemnation because I allowed someone else to make their decision.

I am not here to control the behaviour of other people. It's not my problem. You want to do something? Go right ahead. I'm not going to stop you. It's not my right. The people who run this place are asking me to violate the free will of other people.

"Were you smoking?"

"No."

"Were you smoking? We already know about the cigarettes."

"And your point is...?"

"You are supposed to be the example. You let these people smoke." This coming from the leader who just relapsed, locking himself in Vancouver hotel room, and smoking crack for three days.

"What am I supposed to do? Take the smoke out of their mouth?"

"Yes."

"Not a chance in Hell."

"It's your responsibility to make sure people obey the rules." This coming from the leader who freaked out the other day, took every sharp tool in the shop, and buried them three-inches deep into the drywall.

"I'm not here to control other people. That's clearly your job."

"You are filled with rebellion. Conform," they demand.

"I'm not here to conform," I reply.

David Burton

"We will be searching your room. Please remove the locks."

"What locks? Searching for what?"

"Cigarettes."

"You're fucking kidding me. I don't smoke."

"You're lying."

The two leaders confronting me have less clean time than me, which makes things a little awkward, to say the least. They just can't believe that I turned down the cigarette that was offered me.

I lose all control. Go ahead, search, but our relationship is over. As I am walking to the dormitory, I have the farm police roll up on me in a pickup truck like they were a gang of clan members coming to hang a black man from a tree. They had already condemned me before the accusation was made. They believe I had that cigarette, and nothing will change their mind. Judged, condemned, and rejected in the space of thirty seconds.

These are my so-called 'Christian' acquaintances - raging, judgmental people rolling around looking for conflict because they have nothing better to do. They appear to know nothing else, in spite of the teaching they've had. Or, is it BECAUSE of the teaching they've had?

It all ends with me crying hard, emotions raging inside me like an ocean storm, and I can barely stand in the wind. God starts speaking to me, placing scripture inside my mind.

> "If the world hate you, ye know that it
> hated me before it hated you. If you were
> of the world, the world would love his own:
> but because you are not of this world, but I
> have chosen you out of the world,

therefore the world hates you."

John 15:18-19

I didn't expect this place to be the world, but God has shown me that it is exactly that, no matter what they profess or deception they try cast. The emotional pain causes my spirit to wake up, and through the tears, my eyes change. They start to burn with light. So, for the first time in my life, I try to teach. I walk straight to the leader who condemned me, and say, "Look at my eyes." And then strangest thing happens.

He can't see anything, or refuses to see. I am disappointed, but a part of me is not surprised. I told this man a month ago that he can't truly see me. How can someone read the word, and still have no concept of what 'enlightened eyes' means? How can he be blind when I am staring right at him, revealing myself before him?

Jesus had something to say about the blind leading people, and I trust him completely. He is God after all. So why am I here? I don't know. I sleep at night and fight for their souls, only to awake and be rejected by the people I fight for.

I came here with long hair and a beard, depicting Jesus, as he is visualized in the church. On the first day, they cut my hair, and asked me to shave off my beard. I suppose I should have figured it out right there on the spot - these people aren't interested in Jesus. They are only interested in looking good in the eyes of others, and creating a false image of the real man. I've noticed that many people here still think the outside matters. It doesn't. It's the inside that counts.

What will it take? Even with the book in their hand, they don't understand it. People are using you, Lord, to oppress, create slaves, to judge, to condemn, and to reject. The message is lost. It has been corrupted. Are you listening?

Sunday

I want to leave the second my eyes open. I guess yesterday has more of an impact than I thought. Betrayal and condemnation have a way of doing that to a person. Last night I was dreaming of a room full of people all dressed in white. I walked across the room, saying, "Look at all of you, just interested in looking good." The crowd murmured as I kept walking.

These people think dressing up, and wearing white, is what it is all about. I don't see it that way. One leader yesterday justified everything by saying, "The farm is a place of abuse." What The Fuck!? So I am paying to be abused, that's his theory? How did these people get so twisted? Where does their logic come from?

Our house leader worked all day yesterday, which is our only day off, just to impress the ego maniac who runs the farm. He has bought the lie whole heartedly. He thinks he can earn his way to heaven. I've been taught here that there is a class system in heaven. What!? Do you know how insane that is? Apparently, in heaven, one person will be better then the next. The message Jesus brought to the earth has been lost. It has been taken, and rewritten by the hands of man. Like I said, even with the book in their hands, they can't understand the truth.

My thoughts go like this: What travesty will I uncover today, and how much more can I take before I walk out of here? I have lost all hope whatsoever. Someone else was accused of smoking. They were cornered, hands laid on (not in prayer), pockets turned inside out, and searched from head to toe. Then they demanded to search his belongings. I suppose this violation was too much for him, because now he is gone.

The mentality of this place is that we must all become recovery police officers. However, let's not forget that all of this turmoil has been caused by TOBACCO : a legal drug that doesn't get you high, and is acceptable everywhere except prison. Is this prison? It is starting to look like it more each day. Same mentality; no fence.

Like I said, when are we going to start burning books? They have already placed a book and media ban on us. Media includes: newspapers, radio, television, email, internet, magazines, and unapproved literature. We don't even have access to a phone. They've even tried to extend this censorship to the songs I play on my guitar. I was told that "Stairway To Heaven" is the most demonic song in the entire world, and my guitar will be confiscated if I continue to practice it. I don't even know the words, I just play the melody.

I am constantly told that I have no rights, as if be saying it - it becomes true. I am told that certain rights and freedoms in the real world are considered privileges here. We even have to ask to go to the bathroom. Are you fucking kidding me!?

Monday

Nothing happened today. Thank God. I spend most of the day immersed in anger. It's hard to have peace when the morning is destroyed by the self-centered actions of those I live with. The sad part is that I have given up on them changing. It is I who must change. I have to adapt, or be destroyed. I am all played out, an emotional void, unsatisfied, and unfulfilled with all the farm has to offer.

The progress I was making with God has ground to a halt. I am so distracted and frustrated by what is going on that God is essentially gone from my life. What do I mean? I am so busy doing that I spend no time with God alone, and it is taking its toll on my mental state.

Lord, I can't continue without contact with you. I don't care about this place. It's you I desire. It is you that I want in my life. Please forgive me for falling flat on my face, and giving up. I had a cigarette today. I couldn't resolve the conflict inside of me, and I picked up something familiar to make it all go away. It's stupid, I know. But, my ears stopped ringing, and I stopped hearing the lights. Yes, that's right - hearing the lights.

I have no drugs in my body, and I don't sleep - ever. All I do is walk out of one world and into another. No one seems to understand the fact that I have fully spiritually awakened. It's not a philosophy, or metaphor. I have a spirit, and I know how to walk in it. Freaking heretic.

They could have just turned off the lights, and opened the blinds, but no one is willing to do something different to accommodate me. Who am I? No one in their eyes. They don't understand me. They can't fathom that I am TRULY not of this world, just a visitor in it. How many people have raised their finger to the sky, and watched a star burn up, leaving a trail stretching across the sky?

God has touched my life, and I love him for it. I have always loved him on some level, but the depth of it has changed over the years. I still feel distant from him, and a longing grows inside my heart each day that I am away from his presence. I distracted by daily events here. The farm asks more of me than I am willing to give. No one will work with me. They don't even recognize me. I am no one.

Is that what I have come here for? Is this what you want for me? I am wasting the years of teaching by staying here. Is it me? Have I walked away from you? I think it is the ways of the farm infecting me with a virus.

David Burton

6 Months

Chapter SEVEN

I have nightmares about staying here. Every night I pray for God to guide me, and I have these nightmares about me trying to break free from the farm. The people here are not changing. They remain the same as they were before coming. The only difference is that there are no chemicals in their blood, I hope.

This place is quite cunning, the way they teach you their language, how to say all the right things, and respond to the right cues. It is producing people who are actors, knowing nothing about God. There are a few who truly search, but I don't know how successful they are. If they are just going through the motions, nothing will happen. This is not the place for me, no matter how much I want it to be.

Many people have asked me why I am still here. No one seems to understand, I'VE TRIED TO LEAVE. They will not allow me to use the phone, or give me a ride. I am trapped. They won't even help me find another recovery house. They would rather see me on the street then at another treatment center.

They have lied to me the entire time, saying they will help. I have received no help. This is a cult where evil is rewarded and good is punished. The only way out is to walk, and I have no idea where to go. I have a document in my hand that promises me their help in transitioning. It is all a lie. The only help I will receive is a finger pointing to the driveway.

I have been told that I am the most negative person living on the farm, and that I have affected other people. Apparently, I am the plague, and I will be asked to leave if I continue this behaviour. How ironic. The amusing part of all this is that I've been threatened, assaulted, intimidated, persecuted, and accused, but all of it is ignored when I mention it to leadership. They just tell me I'm being negative. What? All the evil is justified, but my words are forbidden.

Today, I sat in a chair as far away from the dining hall as I could get, so that I could journal in peace. The leaders of the farm decided to have a meeting near where I was journaling. So, while I was mopping the dining hall, they all piled into the room near my chair, and closed their divider. When I finished mopping the floor, I returned to my chair, and my journal. As I am writing, the divider suddenly opens of its own accord. When I turn to find the source of the noise, I find myself staring into the eyes of the farm's director.

"Why are you sitting there?" Condemnation is not easily disguised, especially to me. He stands up and quickly walks over to where I am sitting quietly. "Are you listening to our conversation? You are sitting here so that you can hear us."

"What?" I was sitting in this chair long before their stupid meeting started, and the idea that a cloth divider is going to offer privacy is ridiculous. I stand up, and walk away.

Did I hear something? Yes. Was it my intention? No. I am tried, convicted, and executed in the space of sixty seconds. And these are the people who are supposed to lead me? No way. Things look good on the outside, but death reigns within. The director is a fitness junkie, and in the best physical shape of his life. I've seen him in the gym, and the guy is a beast. He is the lead guitarist of the worship band, and has so much charisma pouring out of him that it is sickening. He smiles, shakes hands, and greases all the right wheels. On the other hand, he is a paranoid fuck who thinks I'm listening in on his war council.

This morning, I was told that I am "overcome with rebellion" because I sat down during 'morning prayer,' and read Psalm 119. During prayer we must stay on our feet, and we are not allowed to sit down. Remember, this all happens at six in the morning. This place is insane. After prayer, I had a counselling session. I didn't let him speak. I just talked the whole time.

I think I'm going to snap, either in psychosis or anger. I'm burned out, and tired of trying to communicate. It's futile. Nothing is resolved, and nothing changes. Tomorrow will bring similar challenges, if not the very same ones. I will ask myself the same questions about my motives for staying, my aspirations for leaving, and examine my thoughts all day long. I will wonder why God tells me one thing, and why people tell me another. I will question my hearing, dreams, impressions, irritations, and feelings - inevitably coming to a place of indecision, where I can neither move forward or backward. In utter frustration, I will attempt to appease this inner turmoil with a chemical fix. I can't help but come to the conclusion that this place is going to wound me deeply.

Six thousand dollars cash, and four thousand dollars worth of labour later, these people won't even give me a phone call. I am a prisoner, an addict with no rights, and not even a human being in their eyes. I have become simply a commodity.

Wednesday

I despise the morning routine here, and whatever peace I had upon waking is stolen from me. It's like this every day. These people think they know what's good for me, but they are mistaken. I looked at myself in the mirror today. I truly looked. My eyes have dark circles beneath, and anger, frustration, and disgust covers my face. This is not helping me. I can't find the inspiration to make it through the day, so most of my time is a total loss.

David Burton

Another person left the farm today. He relapsed once already, and came back to try again. He lasted less than two weeks. An employment insurance cheque came for him in the mail. The farm asked him to sign it over to them. He couldn't do it. The call of the addiction was just too great to overcome. He took the money, and ran. I hope he lives through this relapse, because the last one almost killed him. He locked himself in a hotel room for a week, and became so paranoid that he couldn't leave the room. Brutal.

We had a visitor come to the farm tonight, and share his testimony. He left the farm quite some time ago. He didn't finish the program, and he appears to be doing alright. I think this message is a gift to many of us who are struggling with leaving. He brings a ray of hope, proving that we are not cursed if we leave the farm. I want to leave, but I've been resisting and doubting my motives. The chaos I have to face leaving here is not appealing. He had to walk out of here as well, because no one would help him. I've already stayed three times longer than this guy and he is telling us that his life is wonderful. It's time to open my mind, and stop being so rigid in my thinking.

I approached him after the meeting, looked into his eyes, and saw the truth: no spirit. Very disappointing. I almost bought his lie.

Thursday

For thirty seconds, I am at peace, and then the events of last night come back into my memory like a wave of destruction. I can't believe it. Now I'm waiting for a chance to brush my teeth, and using the time to write these words.

Last night, I was laying in bed, past *lights out*, with my ear plugs in. I can't sleep without them. I am ridiculously sound sensitive, and when I hear people breathing I want to smash chairs over their head. I had worked all day, and was exhausted as usual. Through the wall, I could hear people talking loudly, in spite of the sound protection. I waited. They didn't stop, so I hit the wall with my hand. It's a pretty common gesture that means: shut the fuck up.

In apartment buildings, people use broom handles to pound the ceiling above them, indicating that the noise level is unbearable. As soon as I hit the wall, the person on the other side started yelling, "Do you have a problem!?" Yes. Yes, I do. Then he started pounding back on the wall, out of anger I suppose. I thought it was over, and silence would descend. How wrong could I be?

The man came raging into the dormitory, throwing open the door with a crash, turning on the lights, and walked quickly across the room. He came and stood over me, while I was laying in my bed. I thought he was going to pull me out from under the blankets, and punch me in the face.

"Was it you pounding on the wall?" he asks me, glaring.

"Were you pounding back?" I ask him, standing resolute.

He turns, and walks away. Everyone in the room, all being awakened by the door and lights, say goodnight to him sweet as candy, as though these events happen every night. The dormitory sleeps eight men in one room, and no one has privacy. Two of these dormitories are side by side, with an office and washrooms in between. The man pounding on the wall, and screaming at me is a leader who has just relapsed, but somehow retains his power of authority on the farm. He has lived here for years, and knows damn well that the entire farm is asleep by nine-thirty at night. Everyone has to get up at five in the morning.

Knowing this, he is talking loudly, keeping me awake with his self-centered stupidity. I am abiding by the farm policy, and going to sleep early, but even when following their rules, I still manage to offend everyone.

Choir was good today. I closed my eyes, and came to a place within that I can't define. In this place, I talk to God, and he responds. I can't remember the words, but my heart was touched by powerful and overwhelming emotion, like the waters of an ocean. The pounding of the waves is calling me home. The sea is crashing against the shore within. God has taken me from darkness, and given me light. Nothing compares to this amazing relationship and connexion. Nothing is of any value, or importance, beside it.

I've been clean for six months. I haven't had this much time clean in the last ten years, a decade of addiction. I have a PHD (doctorate of philosophy) in addiction, and this is my thesis.

Friday

I woke up this morning, and I thought it was time to get up. I was on my knees in prayer for quite some time before I looked up, and saw the clock: 4 in the morning. I returned to sleep. I awoke once more, got on my knees, said Good Morning, and walked to the barn. The morning sky was beautiful and I immediately felt peace in my heart. I knew that today was going to be a good day.

I saw the calves, cows, baby pigs, huge pigs, cats, and kittens. All amazing creatures at home in the barn. I poured the feed, mixed the milk, and sang the whole time. I feel alive again. It wasn't my day to feed the animals, but I knew God had something in mind, because the other farmhand showed up late, apologizing profusely for sleeping in.

I have been renewed and strengthened, but I still have hesitation, because I don't know if I can maintain this peace in the face of adversity and conflict. I will do everything I can to hold on to this tranquility. Lord, create a shield of light around me that no darkness can penetrate. God, I give you my heart.

> "I am the door: by me if any man enter in,
> he shall be saved, and shall go in and out,
> and find pasture."

John 10:9

As I lay in bed last night, this scripture entered my mind. I had spent time on my knees in prayer, reflecting on the beauty and love I have for the cross. It is not a symbol of execution, but a symbol of powerful love, grace, mercy, and forgiveness. The amazing power displayed on that day, was this – he laid it all down, and became a man. The pain and agony of true suffering came, and he endured it because of his drastic love for all of us.

This message he gave me last night in prayer, but this morning the very same passage is our devotion for the day. I have no idea how he does this. I am learning to hear God's voice, and he confirms it in ways only he can.

During worship, I felt the change within. I am standing in a place I don't fully understand, tears falling from my eyes, communicating with a spiritual being. Suddenly, I perceive someone is standing beside me, and I cry harder, embracing the presence of the Lord. There is a depth of communication here that I've never experience before.

Later in the day, I walk to private place alone, and speak with God. For a moment, I am convinced he will appear. I see the air shifting and the light changing. I sense him, but can't see him. I can hear his voice, but my eyes remain blind.

David Burton

Being human is painful. I take my will and sin, which hurts him just as much as it hurts me. I just can't bring myself to realize it at the moment of my sin. It is only later that I understand what I have done, and only when he reveals it.

Saturday

I awake to the morning light, wondering how it has come to this. How have I fallen so far? The earth assaults my senses, and I hold on to God for dear life. I've been banned from the Hastings outreach again, and the leaders have decided to punish me some more by forcing me to work in the greenhouse. Are you seeing a pattern?

Saturday is the only day of the week when we have a few hours of free time. If we commit an offence against the rules during the week, leaders submit a punishment to the executive branch of leadership, for approval. For each offence, one *chore* is awarded. A *chore* is two hours of forced labour, to be served during the only free hours of the week: *Saturday*.

Yesterday, when I found out I'd been *chored* twice, I lost it. They have decided to drive a sword through my heart. I went straight to the leader who approves this shit, and raged on him. I am cut deeply by the blade of my anger, and the sense of rejection. I have developed a relationship with the leader who gives his seal of approval to my punishment. I have gone to this man in the past, opened my heart, sought fellowship, and listened to his counsel. I shared intimate details of my life with him, but he has betrayed me.

My words were for nothing, and my attempt at communication has failed. They see the man, not the spirit, and sometimes they see nothing at all. I am as outcast here on the farm, as I ever was in the world. Words may be just words, but the pain increases when they are followed by actions, which say: I hate you, I reject you, I punish you.

"Why have you done this?" I ask. He squirms, and begins his rationalization.

"I understand," he says. "You don't like being punished, but this is the way we operate." And that's it. Nothing.

This place is insane. The leadership here is so deceived that only an act of God, who they profess to follow, can remove the illusion. I have been 'punished' enough by the demons sent after me, by the dealers I bought from, by hateful people in my life, by my family, by the drug I used, by the paranoia I experienced, by Satan himself, and by myself, FOR NOT BEING ABLE TO DO ANTYHING ABOUT IT.

If I desired, or needed, 'punishment' I would pick up a drug, write off my life, and go to the street. I've had enough. I came here to heal, and these people find it necessary to abuse me. I am clean and sober, healed and restored, free from addiction. I am forgiving myself. I want people in my life who are for me, not against me; people who want to help, not harm; people who want to forgive, rather than condemn.

People who are willing to stand on the grace of God. Grace, love, and mercy: these are the traits of Jesus Christ. I pray I don't think of myself more highly than I ought, but I'm not a piece of garbage either. I used to think I was worthless, but not anymore. My value comes from nothing I have done, or will do, but from the fact that God loves me.

What a nightmare. I have had to stand against these people in order to keep my sanity. I am unwilling to sacrifice truth, in exchange for a falsehood. I don't want to be sucked into someone else's problems. In the greenhouse, there were several problems that need to be solved, logistical things, business things. I'm not here to solve the problems of the greenhouse, or allow anyone to trample on me. I am not a worthless, useless person, whose only ability is to be a slave to man. I will not believe the lies spoken about me. These people have no say in my life.

> "But the annointing which ye have received of him that abideth in you, and ye need not that any man teach you: but the same annointing teacheth you of all things, and is truth, and is no lie, and even as it hath taught you, ye shall abide in him."

> 1 John 2:27

I believe this scripture. I only found this verse recently, but I understand the concept, because God has been teaching me in this method for years. The teaching has been in progress for twenty years. It is not something to ignore or forsake. It has been a ray of light in the darkness of my life.

Sunday

Another dream stolen, snatched away from my mind. It is very strange to me, especially the frequency with which it has been happening of late. To most people, having a dream is rare; to me, not remembering the dream is rare.

I awake early to work in the barn. The sky is filled with white clouds, sun rays piercing the overcast, and shining on the mountains. The air is warm. I want something, but I don't know exactly what. The Island is calling to me, but I am hesitant to go.

228

In some ways, it is easier to stay here, but I have to face my life. I can't hide in here forever.

This is the most amazing day I've had here. A day where nothing went sideways, or collapsed around me. I experienced peace, contentment, satisfaction, and fulfillment. Perhaps it is because I was working in the kitchen, reclaiming my culinary art; perhaps it is the sun shining brightly in the sky, lifting my spirits; perhaps it is the people walking around, smiling quietly. Whatever the source, I am grateful for it.

The farm held its Annual General Meeting today, which was less of a meeting, and more of a gathering. Hundreds of people came to visit the farm. Anyone who has been touched by this place: families, men, women, and children. For the first time, I saw this place as a community of healing and spirituality. I saw something real and tangible, which has given me hope. I worked the grill, barbequing for the visitors, and watched the cottonwood drift across the sky like snow. A pristine day.

I am standing beneath a tent covering, singing to God with my eyes closed, and the spirit giving me the words. A flash of light pierces my vision in a horizontal line. It is so bright that I open my eyes, completely in shock, and I search for its source. There is nothing to explain this beam of light; no visible or possible source. For a moment, I am tempted to let the whole thing slip from my mind, until the person next to me asks...

"Did you see the flash of light?" And suddenly I understand.

"Were your eyes closed?" I ask.

"Yes," he replies.

"Ask around," I say. "No one who had their eyes open saw it."

David Burton

We asked the people around us. No one saw a thing. It was bright; and, I mean, BRIGHT.

Monday

I am about to walk away from everything. I am standing in my room, contemplating, when I notice a girl looking at me from the doorway. She catches my eyes, and walks into my room.

"Why are you going?" she asks. "I come here every night to listen to you, and speak to you."

My mind suddenly opens up within me, and I am staring at a memory. I see her laying on the bed, while I am on my knees in prayer with my eyes closed. Her hand is on my arm, and she is staring at me intently. The depth of connection I have with this girl is beyond any earthly realm. We have known each other for an eternity.

I am standing in my room, staring into her eyes. I pull her close to me. I am completely in love with her. She is the most beautiful, spiritual, pure being I have ever known. She is the only one I have ever truly wanted.

"Who are you?" I ask, awaking as I speak.

From the moment I opened my eyes, I have been in motion. I volunteered to cover for someone in the kitchen, and started the day in that I enjoy. I have become a part of the kitchen team here. Mainly, two people are responsible for maintaining everything related to the kitchen. Including, meal planning, picking up donations, inventory, keeping the walk-in freezer stocked, organizing the walk-in cooler, equipment maintenance, and work program oversight. I have built relationships with both, and grown close to them. These men have become my confidantes, and I seek counsel from them. I trust only one other man's counsel, even though many are trying out for the team. God has truly blessed me with these men. They have become my support network, even if they are unaware of it.

The farm is good for me in many ways, but there are things I have to accommodate, personalities I must accept, sorrow I have to acknowledge, and disappointment I've experienced. To continue, I must sacrifice – and, it hurts.

Yet, all of this is turmoil is nothing compared to the truth of my life. What is the truth? **She** spoke to me last night, and it's been awhile since I've heard her voice. I have been at war, caught up in the flash of fire, consumed by the search, and I've forgotten myself. How did it happen? How could I forget?

Why is my memory so distorted? It's the shifting between worlds that is causing this, in complete certainty. When I am in human form, I search for all things human, and forget the true nature of my soul. Does this make sense? Sometimes, I think I have a clear picture of my belief, understanding, and level of comprehension; then **she** comes and radically changes my perception. My priorities quickly change, or are aligned properly.

Who is she? She is a sentient being, a living entity, and her voice is hers. She is who she is. I can tell you who she isn't. She isn't a figment of my imagination, a creation of my subconscious, or a fever dream. She exists entirely independent of me, and for some reason, she has chosen to communicate with me.

My prayer is changing. I reach for God faster when situations slip out of control. I act quickly, respond furiously, come to the Lord in whatever stat I find myself in. These words are not relaying the power I am trying to capture, or the content of the images inside my mind.

Language is useful, and useless, simultaneously.

David Burton

Tuesday

And, it all comes crashing down. I have to get out of here. It may look alright on the outside, but my spirit is at unrest. Why should I stay? Where will I go? So frustrating. I get into an argument with a resident before seven thirty in the morning, and two hours later, there is another confrontation. I freak out, and walk away, searching for a counsellor. At least I didn't leave over this stupid conflict.

Afterward, the day got better, but the whole cycle will repeat tomorrow with another set of problems. Conflict over and over again, with no resolution in sight, because people essentially remain the same. A few spoken words from me means very little to these people, and I know it is only God who can spark the fire of change.

Anyway, let's carry on to something more interesting. A story I have to share with you. About a month ago, I brought a book with me on a walk off the property, and I lost it. It was a book about prophecy. The book fell out of my jacket, and search as I may, it was gone. Today, I found the book beneath my bed. Returned to my possession, and not the first object in my life to go through this process. Strange, eh?

Several years ago, I was living in a community. The building I lived in had three levels. The top two were lined with single rooms, and each room had a separate key. We guarded those keys quite carefully, because losing it meant being locked out of our rooms until someone could be located who had a master key. As a result, many of us attached lanyards to our keys, ensuring their presence in our pockets. The ground level was the common area, coffee bar, and lounge.

One day, I lost my key. I couldn't believe it. I retraced every single step I had taken since I awoke that morning. I searched every hallway I had travelled, place I had been, and chair I had sat in. On my second tour through the common area, I did something different. I closed my eyes, and extended my hand, as I was walking.

My key appeared in my hand.

Anyway, I got right sideways in class discussion today. A leader opened up a topic, and closed it, without discussion or resolution. He simply shut it down, and refused to hear anyone's comments. What kind of open discussion is that? Well, it didn't stop someone in the front row from standing up and attempting to teach the rest of us, imbuing us with his vast knowledge. Like he is the only one qualified to speak.

I am tired of people thinking that they have what it takes to run my life. My life is in the hands of God, and people need to stop interfering. I am tired of being told what is right, by people who think they know what right is. I am tired of people justifying their positions by using scripture. There is a lot of scripture tat is fairly disturbing, and I could use it to justify anything I want.

Am I the only one who sees this? What did Satan use to attack Jesus!? SCRIPTURE!! Why!? Because it is easily twisted. Let me rephrase. Words without understanding can mean anything. Prophecy without vision is just words on a page. A sword wielded to slay the innocent and the guilty. A sword does not have a voice, to say to the one who wields it, 'Turn this way, or that.'

I am at the point of writing off all further teaching from this place, except that which comes through the heart of man, of the voice of God. Emotion, or spirit; nothing else. Don't misunderstand my words, because they are not just words. There is a depth I am speaking of, a connection, a reshaping of my physical reality. Words are failing me. I can no longer express what is happening inside of me, and this place is starting to annoy me.

The cycle has repeated, and the day isn't even over.

Wednesday

Sex, sex, and more sex. Girls throwing their panties at me, and smiling seductively. I awake exhausted. Six months of this schedule has devastated me. I've had enough. I'm leaving. Where, and when, are the only questions that need to be answered. It's too bad this place wasn't more of a community, and less of a concentration camp. This place is like a military academy. If I wanted to be in the army, I would have joined the army.

The class content is based solely on one man, a prominent pastor in the church, with a far reaching ministry of videos, books, and speaking tours. He looks good on the outside, but his teaching leaves me sick to the stomach. There are many great pastors, and great teachers, in history that we could be studying, but we're not. It hurts inside. Even when I am doing a simple task, such as cooking, I check multiple recipes.

I took a trip to the slaughterhouse. One travel companion dropped fifty dollars somewhere on the ground. Lost forever. I had an alright day, even though a resident tried to start a fight with me. I just ignored them, and walked away. What's the point? I don't understand what is going on inside his mind, and honestly, I don't want to.

Thursday

I learned a new song last night. Three of us have formed a worship team, and we are leading this *Sunday*. It gives me purpose, and a reason to remain. However, the treatment of another resident on the farm has me ready to visit the Board of Directors.

The resident has started working for one of the leader's private company. The leader runs a business on the side, of course. Charisma, power, money, and the spotlight, isn't enough - he needs to run a company as well. And, guess where he gets his labour pool? The farm. So, this resident has been working for the company for several weeks. Each day the spend a few hours working contracts off property.

Yesterday was different. They worked a fourteen hour day. It's been moving in this direction for quite some time. What's the problem? Everyone works. Yeah, but hear me out. They pay this man NOTHING, and tell him he is working for the Kingdom of God. That's an abuse of scripture.

Volunteering is one thing, but this is quite another. Why? Because someone is making money. It is a profit driven enterprise, unless I am entirely mistaken. Which I am not. The company bills its clients. People who work for the company are employees, and need to be treated as such. In other words, pay the man.

Insecurity plagues me. It threatens to take hold of my mind. I need to be the strong, confident, being that God created me to be. We are all different. No two people are the same. Each one is created for an individual path. Standing in confidence is especially required while singing with others in a choir. I can have no self-awareness, or the whole process shatters. The only way to sing is complete abandonment of myself into the hands of God. I close my eyes, connect with God, and let go of the world.

Class is a waste of time. I have lost all faith in this video preacher, and want nothing to do with his teaching. However, as always, I must attend or leave the farm. They play the sound system so loud that I literally sit here in agony. The sound quality is poor, but they crank it up anyway – oblivious. I hate it.

I don't think people understand how sound works, or what it is like for me. Sound is a very intriguing part of my life. I hear things other people can't. I hear things that most people assume make no sound at all.

The video preacher is confused. He makes no sense. I can't believe we only listen to one preacher. It's insane. And disturbing. Who does this? Who paints a picture with only one color? An immature artist, that's who.

I'm exhausted. I just want to sleep. Next time I'm bringing ear plugs to class.

Friday

My body is aching when I wake up. I am burning out, living this works based program. For what? Nothing. Just one more fight with a resident, and a nightmare when I fall asleep. My dreams have taken a turn for the worse. My body is sore from lifting weights yesterday morning, but there is no rest, no time to heal, and no peace. It's off to the next thing. My physical being is a complete disaster, and everyone keeps telling me how good it is for me. Crazy.

How about rest, healing, relaxation, and balance? I'm tired of writing about it. These people don't understand, and probably never will. I can't stay here and physically maintain, let alone the mental anguish, and emotional trauma I'm putting myself through.

"The Farm. We're not happy, until you're not happy."

By nine in the morning, I've witnessed several people losing their minds: yelling, swearing, and plain falling apart. Thank God it wasn't me today, because I can't take it. I want the solution to my problem, not cause more. I'm not getting involved. That's my stance today. I am merely an observer.

However, I have drawn the line. I won't allow people to speak lies about me, over me, or to my face. It ain't happening. Why? It's like people casting spells at me. I'm not just going to stand there and take it. I will fight back because I have no fear of engaging in war.

Saturday

I played together with other musicians this morning, and I've found the love that misplaced somewhere along the way. I feel lifted up, higher than the sky, flying on wings of musical notes. Playing with other people brings to life a part of me that has been lost for a long time.

God gave me a vision, a long time ago, of what today will eventually lead to. At the time, I thought, "How is it even possible, Lord?" It seemed distant and unattainable, yet here I am, standing inside of it, at the very beginning.

I don't know if other people experience this. I dream every night, and I have visions of future events. Sometimes, God promises something. He shows me days, months, years, in advance. It seems impossible. Sometimes, I am confused, because the events are so far removed from my current situation, that my mind struggles to accept the truth of it.

The gift has nearly destroyed my life. There is no one left to teach me, except God. That's my reality. I've been labeled everything from schizophrenic to psychotic. With the world lying to me in every direction that I turn, it only makes my task more difficult. However, when the vision manifests in the physical realm, all doubt, fear, and insecurity, is washed away.

There is a train passing through my life, and I don't want to miss it. I will do anything it takes to catch it, even if I have to run through the brambles at the side of the track. The visions I've seen would shatter the mind of the average human being, but that's for another book.

I need to see this place as a school, not wat it is now, but what it could become. There is no worse deterrent to progress than seeing all things remain the same, with no hope of, or inspiration to change.

Sunday

I run, breaking through the barrier, and leaping into the sky. I am descending in the air, over a flight of steps, wings extended to each side. They have tried to stop me, but I refuse to listen. I see a soldier ascending the steps, intent on my destruction. I land in front of him, and throw him to the ground when he attacks. I run, and leap into the sky.

--- Include the rest ? ---

I awake, and know I must write. I can't find the light, so I walk to the washroom, and start recording the vision. I've only been asleep for a couple of hours. This one was intense.

I called my home, and my Mom answered. I told her about my frustration with being here, and my desire to leave. "You just want to smoke crack," she says. That's fantastic. My parents will never see me as anything other than a crackhead. My heart is being torn out of my chest. Will I ever be good enough for them? I don't think they will ever accept me.

God, I pray that you accept me, and love me, for the fallen, mistaken, sinful man that I am; and not for the man you want me to be. I may never become what you want.

My family doesn't believe in me. As far as I can tell, they think it is the farm that has achieved the sobriety in my life. They give the credit to the farm, rather than to God, or to myself. I made the play, and God backed it. I got on my knees, God stepped in, and set me free. It seems that my parents want me to stay here forever. Apparently, my life is over.

Why is this so painful? What happened to the dreams I had for my life? They are gone – taken from me. Did you save me only to have my heart broke over and over again?

I finally prayed the prayer I never thought I would, and, well, God answered. He spoke to me four times in the space of a few hours. Each time the message was the same, but each time, it came from a different source.

"I am changing you from the inside out," he said.

It started with a song I learned, called, Inside Out. I've never heard it before. The message in church service was about the heart being changed by God from the inside out. On the phone, my mother told me, "God is changing you from the inside out." Finally, I went to a church service this evening, miles upon miles away from the farm. The pastor stood up, and said, "God is changing you from the inside out."

You've got to be kidding me. Seriously!? OKAY. I hear you. When God speaks, he makes it so that there is no mistaking it. I get it. Now, teach me what it means. The EXACT same words from so many different people in a single day? Lord, how do you do this? The Spirit. It's the only answer I have right now.

Anyway, I listened, and paid attention. The dream last night scared me. I don't want sin to attach itself to me. I don't want to be in opposition to God. I need Jesus and his power – DESPERATELY.

Monday

Nightmare. All. Night. Long.

I smuggled a pack of smokes into the farm. Every morning, I've been smoking behind the barn after I feed the animals. Last night at church, I threw them away at an alter call. It seemed like the right thing to do at the moment, but now I am wondering if I acted out of emotion rather than reason.

Well, today was interesting. There's nothing like being left on the side of a highway to get your confidence up. The farm sponsors a street just outside the property. It means that we are responsible to keep it clean, picking up litter, and such. I was part of the work crew sent out, which was alright with me. They drove us up a couple of miles, and dropped us off.

It's summer, the sky is clear, and the air is warm. The plant foliage is beautiful. The trees are covered in leaves, the grass is long, colorful flowers are interspersed amongst the blades, and berries cover the brambles. I remove the refuse from the plants, and I'm pleased.

And then I realize I've been left behind.

No one returns to pick us up. For awhile, we stand there wondering if anyone will come, then we give up and walk. I arrive hours late. Supper is over, and the leader just laughs at us. I suppose he is amused by all of this. So, who cares? I had to talk a walk on an amazing summer afternoon. What is really disturbing me?

I view my life in sobriety as a war. Today, a commander sent a few soldiers out into battle, told them he was coming back for them, and then abandoned them. Why would I ever follow that commander again? I have a hard time extending trust to these people already, and this is just another slap in the face.

Today, it cost us nothing. It's not the end of the world. The incident is insignificant, and the consequences small. However, if he does this with a small responsibility, he will do it with a larger one. In war, it could cost me my life. I'm already struggling, and my mind needs to be focused on defense. This is an unwanted distraction.

When people who claim to play on my team, score in our own net, it sets the game back. I don't need to be wasting my time defending against my own players. Let me assure you, my life is not a game.

I found a pair of purple lace panties on the side of the road, and it set me right off, more than the empty liquor bottles and beer cans. I could care less about the alcohol, but I want sex, and I'm tired of living a life of enforced celibacy. I am a complete sexual mess. I have sexual desires raging inside of me. It is not natural for a man to live without a female sexual partner, and it leaves me open to attack. Demonic attack. I will accept a demon in female form because I have unfulfilled, unsatisfied desire.

I have a key, and being denied its true lock, I open doors I know are evil, out of sheer frustration. Do you understand?

Tuesday

David Burton

It's been a good day, all in all.

I have fought hard against temptation today. I tried to do it on my own strength, and failed, no matter how hard I tried. Suddenly, I called on Jesus, and tore the temptation in half, bound the demon, fell on my knees, and cried out to God. This is war. I'm serious. I am tired of accepting the lies of Satan. I am tired of falling, rather than making a stand. No more. That's the end of staying silent. I am making a stand, and taking back the ground. I about to engage in battle, and I WILL NOT HOLD BACK.

What's the lie? Let me lay it out for you. He whispers, "It doesn't matter. It can wait. Compromise. Negotiate. Be flexible." Lies. All lies.

I will move like the ocean: powerful and graceful, gentle and furious, ebb and flow. I will become the tidal waters. It's time to wake up. It's time to arise. It's time to shine light. I am attempting to remain calm, but these words stir the spirit within me. I am not an unlearned man. I understand what I am saying. I say it in faith. The world is changing for me, and nothing will be the same again. I am beginning to manifest the light.

Wednesday

I am walking up the street toward home. There are trees ahead of me and houses on either side of the street. A ball of fire, flashing with light, passes overhead and crashes in the distance, over the mountains.

I stop dead in my tracks and stand still, my eyes turn toward the crash site. I watch in silence as the clouds are pulled inward; storm clouds, black and white, rolling quickly: compressing behind the mountain.

The sky is empty for a moment and then there is an explosion that rocks the world. At first, I think it is a nuclear weapon. A huge ball of darkness appears near the mountain; it pulses waves of dark fire, upward.

I look to my left and see a young girl standing in the doorway of her house. I run up the pathway and enter the house with her. I take her in my arms and pull her back from the world. I fear the atmosphere has been contaminated or destroyed. We close the door and look out the front window.

I see the plant life turn into a black oily substance and melt, oozing into the ground. I am scared. Soon, we witness an army of soldiers encased in machines, a mechanical suit of battle armour: they are destroying the houses around us, tearing them to pieces.

I begin to wonder why these men have joined the enemy; then I wonder if they are even human at all. Our house will be next – I open the door and flee, hoping to outrun the destruction and find a safe haven; but, I fear there is no place left on earth to find.

I awake with my mind destroyed, trying to comprehend how all of this information was compressed into fifteen minutes of the physical realm. I haven't even written all of it, only the most vivid scene. The one that has been engraved inside of my mind.

> "But the day of the Lord will come as a thief in the night; in which the heavens shall pass away with a great noise, and the element shall melt with fervent heat, the earth also and the works therein shall be burned up."

> 2 Peter 3:10

> "And the stars of heaven fell into the earth, even as a fig tree casts her untimely figs,

> when she is shaken of a mighty wind. And
> the heaven departed as a scroll when it is
> rolled together; and every mountain and
> island were moved out of their places."

Revelation 6:13-14

The source of these two prophecies is Isaiah 34:4.

I watch the coming destruction of earth as a living soul, experiencing the emotional upheaval of the event, and awake - surrounded by people who think whether or not I wear my hat during group is the most important thing in life. And, they want to fight about it, all in the name of 'trying to help me.'

These people have no concept of what VISION is. They use the word carelessly, in near profanity. English is a whore, who switches the meaning of her words like sexual partners. All is lost. I explain the best I can, but it is like explaining a space ship to a cave dwelling man. They may be able to pronounce the word and mimic my speech, but they will never grasp the concept. NEVER.

Some people on the farm are messed up. It's not a judgement - it's the truth. Several people try to teach me a concept they don't understand, and it is tiring. I need someone who can relate to what I'm going through. It has nothing to do with addiction. I feel alone, and no matter how many times I explain it, the people do not understand, nor can they.

There has to be others with the gift. I can't be the only one. My eyes are burning, and I can't seem to find the power to sing. I'm burned out. How did it happen? I need guidance. I spent the morning in tears, crying for the innocent that were slain in the vision. My heart is torn, my body broken, and my spirit weak.

I need you, Lord.

Thursday

"I have had a vision," I say, within the dream. I am told that certain people will attempt to take control, but the creation must stay in my hands, or it will fail. I awake with the images burned so crystal clear inside my mind, that I could draw the images.

And then, the world infringes upon the clarity, attempting misdirection, and trying to take my eyes off the truth. I feel frustrated, but remain calm. The world is a mere irritation. People obviously don't understand, so why freak out. My anger is motivated by sadness. Sorrow for what will come to all of them.

Friday

Another day has come, and this one has hurt since the moment I awoke. The dream slips away, I'm exhausted, and I can barely get out of bed. I fall to my knees, and cry out to God, quietly. I'm reasonably sure that the people I live with don't want to hear me screaming at five thirty in the morning, but that's how I feel.

I suppress my true nature, because it is unacceptable in the eyes of man. I will try, for one more day, to do it their way. The first tragedy is that I get off my knees, leaving prayer, to listen to a devotion written by a man. I exchange the reality of God for a forgery, and I am sick to my stomach. I can barely walk this morning, and my balance is all fucked up - this is not a good sign.

I have a strong presence within me, fighting against the forgery. The voice warns me that what I am doing is wrong, dangerous, and unhealthy. Everything within me says, stop and pray, but I continue onward because the schedule forces me. If I stop to listen to God, I will be reprimanded by leadership, and evicted. By trying to please men, I walk into a disaster. How could it end any differently? I am now standing in enforced 'morning prayer,' and I'm freaking out.

Satan is in my head, screaming at me, playing on my weakness, frustration, and anger. I visualize running from the room and screaming, "SHUT UP!" I collapse to my knees, screaming at the top of my lungs, "I CAST YOU OUT IN THE NAME OF JESUS CHRIST!" My eyes are closed, face screwed up in concentration, and my fists clenched. It hasn't been this bad in awhile, and I know it is because I am stressed out, at the point of exhaustion, and trading a truth for a lie.

Satan continues to whisper, because I'm still standing in the room, rather than walking outside and fighting, as I know I must. I am at war within my mind, desperately trying to protect the people around me from the torment I am experiencing. No one knows what is happening, and I attempt to keep it that way.

In a few minutes, I can't take anymore, and I have a complete melt down in front of everyone in the prayer room. I lose it, and walk away (which is forbidden). I need to be alone. The second I am alone, I start speaking to God, vocalizing everything that is happening. I am immediately drawn to higher ground, and start walking up the mountain.

With each step I take, my freedom increases. I become aware of the sickness inside of me, and I pour out my heart to God. I want to throw up all over the road. I reach the plateau, rip off my jacket, and throw it on the ground. I start screaming as the rain begins falling. As I look out over the valley below, a sense of peace quickly descends. Suddenly, something changes inside of me.

THIS IS WHERE I AM SUPPOSED TO BE.

God has been calling, the farm interfering, and it becomes painfully obvious. A leader arrives, and tells me, "You are doing you own thing. You need to pack and leave the farm." I ignore him, because I know God has sent him to listen to me, even if he doesn't know it yet. I know this man, and I've spoken to him many times before. He isn't like the others. As a result, my defenses remain lowered, and I start talking to him about how I feel.

I am still in prayer, and in a few moments, I am crying. I widen the circle of prayer, and allow him to witness. We talk quietly for quite some time. It is difficult for me to open up, because there is a voice in my head telling me: I'm not worth the time, he is only listening to me because it is his job, my problems aren't big enough to deserve attention, I am a stupid child, I am insane, none of this is real, it's all in my head, I'm a failure, I'm lying to myself, I'm not good enough, it's all hopeless, and I may as well give up and get high.

I keep talking, in spite of the distraction, trying not to hear the voice in my head. This is hell. The time we spend together helps me, and I find a reasonable explanation for why I am ultra-sensitive this morning. My parents are coming tomorrow. My pattern is that I get high, usually the day before they arrive. This is that day.

In the eyes of my family, I am a drug addict. It will always affect their perception of me. Everyone in my family is employed, successful, married or moving toward it, has money and material possessions. I am a homeless crackhead, who can never get his life together, and experiences failure upon failure. Our two views are in stark contrast.

I see myself as a spiritual being, and they see a human being.

Well, this is shaping up to be a fantastic weekend (sarcasm). My parents called and bailed on the visit, and I've been banned from attending the Hastings outreach - yet again. Just one more bullshit excuse from the leader in charge of the outreach. He's a write off. The Hastings opportunity door has slammed closed in my face, permanently.

Satan is using an interesting tactic. All things human have failed. My anger has surfaced and is raging, wreaking havoc inside of me. I can feel my heart pounding, and my blood pulsing. I am responsible for what I do now. Thank God I have a choice today, and I don't have to walk blindly into stupidity.

The leader is an ant with delusions of power. An ant speaking with a loud voice to the anthill, grasping at straws, while trying to describe aircraft. He will never see an aircraft, or understand how it works, let alone pilot one. Suddenly, sadness overwhelms me.

> "For in much wisdom is grief: and he that
> increases knowledge increases sorrow."

> Ecclesiastes 1:18

Laugh or cry? Someone once told me to try find the humour in every situation. I have become very good at seeing the tragedy and disappointment, uselessness and stupidity, bitterness and travesty. So, let's see if I can find anything to laugh at in all of this.

Nope.

I'm starting to get sick, and I need to go to bed. I lost my voice this morning, and now I can feel the disease taking hold in the back of the throat. Instead of staying in bed, as rational people do, I was forced to rise and face the day. Now, my condition has worsened. My health suffers because of the intense schedule here.

Our alarms pierce the stillness of morning at 5 AM. We have

fifteen minutes to shit, shower, and shave.

5:15 AM we meet with our partner, and read the corresponding chapter of Proverbs out loud to each other, alternating verses. 31 days in the month; 31 chapters in Proverbs.

5:30 AM we gather as a house and read a devotion from a prosperity gospel pastor, and a short section of scripture. We write a *seven point study*, identifying the commands, promises, ... , and the message we received from the passage.

6 AM we meet in the New Life Center basement for 'morning prayer.' Slides are placed on the projector, and we pray for different topics while walking in an endless circle. No one is allowed to sit down during this time, and we have to pray out loud. Silent prayer is forbidden.

6:30 AM we disperse into various groups for physical training. Walk the track, run to the stop sign, work out in the gym, or do calaesthetics in the prayer room. 7 AM we gather for breakfast in the dining hall. 8 AM we begin our classes, which usually consist of video preachers. 9:30 AM we split into journal groups, and read the previous day's entry to the small group. 10 AM brings us into worship (twice a week), or another class (twice a week). Every Wednesday work program begins early. 12 PM we gather for lunch, and are granted one half an hour to prepare for the afternoon.

1 PM we all gather in the dining hall for work program, where we are given our assigned labour for the day. This mainly consists of sending people to the industrial greenhouse, where we work until supper.

5 PM we come together to break bread and bitch. 6 PM we attend evening classes. 8:30 PM we are dismissed and sent to our respective houses or dormitories. 9 PM we gather for warfare,

which consists of praying out loud for fifteen minutes. 9:30 PM is lights out. No one is to be caught awake past this time.

Every resident on the farm has a partner, and can't go anywhere alone. We must ALWAYS be in the presence of another person. In the case of an emergency, a leader can release you (which is permission to travel alone for a few minutes). If caught alone, you are immediately reprimanded, and *chored*. If you complain, you are *chored*. If you question the authority, you are *chored*. If you sleep in, you are *chored*. If you are thirty seconds late for ANYTHING, you are *chored*. If you talk back, you are *chored*. If you are sarcastic, you are *chored*. If you express an opinion not aligning with the farm doctrine, you are *chored*. If you fail to complete your daily journal entry, you are *chored*. I've even been *chored* for taking a shit during a lecture.

For every *chore* you earn, you spend two hours working in the greenhouse during the only free time we have all week. Saturday. As you may have gathered, time is precious here on the farm, and they love to take it from you.

As if this wasn't enough, allow me expound some more of the inner workings of the farm. In order to access such things as medical services, dental services, essential phone calls, receive mail, or play a musical instrument, we must fill out a permission slip. Permission slips can be filled out and submitted all week long, but they are approved and returned only once a week. Only two phone calls are allowed each week, and only if they are approved by leadership. Calling a treatment center, or recovery house, is forbidden. Calling for help to leave is forbidden. There is only one phone that can be used to place outside calls. It is in a locked office, and guarded at all times. Any mail that is received must be opened in the presence of leadership, and screened. If the envelope contains a cheque, it must be signed over to the farm, or you are evicted.

Musical instruments can't be played for the first three months. If you are caught playing an instrument without a permission slip, you are *chored*. No secular music can be played on the property, either on the radio, or by your own hand.

All literature must be screened and approved. No books outside of their particular doctrine are allowed to be read, at any time. There is no room for philosophical thought in this place. You literally have to conform to their conditioning in order to maintain your residency.

There is some slight variation from day to day, but generally the schedule remains the same.

You've got to be fucking kidding me!? I am tired of fake people, who wouldn't know God if he was standing right in front of them. What do I say? What am I supposed to do? Am I to remain motionless? Am I to sit here intently listening? BLAH. BLAH. BLAH. Words with no meaning. That's all I hear. Twisted words, broken concepts, and lies, mixed among other lies for flavour. What an utter waste of time. Anything is better than this. Shoveling shit in the barn is more interesting than this.

I've seen this act before, and that's exactly what it is. An act. I see what is happening here. They are asking me to exchange the truth of God for a man-made concept. Grace, for law; power, for the delusion of it. The people listening to this crap accept it because they know nothing better. In fact, they know nothing at all.

I'm not sure of what to do in this situation, or how to proceed. The teacher is yelling at the class again, and I'm ready to lose my mind. It doesn't seem to matter who I talk to on this farm, leadership allows this man to teach this class, with no oversight. Here's a class, do whatever you want. The person teaching this class is a lunatic.

I can't stand it. I am going to lose it. Either I speak up, or throw up.

Okay, it passed. Heavy breathing and some mental gymnastics. I think I'm going to make it through this. What a lovely place. I can't contain myself. I am going to rip this man apart. My hands are shaking, and my heart is skipping beats.

The entire time, I have sit here quietly, and stared out the window. I draw no attention to myself, but he places it on me, in total disregard of the other thirty people in the class. I gave him the gift of privacy before class while he was in deep thought, and he returns it with a public verbal slap in the face.

He is a mess. He is making a joke of God, and the message of Jesus Christ. He doesn't even understand the scripture he is reading. Misrepresentation. That's my conclusion. I wonder how God deals with this kind of blatant disregard of the truth. Is this why he brought me to the farm? To correct this guy?

Let the people discover the truth for themselves. Have I become that jaded? This leader is a lunatic. Did I mention that? Probably, it's the main theme of this literary tirade. Honestly, I don't know how else to express these emotions that threaten to overwhelm me.

Well, I finally found the humour. Ready? He is constantly hoping for a manifestation of God's power while runs the outreach on Hastings. God sends me, and this teacher bans me from going there. Do you see it? It's so ridiculous that I can't help but smile and laugh. Sadly, it is killing the people he wants to save from destruction.

This class is a nightmare. I've never seen a man lead so many people astray as this one has. I have refrained from all-out war in the classroom, but I have recorded my thoughts here, in these pages.

I saw the kittens playing in the straw laying on the barn floor. A ray of sunlight pierced the ceiling, and fell upon the straw. A single beam of bright light. A kitten noticed, and crawled up to investigate, pawing at it gently. In the blink of an eye, a couple of them were rolling around in the warmth of the light, playing. God Is Good. All The Time.

Saturday

I made a lot of mistakes when I left the farm, to visit the city. I smoked, I stared at women with lust in my heart, I drank espresso endlessly, and laughed at stories of my past drug use - stories only an addict could laugh at, because they are truly horrifying. I did not control my eyes, or my imagination.

I fell hard, and even as I was falling, I justified it by saying, this is the way of the world. Everyone does it. It is obvious that our culture has fallen, and me right only with it. Satan has this world in his grasp. Am I to be driven by lust and material possession? No. There is a higher calling for my life. I tell no one the truth. I can't even acknowledge it to myself. When am i going to get real?

Today, I am making the decision to stay here on the farm. I am ignoring the confusion and conflict, even though it is difficult. I am acting in faith, and trusting God. I am sacrificing my plans, and laying down my imaginations. My perception of life, and God, is changing slowly. I am coming out of twenty years of addiction. Can you imagine the damage I've done in all those years of suffering?

Satan, I know you will come and speak to me. I know you will try to convince me that I am making the wrong decision. I know you will use the people around me to hurt me. I know you will try to distract me. I know you will attempt to use my anger against me. I know you will show me how weak and lost humanity is. Have I left anything out? Yes. Your tactics are many. The list is ridiculously long.

God, I have a great sadness within me. Where does it come from? Sometimes, I feel frustrated with myself. I have a difficult time making a decision and keeping it. I want to change, Lord. I want to wake up in the morning and know what I believe, understand what I am supposed to do, and the reasons for it. I don't want a man-made set of rules, or a concept of religion. I want to know you. I don't want to ever ask the question of what Jesus would do, I want to know what he would do. Jesus, you did what you saw your father do; you said what you heard him say; and, I want to be the same.

Sunday

I dream of evil people, in evil circumstances, doing evil things. There is no point in describing it. I am still shocked by the decision I made yesterday. I made the choice, and I relate it to selecting a major in university. This is the first day of class in a new semester. I didn't do much in the first six months, except remove the narcotics from my system. Now, comes the next stage of development.

I've identified certain qualities that I need. Now, I need to refine them.

Masturbation. Can't avoid it, so let's take a look. Masturbating gives me a false sense of power and release. I feel power flow through me, but it leaves me with less than I started with. The thought of taking a woman against her will, and forcing her submission, excites me. Humiliating her brings me release. Nothing is more arousing than forcing my will upon her.

How did I become this way? I have twisted my mind through the pornography I've watched, and completely corrupted my sexuality. I've become conditioned by endless hours of video pornography. I didn't start out like this, but here is where I've ended up.

I want to take a woman, regardless of how she feels about it, and have my way with her. It is mental stimulation. My mind has cut out my heart, and all that remains is a cold sexuality. Anger, sex, and power have all mingled within me. I don't just want sexual release, I want to dominate and humiliate my partner in order to obtain it.

Monday

I am lifted into the sky, soaring around a huge storm. White clouds surround me, with lightning flashing inside. I see the earth far beneath me.

I awake, and my body is weak. I've lost my voice, my lungs are infected, and I'm running a fever. I rise and face the day, hoping it will pass, but I only get worse as the day progresses. I am so tired that I do not have the strength to embrace my anger.

I've tried to become involved with the worship here on the farm. I've built relationships with all of the musicians, but I've discovered it is a club with a hierarchy. It aggravates me, but it's not the first time I've had to start from the bottom, and work my way up. It's not a new concept for me, and if this is what God wants me to pursue, no obstacle will be too great to overcome.

As disgusting as it is for me at the moment, I must play politics. I can't access the equipment unless I follow the unwritten code of these musicians. I'm not the only person on the farm that plays an instrument, but I play it for a different reason. It's not a show, or a performance; it's like breathing air. I need to breathe in order to live.

I am really sick. My lungs hurt, and my sinuses are filled with liquid. That was fast. Saturday morning, I felt the first symptom, and today I have a full blown infection. I am weak, dazed, and extremely calm.

Tuesday

Still sick, in spite of the healing I experienced during the night. I dream of music and the ocean. I didn't sleep well, and this morning I'm told I have to walk halfway across the farm just to get permission to go back to bed. My voice is gone, lungs in agony, and sinuses destroyed. Fantastic. I have no energy to face this day.

Somehow, I am making it through the day. Slower than usual, but I believe God is in the process of healing me. Last night, God showed me how bad my life was before coming here. He showed me how I was trying to create a life on my strength, and in my own way. I used to feel empty, alone, hopeless, and in despair, constantly in an altered state induced by prescription medication or illegal drugs. I had no one in my life, and was existing for only one purpose - to get high, whenever the chance arose. I was lonely, and the only contact I had with people was when I was loaded.

I have come to the conclusion that judgement and offense are linked. I judge a person's actions, behaviours, mannerisms, methods, beliefs, or even tone of voice, as inappropriate or unacceptable. Then I am offended when they continue in this inappropriate or unacceptable way.

God has taken the blinders off my eyes.

Wednesday

I am in a house, in a bedroom near the back of the house. I am looking through the window, and listening to someone tell me a story. "He put his fingers in his ears. He did not want to see what was entering the room. He was terrified. He tossed aside his blankets, and tried to run. He fell. He could not escape, and he died horribly." I am shown in a vision, what entered through the door. A demon, in the form of a man.

I awake. I work all day, and can't even find time to have a shower. I make some mistakes, but I let them go. The men on the farm have been showing me grace, but it's taken me awhile to see it. I think I am finally beginning to change, and making the decision to stay has opened doors. I can't believe how close I came to leaving. God intervened and rescued me, when I didn't even know I needed help. Conflict will arise, difficult situation will arrive, but God will see me through.

I don't know everything, but I know the one who does.

The person sharing their testimony during peer review this evening touched a chord in my heart. When he arrived on the farm, he caught my attention. I've been monitoring his progress from a distance, careful not to interfere. I've seen the light come into his eyes. I hoped for it, believed in it, and I've seen it come into existence. This is a beautiful thing to witness, and better than listening to a thousand sermons. Not many people understand what I'm talking about. I don't even think I could explain it effectively, because I'm still walking out the process myself.

A song has risen within my heart, and is beginning to take shape. I didn't know if they day would come, that I would begin composing again. Something has changed inside of me. This day continues to bring a sense of purpose, direction, and hope, to the edge of my perception.

Thursday

The earth is dying, but several people are escaping the destruction. I am one of them. We rise into the sky, aboard a ship, into the darkness of the sky. I am hidden among the people, and no one knows who I am. It remains that way until I begin to reveal myself. The people are angry because of what I am, and the power I have.

I awake, rise, and walk the earth. I am dismissed early from morning class, so that I can rest. I crawl into bed, and fall into the dream world.

I am standing on the hillside, wings extended to either side. I launch myself from the earth, and glide into the valley below. During the flight, I notice a black weight chained to the edge of each wing. I am disturbed, but it does not interrupt my flight. I land, walk into a crowd of people, and confront a man hiding within them.

"You have lied to me," I say. "I am leaving this place."

I awake, reeling from transference. In other words, I am not fully returned. I am still in the spirit. I look at the world as an alien angel, walking in human skin, looking through human eyes. My sight is clear, and crisp, sharp like the sight of a bird. Even the light appears different. I have lived on the farm long enough to have some small recogonition of my surroundings. I hear a choir of voices singing in the distance. Something within understands that these men are singing to God. I am pleased, and walk toward the sound.

I am a traveller between worlds.

Friday

She walks my dreams. I awake with my eyes burning a deep blue, and a peace in the depths of my soul. She graced me, as tempermental as she was.

Today, we are given a day off. For some strange reason, they have decided to give us some rest and relaxation. Everyone is loaded up into the farm vehicles, and we head for the community tennis courts. We bring all our ball hockey equipment with us. It was the perfect opportunity to talk to some people, and get some counsel; however, I ended up giving more counsel than I received. Something inside of me is changing, and I notice it most in the area of communication.

It is summer, and there are many young women at the park. They are young, fully developed women, with hormones raging inside their bodies. I sense it like blood in the water. It drives me insane. I've been celibate for over a year, maybe two. My eyes are drawn to these women, and I can't help myself. There is no inhibition within me. The director notices my gaze, and decides to confront me.

"Are you looking at them?" he asks.

"No," I lie.

They enforce celibacy on the farm. No one is allowed to even look at a woman, let alone touch her. Relationships are forbidden. Socializing with women is banned. I'm surprised they don't ask us to castrate ourselves. Discussing the topic with leadership will just lead to punishment by the thought police. In my opinion, it's just easier to lie and avoid the conversation.

The sick and twisted part of all this, the director is married. As are all the other leaders. They are all free to fuck their brains out with their wives, but all the slaves can't look at women, talk to women, or masturbate. All self-gratification is from hell. Honestly, who even wants to try masturbate on a farm surrounded by men?

Saturday

Powerful dreams.

Sunday

I am learning about being in relationship with people. I've come to understand that there is another level to playing guitar. It comes when two musicians play together, who understand keys. I played rhythm, and someone else played lead. The two of us blended our sound together to create something new. I was able to play some songs I've written, while the other musician used a scale to play along. I was still able to convey the message of the song, but the second guitar added a depth to the composition.

Addiction has destroyed my life, and stolen everything from me. The pieces of my life that I have left are stored in a few boxes. I had them delivered to the farm yesterday. All of my writing, and artwork, are now sitting in my room. Most of the work was created in my addiction, in suffering, pain, and sorrow.

I think someone has sorted through the pieces, and assembled parts of it, but I don't mind. Only someone who accepts me as I am could have done this. My family has earned my trust over the years. They could have destroyed my work, or thrown it into the garbage, but they kept it and protected it. I am grateful.

My description is inadequate. The words contained on these pages, laying inside the boxes, could destroy the way a person sees the world. Certainly, it would change their perception of me forever. When I read the text, and see the images, that have come from the depths of my soul, I am in shock and awe. I can't believe that I've created them. There is more to myself than I understand.

I've been a small pieces of a large puzzle, but as the pieces come together a painting is revealed. I am scared to admit to myself the truth that is displayed before my eyes. I don't think anyone will understand.

Monday

I found an old photograph, torn out of a pornographic magazine. Of course I looked at it, then tore it into tiny pieces, and tossed it into the garbage can. I don't want this in my life anymore. It has no place within me.

I stay up late reading the words I have written in the past, and even later trying to understand what it all means. It appears that I have left a message for myself. I hope I am prepared to receive it. Among the scattered pages, I find an old manuscript. I read the entire book. Segments of it are amazing, but some ideas are so compressed that they make no sense. A single theme stood out. I wrote these words because I would need them in the future. I need to remember what has already happened, in order to see clearly the events ahead.

Some is prophecy, some is truth, some is for me alone. I can see several books, contained in one. All I need to do is extract the information. Eleven years have passed since I wrote the manuscript, and at the time I was still learning how to write. I can see the inexperience in the way I assembled the words. However, I think I can create a coherent vision out of it. A book that people could understand.

David Burton

I can see the indecision in my writing. I was faced with a choice, but didn't want to make it, fearful that I would choose the wrong pathway. I suppose the indecision itself has cost me years of my life.

Tuesday

I awake, and rise from my bed, exhausted. I never get the rest I need here. Last night, someone was snoring so loud I put a pillow over my head, and pushed my ear plugs in as far as they would go. I could still hear the person, and I keep waking up all through the night. I can't remember the last time I've slept through the entire night.

I get up, grab my towel, and head for the showers. Only the scalding hot water scorching my body will wake me up this morning. I can barely keep my eyes open, and it's only the second day of the week. This madness is endless. The schedule is brutal.

I attend morning prayer in frustration. It's a complete waste of time. It's difficult to concentrate while thirty other people are talking at the same time. Most of them are just making conversation, rather than actually talking to God. Yesterday, I was deep in prayer, connected with God, tears streaming down my face, when suddenly the person running the prayer session claps his hands and says, it's time to pray for a business. I was a complete mess, heart torn open, standing there, and unable to contain the emotions raging inside of me. I was praying.

Like so many other things here, they don't want prayer, they want the image of it. They want to go through the motions, but fail to find the power. The divide morning prayer up into small segments. They set a timer, and when it goes off, we change topics. It's ridiculous. They think prayer can be boxed, measured, and contained. Guess what? If you come into the presence of God, you will be blinded be tears and unable to speak.

They teach what I call 'slot machine prayer.' Approach God like a slot machine. Safely stand outside the box, drop in your coin, and wait for a response. Perhaps you will win what you hope for, or simply lose your coin. Understand? There is no relationship with a slot machine. The machine isn't going to talk to you. You can stand there all day, dropping coins into the slot, but nothing will happen.

It is amazing how quickly my thoughts fall into old patterns. As though roads have been cut into the forest of my mind. I have walked off the known road, and I am cutting new trails to follow. I don't want to return to my old ways. I don't want to spend my time being miserable, and hating every day I spend here. Sometime, I become irritated with the people here, but I can't let this ruin my day. I have been set free, but there are certain things I must do to maintain this mind set. When offense arises, I must use forgiveness and grace to fight the war.

Forgiveness isn't just a theory. It has practical application. To understand forgiveness, I must forgive. To understand grace, I must give it. Jesus says I can't expect to be forgiven unless I forgive others. I get the concept, but actually practicing it is hard. I don't want to forgive the person who has offended me. I want to see him held accountable, reprimanded, and receive the punishment he deserves.

The way I understand it, forgiveness isn't making an excuse for the other person's bad behaviour. They did something wrong. Truly. And, they will answer to God for that someday, but if I don't forgive them, I am the one who suffers. The poison is in my own soul.

Wednesday

A girl is standing in front of me, facing away. She bends down, and her panties slip out of the top of her jeans. She's wearing a pink thong. I take her in my arms, and reach between her legs. She is soft beneath my fingertips.

I awake, and I'm not impressed. There is no girl in my arms. I am laying in bed, alone in the darkness.

"Not again," I whisper.

I am yearning for a female to spend my life with. I can't take this. I start praying as soon as I return to my body. My eyes aren't even open yet, and I'm not on my knees, but it seems right. I grab my towel, and head for the showers, knowing the hot water will wake my soul. After inserting my contacts into my eyes, I realize that my eyes are refusing to wake. Sleep covers the lens, but I try to blink away the blur so that I can read.

I'm tired, but determined to continue. I feel a new presence within, carrying me forward. Sometimes, the pathway is hard and slow, but I trust the guidance within me. I have made a decision to do something each day that moves me forward, toward the future I can't see or understand. I keep walking, no matter what. There is a war being fought, ground being taken back, new strategies formulated, and old images being transformed into new visions.

I don't know what to expect, but there is light in my eyes.

7 Months

Chapter EIGHT

I awake from a nightmare, unimpressed, and angry. Several nights have passed with these faded impressions passing through me. They slip through my fingertips like sand. I can't examine the images, because they flee from my consciousness. I know something is wrong, but I can't identify the source. I have a theory. Satan is interfering.

I found several documents, among the others inside of the boxes. They were a personal message, written years ago, because I saw what was coming. It is time to rise. I've wasted enough time. I must complete the work that has been given me by the author and finisher of my faith.

This farm is ridiculous. Let me demonstrate. During class, the blinds were open, and the sun shining bright in through the wall of windows. Not needing the overhead lights, I flicked the switch, and turned them off. When the teacher entered the classroom, he turned the lights back on and closed the blinds. Several people groaned.

"Are you seriously turning on the lights? Look outside." I said.

"Be quiet," replies one of the residents.

Then he turns in my direction, and threatens me. He supports the stupidity of the teacher, and is ready to fight in order to protect the idea. With both doors standing wide open at each end of the classroom, I finish my critique of their uselessness.

"We might as well turn on the heat," I say.

Several people laugh, understanding my point, but it only

aggravates the teacher, and his mindless followers. They are invested in defending the use of lighting on a sunny day. There is a consistent lack of common sense here on the farm, and it scares me.

The way something is said can carry as much weight as the words spoken. Tone of voice, word placement, and body language, can convey condemnation easily. A single line of speech can tear someone apart, or lift up their spirit.

I am exhausted to the point of collapse. I approach leadership for help, explaining the fatigue I am experiencing, and looking for a solution. Why am I exhausted? Sleep is denied me, meditation is nearly impossible, and I have a thousand images inside my mind, passing through me like the hail of a coming storm. I am overwhelmed, and having a hard time breaking down the images into segments that I can handle. I've found a river, and I can't stop the flow. If I try to stop the water, I will likely drown.

I've figured out a way to assemble one of my books. I will weave the story using an abstract method. It's not the way literature is written these days, but I think I can make it work. I will present the pure information, and allow the reader to drawn their own conclusions.

Friday

I awake, surprised that morning has coming so quickly. The sun is shining brightly in the sky, and the air is crystal clear. This is the kind of day that inspires me to travel. Something in the air calls me to destinations unknown. There is a sense of mystery and intrigue, excitement and preparation, longing and fulfillment. I want to walk the world, experience the culture, visit foreign lands, and find what I am looking for. I don't want to just hide here on the farm.

David Burton

I could be working, creating a life, with a woman at my side and in my bed. My mind begins to visualize the old ways. I see myself sitting on the patio of a pub, enjoying the warm summer evening, a glass in my hand, and a strange woman sitting with me. We talk quietly as we sip drinks, conversing about philosophy, hopes, and dreams. Slowly, we lean in closer, our hands touch, our eyes lock, and we know where this will lead.

Nope. Instead, I live with thirty men, and can't remember the last time I got laid. On the bright side, I might be able to join the Hastings outreach. I seem to have repaired the relationship with the leader in charge. Strange, considering I had written off ever going there again. I don't understand these fluctuations in relationships. What am I supposed to be learning?

Worship opened my heart again today. I reached out, and God reached for me. Tears are blinding me as I write these words. I stood in worship, with my eyes closed, singing. Suddenly, God gave me total recall of a dream I had many years ago.

I dream of my daughter. She is standing next to me, tears in her eyes, with her arms stretched up to me. I reach down, pick her, and wrap my arms around her. "If you wanted up, why didn't you just say?" I ask her. She wouldn't even have to ask out loud. I love my daughter, with all my heart. I want to her to be at peace. She is safe in my arms.

For years, I have thought that I am the father picking up my daughter, but today God showed me something different, and my perception altered. I am the child, and God is my father, lifting me off the ground and into his arms. I am the child, reaching out in agony, not knowing how to ask, "Father, lift me up." The feelings I have in the dream, are the emotions God has for me. The love I feel for my daughter, is the love he feels for me.

So, today I raised my arms to him, as she did to me, and he picked me up. He wrapped his arms around me in love. The peace and presence that surrounded me was amazingly indescribable, beautiful, and powerful. The contact and presence of God remained within me, and it did not break - as long as I reached for him.

Thank you, Lord.

Saturday

I lay in bed, preparing my mind for what is coming. Today, I return to Hastings, to face the darkness. I rise, shower, get dressed, and head for the team meeting. We pray, mount up, and fly down the highway. When I arrive, the streets are quiet, but they explode into a flurry of movement only a moment later. I feel called to walk the streets, and talk to the people trapped in their addiction. I assemble several others, and we are quickly moving toward the back alleys.

"Why are you here?" A girl asks me, huddled in a doorway.

"I was addicted to crack," I reply.

"You were a crackhead!?" she asks, incredulously.

"Yes," I say hesitantly. "Jesus Christ has set me free."

I don't have the words to explain what has happened to me. I don't even understand my freedom. I just know that it exists, and I want to give it to others. I want to give those in the darkness the light that I've found.

"I don't see it in you," she says, "At all."

"I know," I whisper.

David Burton

The people I am walking with don't understand what is happening. They are awkward and unsure of themselves, not knowing what they are doing here. I am learning as I speak. God teaches me with every step of faith I take. As usual, I learn in the moment of greatest need, and this is one of those moments. Suddenly, she turns inward, toward the cloud of smoke she has just inhaled, and disappears.

Good-bye beautiful girl, I say quietly. I turn and walk away. I make several other connections as I walk the alley. I seek the people. Every chance that God gives me, I take hold of and refuse to let go. I am standing in the alley praying for a man as he injects a syringe full of heroin into his arm. The girl's voice returns inside my mind.

"Get out of here," she says. "This will trigger you."

"I can't be triggered," I respond. "I've been healed."

Lightning flashes in the sky above me as I write these words, and thunder echoes from the mountains. I am trying to teach the people around me that I have come here for one purpose. To talk to the people.

On the street, many things are happening at once, and I become distracted. I can see the increase of the lost on the city street, and I am suddenly overwhelmed. The darkness seems so great, the situation so hopeless, the war so overwhelming, that for a moment I lose my concentration. I can sense the impatience of the people I am walking with. They don't want to be here. Being a missionary is a noble ideal, but many are unprepared for the reality of it. I acquiesce to their unspoken request, and return to the church.

As we walk toward the vehicles, I see two people walking up the street. Their hoods are up, evil consumes their eyes, darkness and hatred surrounds them like a blanket. They are not what they appear to be. Satan makes himself known. I don't think the people I am with understand the theory of a spiritual world, let alone believe in it. They see with physical eyes, while I see with spiritual. I am aware of things others are simply blind to.

As we walk the alley, I am familiar with the surroundings. Not because I've been here before in my physical form, but because I've walked this alley in a dream. The dream was filled with darkness, but the sun shines bright this morning. I am to drawn to an old doorway, now covered in bricks. I can see the outline of where the passage used to stand. On these old bricks with broken mortar I find three small pieces of paper, taped to the wall. The name of my Saviour is written on one, and a question written on the other, scrawled in a black marker.

"Where are his disciples?"

I am the only one who sees the writing.

Sunday

This morning my books are searched, and confiscated. Rather than give into the anger, I take my guitar and walk outside. I place my music sheets on the cold concrete, and start singing to God. I may not have the answers for today, or even the hope I require, but I know the one who can heal me. I raise my voice to heaven, and trust in the unseen. I know he is watching, and in my more human moments, I must trust him the most.

Service is interesting. A pastor from a local church comes to deliver the message. He is quick and concise. He captures my attention, and find myself listening carefully to the words he speaks. I want to understand what he is saying. This man is a welcome change from the way things are usually done here. We have had some really long winded people speaking on *Sunday* morning. They have a strong desire to preach, but absolutely no talent. This visiting pastor is a breath of fresh air.

Monday

Six in the morning after six hours of nightmares. I wake up into the cold night air. I walk across the farm and into the classroom. Some idiot decides we should all worship the video screen this morning, as if God was impressed by our vocal talent. Thirty men standing in a room, staring at a video screen, while God's beautiful sunrise lights the sky two feet to the left, outside the window. I feel nauseated, and I want to throw up all over the floor.

The last images in my mind before waking up consume me. In the vision, I see two people from the farm, locked in room, smoking crack. One watches television, while the other melts crack cocaine into a pipe with a torch lighter.

I awake disgusted, literally wanting to puke. I grab my towel, and walk to the shower. My eyes are still blurry from sleep, the soles of my feet hurt, and my bones ache. What a lovely sensation to have every morning. I thought the disgust would pass, but it;s the same every morning. My tiredness give way to rage.

I can't stand being forced to work in the greenhouse. I hate it. It's not the plants, it's the concept of slave labour that disturbs me. I love gardening, but this farm has destroyed what I once enjoyed. They have taken a peaceful activity, and turned it into a profitable business, only concerned with production.

Ultimately, it comes down to this. "Do not be overcome of evil; but overcome evil with good." Even when there is darkness all around me, I will not be consumed by it. I will stand in the light and draw power from its source. My peace remains within me. It can't be stolen by circumstance, but I am free to give it away. I don't like falling into holes that I should be able to see and avoid.

Another leader has disappeared into the darkness. Interesting that the vision of last night is proven so quickly. It is too accurate to ignore. The vision is becoming a regular occurrence. Perhaps my sight is being refined for clarity. There is nothing inside me that wants to judge or condemn our fallen leader. I would not wish addiction upon my worst enemy. The sorrow and suffering invoked by using is incredible, and the devastation complete upon waking from the psychosis.

I've experienced it many times.

I spent some time reading a couple of papers I wrote in university. Apparently, I was desperate to prove that human beings have a spirit. Particularly, the conscious existence of the spirit, while separate from the body. My premise is the symbiotic relationship of flesh and spirit. Now, it's quite apparent why I needed to prove this thesis.

I am operating in a spiritual world, and I am using a dream as a doorway.

The papers are years old, written in a sophisticated academic language. It's hard to explain, but at least now I know why it is so difficult to communicate with people. I am attempting to explain an overwhelming amount of information, and complex concepts, in a brief description. The nuances are lost.

A novel will probably be a better delivery system for the manifesto.

Tuesday

Nightmares until the moment I awake, only to rise and find myself in another type of torment. I sense the conflict coming. I can't avoid it. I approach a leader, and offer him my assistance.

"Do you want some help?" I ask.

"No. You're unstable and inconsistent."

In my opinion, I'm very consistent in my instability. He is making excuses, but it still hurts. He doesn't want me near him, whatever the reason. It's the same message I've heard my entire life. You're not good enough, you're useless, I don't want you to be part of my life. I walk away from the conversation in frustration. Seriously - why do I bother reaching out? These people can barely identify their need for help, let alone accept it. They definitely won't accept help from me. I'm an outcast, an untouchable.

I am willing and able to help, but in their eyes I am nothing more than a crackhead, incapable of doing anything except using cocaine. Before I lose control of my emotions, I go to a friend for counsel, and reign myself in. Having hope once more, I reach out to another leader. I suggest using a computer system in the greenhouse, tracking inventory and shipping orders. He becomes angry, and rejects everything without further thought. He claims it will add more hours to his work day, when it will actually save time.

I am starting to lose my patience. These people would rather live with the problem, rather than change and accept something new. Why? They have become comfortable in their problems. Sounds silly, doesn't it? It's true. They continue in false belief because it is all they know. Anything new is considered a threat, and they raise their defenses. Most people aren't even aware of it.

We have to work, hour upon hour, in this greenhouse. After six months of the monotony, it's easy for me to identify some flaws in the system. Rather than just complain about the problems, I am looking for solutions, and presenting them to leadership. Rather than listening to my suggestion, he holds on tighter, and condemns us all to hours of wandering, searching for plants we can't recognize, to fill orders we don't understand.

On the farm, we call this area the greenhouse. It's not accurate description. There are, in fact, seven industrial greenhouses. The plants are in different stages of development. They start as cuttings, planted in fertile soil. As they take root and begin to grow, they are moved to a different greenhouse. In front of the greenhouses, is a large open area. When the plants are able to survive the climate, they are moved outside.

We spend our days planting cuttings, filling endless black trays with soil, moving plants around, and filling orders. The farm has some sort of arrangement with a local distributor, but I'm not sure of the details. I intend to find out. Someone is making a lot of money, and I know it's not me.

Most of the leadership is made up of past residents who have stayed on at the farm. There are a few coveted paid positions on the farm. The greenhouse provides two of these. The leaders here seem to think they will never fall, so they keep their knowledge to themselves. They treat us like idiots, worker drones, slave labourers, refusing to teach anyone what they know.

If they train us, we can replace them. We are given mindless tasks to complete, always denied the knowledge of WHY we do these things. Typical. The farm teaches us never to question, and we are reprimanded when we do.

Today has demonstrated the utter failure of their methods. The leader who runs the greenhouse is gone. He has disappeared. Relapsed, most likely. Does the greenhouse stop production just because he is missing? No. Now, none of us know how to fill the orders, or even identify the types of plants required.

It's sheer stupidity. Children playing in the sandbox, unwilling to share their toys.

Wednesday

An interesting day, to say the least. In prayer this morning I was confused. I walked into the room laughing with joy in my heart, I walked out miserable and angry. It is hard to connect with God while surrounded by thirty men, babbling aloud, and walking in an endless circle. I despise the methodical way in which prayer is approached. No one is listening. Everyone is speaking. They consider this being of one accord. It's shallow, far from intimacy with each other, and not even close to intimacy with God.

Someone told me we do this so I can develop the ability of connecting with God in the midst of distraction. It's a relevant concept, I concede, but I've already mastered it. I don't need any more practice in being isolated. Aren't we supposed to come together in agreement, share our burdens, and pray for each other?

I refuse to be drowned by the feelings of despair and hopelessness invoked by morning prayer. I face the day, and somehow retain the peace I've found. I continue onward, walking to the gym for a workout. Nature calls, and I leave for a few minutes to go to the washroom. As I return, I see groups of people scattering in all directions. I can hear someone swearing loudly inside the gym, throwing a temper tantrum.

"Let's walk the track," I say to my partner, not wanting to be involved in the chaos that has ensued since I left. It's becoming a pattern. The meltdown happens while I'm absent from the room, and I miss the show. It's always exciting here on the farm: sometimes painful; sometimes entertaining. Today, it suits my mood, and I'm suddenly laughing again. I am restored to my previous state of detached perplexity.

For work program, I was sent to the new women's facility to complete some work that was started. The founder and visionary of the farm went with us. He has expanded to vision to include this new development. It's the same model as the farm I live on.

It was tempting to put on a show for him, but I spoke, ranted, raved, questioned, and conceptualized in the same way as I do every day. He didn't reject me, or try to make me into something I'm not. In fact, he listened quietly even when he didn't agree. Something I need to learn how to do.

Peer review was powerful tonight. I heard the truth spoken, and it has cleared my mind. This is a war, and I fight not just for myself, but for the people. Satan has taken captive the people God has set free. He has lied, and abused them, until they believe the lie.

The greatest calling in the world is to set free the captives, proclaim freedom to those who become enslaved, and the broken hearts of the people. Tonight, I bring the war to Satan's doorway, as he has brought it to mine. I'm seriously angry. Everything I heard tonight only solidifies my resolve to rise up.

Thursday

I am in space, far above the earth, working in the depths of night. I am suddenly filled with anxiety that someone below may be in pain. In the blink of an eye, I am returned to earth, and find myself walking down a road. Rain falls endlessly from the sky above.

I awake. My body is aching. After kneeling, and committing my day to Jesus, I attempt to stand. I nearly fall to the floor. I reach out, grabbing hold of the nightstand, steadying myself, and regaining my balance.

How much longer will this continue. My body is suffering, and I continue to torture it because of this schedule. With my eyes still sleep blind, I slowly make my way to the table for our morning devotion. A leader sits down, opens the book says:

"Welcome to Earth." It takes a moment to register in my mind.

"What did you just say!?" I ask quickly.

I sit silently for several minutes, grasping at what is happening. Any other morning these words would mean nothing to me, and I probably wouldn't give them a second thought. For a moment, my two worlds combine in a flash of light, and I'm confused. How could anyone possibly know what I have seen before waking? As I understand it, only a spiritual being could know. Is this God reaching out to me?

I need to find a solution to the pain I am experiencing day after day. I pull a leader aside, but he says he can do nothing to help me. Refusing to give up, I pull the director aside in the gym.

"You're not giving us enough time to heal," I begin explaining. "Every day we come to this gym and lift weight, but it's wrecking me. I am working out in the morning, and labouring the rest of the day."

He turns his gaze to me, with an exasperated look on his face, and his eyes shining bright. He says nothing. I continue speaking.

"What's the point of all this? I'm not interested in body sculpting.

This schedule is killing me, and you're not giving me enough recovery time. I'm not sleeping and I'm exhausted."

His answer?

"Lift more weight," he says. I shake my head and walk away.

Communication is futile, I think.

While on the farm I have felt the sting of betrayal, depth of sorrow, despair of depression, and exhilaration of joy. I've even experienced the pain incurred by using the sword of vengeance. Not once have I had to use cocaine.

Recently, I've had an experience with God that has changed the way I interact with him. In some sense, a lie has been removed. My belief system has shifted. After class, I walked into the so-called '*worship room*,' picked up a guitar and started playing. I began singing the songs I've learned since coming to the farm. Usually I can capture the melody without a problem. Today, something was different. I couldn't do it. I kept missing notes, and using my will to push against the invisible barrier. At first, I simply tried harder, assuming that I just wasn't pushing hard enough. I failed. Now, God had my attention, and I started to listen.

"Don't play someone else's song. Don't perform. Speak to me."

God? Are you speaking to me?

I obeyed, chose a key, used a three chord progression, and spoke to the Lord in song. I closed my eyes, and my spirit left the room. When I returned, I found myself dancing, and experiencing a joy that I've never felt before. I suddenly understood that I was experiencing true worship, and my heart broke. Everything prior has been a forgery.

If you have never tasted wine, I could give you grape juice, and lie to you, saying: "This is wine." God is faithful and nothing will keep him from me, but once awakened, it is difficult to return to sleep. I don't want to. After having tasted the real thing, a facsimile will never satisfy me again.

My heart has changed. It's happened before, but it's new every single time. I can't remember the words I sang to God, but I do remember coming to a precipice. I was on the verge of slipping into a tongue I only use in dreams. A private conversation from one spirit to another.

In some ways, the training has helped me, but the training ground becomes a prison once the soldier has gone to war. The same walls that kept the evil from entering in, become the walls the prevent the good from getting out.

Once a child is born, the womb is no longer required. In fact, once a child takes his first breath, he can never return. The same liquid that once nurtured him, will now kill him - if submerged for longer than a single breath.

Okay, I've broken through the barrier (according to counsel). What I do now is important. I need to be careful. My mind is telling me there is a formula for this interaction with God, turning my life into a science project, rather than a relationship with the Lord. Is is possible to live in a sustained state of what I've just experienced? It's a question worth investigating.

Friday

I night is filled with knowledge that I can't retain upon waking. I see it in the fragments of my memory. During the night, I awake clutching the scripture close to my chest. Something is happening. By seven-thirty in the morning, I've collapsed to my knees on the hallway floor, crying in an agony I don't understand.

Every time I cry, the light becomes a fire in my eyes. Some people can't look at me because the darkness within them can't stand in the presence of God. I suppose that gazing into the light reveals the unclean parts of ourselves. Not for the sake of condemnation, but so that we can confess and receive healing. Satan continuously lies to us, saying the light only exposes the darkness of our true nature.

The light pouring out of my eyes inspires only two responses in the people around me: scatter, or attack. In the past, I've sometimes dulled the shine to gain human relation. It is a sick perversion that I will no longer allow in my life.

Accept me, or TURN AND RUN.

Saturday

I walk through a doorway into a hidden room. Musical instruments are hanging from the wall. I select a guitar and start playing. The words of a song pour through my voice. I sing about a flash of blue-white light, and the coming of something. I can't remember the words, but peace fills my soul and joy rises in my heart.

I awake, alive and refreshed. Finally, the nightmare has ended, and I am restored. I am in love with God, and my eyes are shining brightly. My optimistic outlook ends with journey to Vancouver. I've been given permission to leave the farm.

When I return from the city, I feel dirty inside because of what I've seen, disgusted with myself because of what I've done, and horrified with the world around me. I did a lot of unethical things today, but refused to pick up a cigarette. **SO FUCKING**

WHAT!? I'm sure the next asshole who reads this journal will find something they can use to wreak havoc on my life.

The rain poured down the sky above, and the earth sent up a mist. The last bridge I crossed before entering the city was wrapped in a white cloud. I couldn't see the top of the support pillars.

So what happened?

I was ready for this day. Before walking into the city of darkness, I prayed, and asked God for help. Next time I will be more specific, but how can I pray for something I don't even know I need?

As we walked into the city, I found myself falling in love. There is darkness here, but also beauty. As we were walking the city streets, we passed a music store. I stopped to investigate. With hours ahead of us, I had a chance to reach out to the Lord through song. I took the time to reach for contact, and peace descended. With my foundation strengthened, I continued on the journey.

So many people were smoking that I could taste the smoke in the air. No compulsion or anxiety that needed to be appeased by tobacco. I have found a trust in God that extends to my final place of addiction. When we reached the ocean I was content. I love the sea. I stood for a moment, looking out over the water. I want to breath in the air and sit quietly in reflection, but it is not to be.

We continue walking the seawall, my eyes searching, taking in everything. We finally came to a rally for 'world peace,' but all I found was a demonic presence in the eyes of the people, deceiving and draining them. The evil was apparent, and the demonic influence obvious. I was tempted to enter the war, right there in the moment. I felt sick inside, witnessing how far the people have gone astray with no knowledge of their transgression. I walked away, but my spirit was furious. There is something awakening inside of me.

As we continued to walk the city streets, my attention was drawn to a parade approaching us. The first thing I noticed was the police escort. *What's this?* I asked myself. I walked to the edge of the street, trying to get a clearer view of the banner being held between two women. **"SLUTWALK"** is painted in large black letters on white background. What!? Is this a joke? Am I reading this right?

I look closer, only to discover that the two women holding the banner are most accurately dressed as sluts. Interesting. Okay, you have my attention. For sure. A group of women, dressed as whores, some with the word 'slut' written across their bare breasts, walking down the street chanting: "No means no! Yes means yes!" *Whatever the fuck that means.*

One girl in the center of the group is stripped to the waist, breasts proudly displayed for all to see. *What is going on here?* Many people are carrying signs, and it is very confusing trying to figure out exactly what their message is. One sign says, "Slut does not equal a bad word." Another says, "Have sex instead of making war." At first, I think it is a parade of sex trade workers, but towards the end I reconsider. Many of these women are young college girls. Whatever their statement is, I hope they clarify.

After this bizarre turn of events, I am left somewhat stunned and grasping at the air for an explanation. I decide coffee is the answer, and sit in a street cafe, contemplating. So far, the evil has not touched me, but definitely made its presence known. One of the people I'm travelling with decides to enter the arcade beside the cafe. I follow. We get change at the counter and part ways. He finds a game. I walk deeper into the dim light, examining my surroundings while allowing my eyes to adjust to the light.

At first, I miss the sign hanging above my head. Girlie Movies. What!? I thought this was an arcade. What the hell? Is this whole city fucked!? Everywhere I turn there are sex shops and pornography on open display, completely accepted without any thought. It is so common that I don't think anyone notices anymore - or even cares.

I am enticed.

This journal entry gets personal on several levels, so if any of this writing is shared, I WILL COME AFTER YOU AND MAKE YOUR LIFE HELL. It's not a threat; it's a promise. I am sick of this shit - where people invade my private thoughts, and then discuss it over coffee. Don't violate the trust I am showing by allowing you access to this. If you can't handle it, THEN STOP READING. Final warning.

I see a row of gray box like compartments. My mind snaps and I remember the vision I was given of this several years ago. *This can't be possible*, I think quickly. *It's too soon. The time reference can't be right, but here it is.* I know what these gray boxes are the moment my mind reveals the dream to me.

There is a screen in each of these shielded compartments, and pornography plays unabated. Privacy in public. I can't resist. The combination of watching a dream manifest before my eyes, and having lust burn inside me - overwhelms me. I fall. I walk straight into the darkness without another thought. Pornography is familiar territory. I used to watch it every day, even when I was disgusted by the depths of my own depravity.

I walk into the compartment, searching for the screen. I begin to see the differences between the dream and the reality. In the dream, the booth, equipment, and interface are far more advanced than the primitive models I stand staring at. I learn quickly. There is a small glass window for viewing. The moment I look inside, darkness descends around me like a cloud. The world is gone. I drop a quarter in the slot, and in the next moment, I'm watching naked girls getting fucked.

I haven't seen anything like this in over a year. I'm seriously aroused. I don't care about the ethics of the situation. My flesh desires what my eyes see. I can't keep watching. I'm crashing hard. I know I'm falling. The next step is a crack pipe. FUCK!! I tear my eyes away, and try to leave. Not happening. I want satisfaction. I see a washroom six feet to my left. It's all too convenient. Satan has planned well. I don't want to write these words, but I must. The thirty seconds of imagery I saw is BURNED into my mind and I WANT IT GONE. **FUCK!!**

I dream every night, and these dreams unfold before my eyes. Sometimes the same day; sometimes years later. I knew what lay within those gray compartments, but my curiosity overruled my intellect. In that moment, I forgot that the image I was about to gaze upon would be SEARED into my memory.

I know where I come from, but everyone around me treats me as a human being, and I fall for their lie. I am finished with apologizing for who I am, or what I am capable of. I'm done with embracing stupidity just because the people around me are confused and intimidated by genius. I will not embrace ignorance to appease the people in my life. I am at war. This war will not end any time soon (that I am aware of), and although some may walk with me for a moment of time, they will pass away. Once again, it will be me, standing alone with God.

I need access to my dream journal. I refuse to walk into these situations blind, when God has given me sight to avoid them.

I walked out of the arcade, and into the sunlight. Later in the evening, we watched a three dimensional film in the theatre. The technology is moving quickly, but has not reached the level I have used in another world. It is coming. I can't take it anymore. I'm losing my mind. I need to understand what is happening, or I will retreat into addiction again.

I am dealing with serious philosophical concepts that no one around me understands, but the simple minds are only concerned with one thought. Did he smoke? No, I did not have a cigarette. So Fucking What?

Sunday

For the first time in several years, I can't remember a single event from last night. Surely I have dreamed, but no memory remains. I am shocked beyond comprehension, and left to consider the implications. First question. Have I dreamed and forgotten? Or, dreamed and been denied?

Most people would think nothing of this experience, but I am not most people. I dream every single night, full recall, without fail, every single night of my life. No exception. So what is this empty void? It's a message as clear as any dream. The absence speaks as much volume as the presence.

Still reeling from the events of yesterday, I am dragged from my bed to go pray on a street corner at six-thirty in the morning. The last time I was on the street at this early hour, I was high - and had been for several days. I'm not impressed with the morning's events, and the director notices my seething rage.

"What's wrong?" he asks.

"What the hell are we doing here?" I ask. "I'm exhausted." And then he says something profound.

"Sometimes the one thing that will help us overcome, we reject."

I could say nothing against this truth except abandon myself, close my eyes, and trust God to speak within. In seconds, I am crying, tears falling from my face, as the Lord speaks to me about the freedom his has given. I am beginning to understand that when I am overwhelmed by circumstance, I have a tendency to revert back to deadly and poisonous methods of coping. Sometimes I am aware of what is happening, but unable to pull myself out of the spiral. Until someone helps me. Why? **Trust.** I don't understand the answer, but there it is. I think God has designed this process to help me establish, and build, trust with other people.

A bridge between worlds.

Sunday service has become an excellent opportunity to catch up on writing, or sleeping; whichever is required at the moment. The person giving the message this morning is a terrible speaker, who never makes a point. He uses many scriptures, but none of them connect to each other, and his reasoning leads nowhere.

I don't think he's ever written a paper, let alone delivered a sermon. He continues to speak, even though he has lost the people, and I wonder why he doesn't notice. I could care less, but the other residents have a point. This is not good for us. We are not receiving what is required to sustain us. This service (if I can all it that) is a lesson in patience and forgiveness, if nothing else. Do I continue to ignore the problem? If I speak up, his feelings will be hurt. This person is not called to speak, or preach. It is ridiculously obvious. Is it a kindness, or condemnation, to tell him the truth of the matter? Many people are simply falling asleep. Nothing this person says makes any sense, and I would hazard a guess that the other people in the room feel the same.

Another person is in the process of walking away from the farm, and it hurts to watch. I've hated and despised this place at times, but I also recognize its potential. Some people see a pile of rocks -

I see a stone wall. Understand? I know the history of the man who is leaving. I know the life he has come from, and I don't want him to return to the darkness. I want freedom for him, not captivity. He has a beautiful family. A family that he can strengthen and protect, if he comes to God and makes a stand.

How do I give away what I have been given? How do I share the light?

Monday

I am not impressed upon waking. At first, I am shocked to find myself laying in my bed. Then the rage sets in. It's not like the emotional connection of a dream fades with the morning light. I lay in my bed for several minutes, just trying to understand the imagery of the night. Was the entire dream an attack of the enemy, focusing on my feelings of rejection and betrayal? Why does God allow this over and over?

I kneel beside my bed, but I don't have the words to pray. I rise to my feet, but my body is filled with pain, and I find it difficult to acquire my balance. It's like teaching myself to walk, for the first time, every day. I take a few steps, and my muscle memory takes over.

I'm completely fucked up right now. Someone approached me today and told me to pack my bags. They pointed to the driveway and asked me to hit the road. I refused. Later in the day, a leader told me to stop speaking, or leave the farm.

Fuck this place. I found a copy of their financials, and I asked the founder exactly how the greenhouse operates. How much money do they generate, who benefits, and what does the arrangement with the distributor looks like? I feel sick to my stomach. I've been lied to the entire time I've been on the farm. Like so many other times in my life, I have believed in a lie. I keep thinking that people are essentially good and moral at their core. This hypothesis has proven invalid time and time again. Especially within the recovery industry. Addicts are a commodity – a way of generating income. Period.

To seal the conclusion, I have discovered that the farm has solicited hundreds of thousands of dollars in donations every year. They ask for this money on my behalf, and the behalf of other residents, but we never see a cent of the money. The farm then pays out more in wages than the income it generates. I'm not stupid. I know that what they are doing is wrong – on many levels.

I've lived here long enough to see how this place operates, and I question the validity of their expenditures. Basically, I'm saying: there is something wrong here. Red flags everywhere. I've asked questions about the financial position of the farm ever since I've arrived, and I've been fed a lie from day one. They have continuously held the position that the farm costs more to operate than the income it generates. This is the reason they ask for donations.

It's an outright lie.

Anyone in leadership has to maintain this lie, or they are banned from the farm. Any resident who questions the financials is told to focus on their development with God, and ignore where the money goes. I should have recognized the standard company answer before this, and investigated earlier. As foolish as it may seem, I believed in this place.

We are not talking about peanuts here. This farm generates nearly two million dollars a year, and I'm sure this figure will only increase as the years pass. They generate a lot of money from the connections they have built over the years. All in the name of helping the lost, broken, and addicted.

The residents who come here pay a thousand dollars a month to stay. On average, that's forty thousand per month. Trust me, it's enough to keep the lights on. Almost all of the food we eat is supplied by several local food banks, and we raise our own animals to slaughter. So, if their argument is that they are paying out huge food and electrical costs, it's a lie.

The truth is, the money lines the pockets of the leadership. The highest up in the organization benefit, while the residents are left to exist on ninety-five dollars a month (subsidized by social assistance). The clothes we wear are donated. This farm gives us nothing. They are using us, plain and simple.

Don't be fooled by their marketing strategy. I actually live here and know the truth.

I've been asking about the greenhouse operation for months. No one would give me a straight answer, which only fueled my desire to find the truth. And, here it is. The farm receives five thousand dollars a month from the distribution company, paying for twenty thousand dollars worth of labour. The founder of the farm seems to think this is a good deal, which leads me to believe that there is something else going on behind the scenes. Gifts or services exchanged which aren't on the books, or in the yearly financials (but this is only speculation).

I've been told the following:

"When the farm began, they had no way of marketing or distributing their plants. There was no network in place. A private local nursery took interest, and created a working relationship, which eventually developed into a contract. A single monetary payment each month, in exchange for the labour. Funds were provided, more greenhouses were built, and the operation advanced from there."

The farm was probably so happy to finally have distribution, that they failed to see they were being taken advantage of. I didn't come to the farm so that I could create more profit for a local company. I came here for help with my addiction, an encounter with God, and a vision for the future. However, I appear to be generating money for a private concern. I am constantly being fed the lie that I am 'advancing God's kingdom.' Bullshit. I'm making someone's pocketbook a little larger every day. I am told that my labour helps the addicts who will come after me. LIE. It helps the people in power, and businesses connected with the farm.

According to the current financial report, this farm received six times the amount of cash donations than the greenhouse generates. And yet, the majority of our time is spent working in the greenhouse. The greenhouse operation is NOTHING, and needs to be kept in perspective. It provides a valuable opportunity to delve in the dirt and fall in love with God's creation, but the entire process has become corrupt through greed. What was once an activity that provides restoration and relaxation, has now become filled with stress, anxiety, and frustration. The greenhouse is simply about production and the bottom line. It has nothing to do with advancing our recovery. They can tell all the lies they want, and spread all the propaganda they can imagine, but it will never cover the truth.

They love to use the greenhouse as their selling point to prospective donators. They paint us all as useless, dysfunctional people, who don't know how to support ourselves. We need to be taught the value and ability to work as others do in society. Fuck That. We are some of the most productive, loyal, and skilled tradesmen, or labourers, society will ever come across. Sometimes, our addiction is the very thing that produces this quality within us because, at all costs, we must protect our supply of drugs. And, that means working every day, pulling extra shifts, and working overtime. We value our jobs.

Forget the employee side of it for a moment. Many of us have founded, and operated, multi-million dollar companies. We are the employer, and our companies thrive because of our obsession to detail, innovation, and creative thinking. Even if we aren't executives, many of us have risen up within the company itself and hold positions of leadership. We hire, fire, and train new talent.

Even the drug dealers have work experience of a sort. They build an empire out of nothing, working their way up from the bottom, and create a huge network of distribution. At great risk to themselves, they work 24 hours a day, 7 days a week. Whatever their motivation, no one could say they don't have transferable skills, and the drive to succeed.

We're not idiots. We don't need to be taught how to work.

I love to garden, growing produce and flowers. I love the feeling of dirt in my hands, and the beauty of God's plants arrayed in various colors. Working in the greenhouse has stripped me of that love, because it is all about the money. It's corrupt. The greenhouse program isn't about finding the love God gave us for gardening – it's about generating income, and turning a profit. It's hurting the residents, not helping us.

The local nursery is receiving $180,000 worth of labour from the residents of the farm, and paying us $60,000. I've used averages, but the point clearly states itself. Do I really need specific figures to demonstrate was has gone on here!? Now I know why no one in leadership would give me a straight answer. Perhaps they have never even asked the question themselves. Maybe they can't grasp the point I'm making. So, let me clarify.

I HAVE VALUE.

My labour is worth the same as everyone else's. My labour is not worthless because I am a drug addict. I will not allow myself to be used by a corporation in this way. I am not a slave. How this farm is getting around the labour laws that govern our land is beyond me, but I assume they have done so by claiming that the *work program* is part of our recovery.

If that was true, they would pay us.

The word states, "Let him who stole, steal no more: but rather let him labour, working with his hands the thing which is good, and he may have to give to him that needeth." (Ephesians 4:28)

Many of us have stolen at some point in our addiction, and I believe that working with our hands is a godly principle. However, the greenhouse operation is taking this verse and twisting it to their own financial ends. They are abusing the word of God, not embracing it.

The reason this place exists is to employ people, and generate an income for the few. It wasn't always this way, but this is the shift in thinking that disturbs me. **Once upon a time, this farm existed for us, now we exist for it**. Perhaps I could volunteer to run this place and save the farm $500,000 a year, but then again, I'm altruistic – even when people can't understand what I'm doing.

Tuesday

I am in a room filled with people, attached to a church sanctuary. There is a doorway at the far end of the room which people are coming out of. They walk into this room and say a message, speaking into a microphone.

They all talk of God, but know nothing about him. They pass all sorts of nonsense off as divine revelation. I can't stand it anymore. Words are burning inside of me. I take the microphone and begin speaking. I am raging but speaking clearly. You do not understand or have the power of God, is the basis of my speech.

I am walking around the room with a microphone until a man enters the room who has obviously been sent by the church to silence me.

"I am being thrown out for telling you the truth," I say.

I awake in the darkness of my room, and know that I am engaged in battle. I seize the threads of the dream, and weave them quickly into a tapestry. I can't lose this, I scream inside my mind. As soon as I complete the weave, I examine it, only to find that something has interfered, rewriting another weave on top of mine in an attempt to deceive me with illusion. My weave is strong, so I dispel the illusion and find my work beneath, glowing brightly.

Thank you, God. I rise and write. These aren't just dreams. What is happening to me? And, who is attempting to keep this knowledge from being revealed to me? I have just experienced the direct influence of a will that is attempting to misdirect and deceive me. WTF.

I'm getting sick of this place. I have no time to myself so that I can communicate with God, and I am beginning to rage on the inside. I don't need someone to teach me how to pray, or how to have a relationship with God – I already have one. I am starting to lose my composure, and I fear I will soon explode in furious anger. I can see it coming, and I know why it's happening. I don't even want to stop it from happening. It's inevitable.

I have tried to communicate with these people, but they refuse to hear. They have put God inside of a box, and placed the box on a shelf. They point to the box from a distance, saying, "There's God. Let's worship the box." They have created a formula that does not work, and ignore the problem. They window dress the problem, and pretend that it doesn't exist. All is well, they profess.

God, I don't want this empty religiosity in my life. I don't want a life filled with doing things, trying to create a substitute for a relationship with you. I've had enough. I don't want to hang out with men twenty-four hours a day, or be sexually harassed by the gay men who reside here. None of this is alright. There is no justification.

I want the farm to place of real relationship with you, but it won't be as long as they continue down the path they're on. I will not follow the men who lead this farm, because they ask me to betray you, and they are using me for their own gain.

It's the truth that no one wants to acknowledge. They are doing evil things in your name, Lord, and it sickens me. I am constantly being taught that evil is good, and good is evil. They fill my day with useless man-made garbage, and tell me it is from God.

I'm done. I seriously can't take much more of this.

Wednesday

Crack cocaine and pornography, forever interwoven in my mind and dreams. In the dream, I am visiting my homeland, but experience rejection from those who were once close to me. I search for drugs to numb my emotions. Once I score, I lock myself in a hotel room. Video pornography is offered on the television. $1.49 for four hours. $1 more for eight hours. The destruction of my soul comes cheap.

I awake several minutes before I have to rise.

David Burton

The only thing awaiting me today is the monotonous routine that has consumed the last seven months of my life. I'm sick of it. There's a reason I never enlisted in the army (besides failing the drug test). This kind of life is not for me. Going through the useless motions, day after day, is demonstrating the true emptiness of this farm. The empty actions we walk through each day is actually taking away from what I *could* be doing with the time.

Not all is well with me. I was drawn into a conflict, and exploded, when a leader asked me to sacrifice my well-being for one of the new arrivals. It was a powerful lesson. I wasn't a willing participant, but God used the situation to teach me. My sacrifice allowed God to give this man a gift. In my eyes, it was so small that I hesitate to even mention it, but I saw the effect it had on him. The way his eyes lit up and the pain removed.

I gave this man value and validation. I showed him that he has worth in the eyes of God and man. Perhaps, I just showed him a small glimpse of love that has been absent from his life. I don't understand entirely, but I can't deny the fact that something happened. When I think of the power of God, I imagine a physical or spiritual manifestation… this love aspect is strange to me.

An expression of love is powerful. It has impact on the human soul, and it changes people in greater ways than a 'sign.'

I've been offered a thousand dollars cash to walk away from the farm. I don't think it's a ploy or a lie. This person is literally offering me cash to walk away. I think he wants someone to *use* with him, but who really knows.

No one in leadership has come and offered me money to stay, or even given any consideration to what my future may hold. They have offered me nothing except heartache, rejection, betrayal, condemnation, and criticism. When I voiced my concern, the director told me to leave if I don't like it.

"There's lots of places you could go," he said.

I had voiced my concern about the focus that is given to working out in the gym. I realize that physical health is a component of healing, but that worshipping our bodies will only get us in trouble with God.

"Your comments about the gym are getting old," he said.

He judged me. I could see it in his eyes. He essentially implied that my words are worthless when they disagree with farm doctrine. As though 'the program' is beyond question or critique. He knows nothing about me, and dismisses everything that I have to say. His eyes condemn me. He thinks I'm just lazy.

He's wrong. I've always been physically active. I've played on many sports teams, and look forward to ball hockey every *Monday* with anticipation. I've played rugby for years, I'm an accomplished swimmer, I've climbed mountains and crossed glacier, I love hitting the water with a canoe beneath me and a paddle in my hand, I enjoy mountain biking, and for most of my life I've been a runner.

Until a combination of recovery and anti-psychotic medication destroyed my body.

Anyway, my point is, I'm not opposed to physical exercise. However, I am very concerned about sculpting our physical appearance in the mirror. Building a better temple so that we can worship ourselves, rather than the spirit of God. The Lord isn't concerned with our **outward** appearance; he's concerned with our **inward** appearance.

When he told me I could leave the farm, I freaked out. Two

months ago, I was in this man's office for a *counselling* session, asking him about my options. I asked him for permission to leave the farm and seek help elsewhere. I even had a few ideas of where I could go, and find a transition back into society.

After hours of farm doctrine, intimidation, and manipulation – he convinced me to stay. This morning, he casually tells me to leave. What an asshole. What is he thinking? Why didn't he support me when I was asking for his help? He asks me to stay when I want to leave, and asks me to leave when I want to stay. Insane.

Now that I want to stay on this farm, and attempt to change some of the insane teaching, I am being rejected. A few months ago, the director asked me to trust him. I made a decision to believe him, and now I've been betrayed. He is only interested in keeping me here if I agree with everything he says, and everything the farm teaches. There is no room for independent thought, or changes to the system.

I'm starting to think my stay here will end horribly. At the moment I least expect it, I will be discarded like a piece of trash. Ironic isn't it. The moment I decide to stay, they try to usher me out the door. Recently, four people have asked me to leave because I disagree with their version of Christianity. All of them were *leaders*. I use the term 'leader' very loosely. These people are just men, appointed by other men, and that's all they are. Nothing more.

At this point, I'm going to leave unless God intervenes. All I have to do is walk to the bank, and this guy will give me a thousand dollars. It's ridiculous. I could just get the money and then come back to the farm. More than likely, I'll be kicked out of the program because I've left the property. The money isn't worth it. It's probably Satan trying to screw me over. I'm not going to risk losing what I have, just to get some cash.

Thursday

I walk toward a storm, drawn to it because I know I will find something there in the raw power of God displayed in the sea. Waves crash against the shore and the streets are flooded with water.

Someone tries to force me away from the storm, but I kick and scream until I am free. I run to the water's edge through a series of hallways and doors.

I awake. How many dreams will it take before I listen and leave this place? I told God that if he doesn't intervene, I am leaving today. He decided to. Right at the last moment, he came and tore my heart wide open. It was during worship. I reached out and sang to God in desperation. I closed my eyes and surrendered. I connected with God, and as I sang, the words entered my mind. It's been awhile.

Worship has become a **performance**. The musicians practice, and perfect the songs, before starting the service. They plan everything out, and kill the spirit. It becomes nothing more than a concert.

A man, a guitar, a drummer, and the spirit of God. Today was not a performance. It was an honest cry out to God. I could sense the difference right away, and the spirit opened like a flower blossoming. My spirit recognizes the of God, and I open myself up entirely, pouring out my heart. The songs chosen for worship are personal to me. They are songs that have changed my life, and brought me into relationship with Christ again.

While I am singing, I have a vision of myself learning the song, and see the first time I sang it to him alone in my room. I am overwhelmed with emotion. I am crying and tears are streaming down my face. I am singing, but the room has grown silent. I am filled with the spirit and I ask for his healing. For the first time since coming to the farm, I fall to my knees, uncaring of the people standing around me.

I present myself to God, and I see him standing in front of me with his hand resting on my head. I am broken in utter abandonment. I am crying uncontrollably – so hard I can barely breathe. I am sobbing, asking God to take this evil from me. In faith, I come to him. I reach for him in trust and abandon. I give myself to him, and he gives to me.

When the communion is over, I stand up. The room has become clearer, and all evil has fled from the presence within me. I stand in a strength that is not my own.

How did the lie that money has value become so deeply rooted in me? When did I begin to think that money can give me what I seek? At what point did I start believing that money would provide, instead of God?

These questions pass through me, not as a condemnation, but as a realization. God has just given me freedom, and torn out the lies inside of me. As I am standing in awe of what has just happened, and the depth of this relationship with Jesus Christ, the man walks into the room holding the cheques – thousands of dollars.

"I'm staying," I say.

Friday

The dreams of last night fade away. They are not a stunning revelation, and I let them slip from my fingertips. My mind self-destructs quickly. I knew it would be coming because of the choice I made yesterday. However, knowledge of a coming attack does not prevent the attack from occurring.

I attempt to weather the storm, and speak to God, reaching out in faith and refusing to listen to the lie being told by Satan. There is something different in my prayer this morning, and I notice it immediately. I feel my heart turning toward the people, and sense a calling to pray for them. My prayer this morning is not for myself, but for the people. I ask that their prayers are heard and acknowledged. My heart yearns for the uplifting of the people around me.

I see quickly how Satan and his demons are moving in the lives of the people. In their blindness, they are deceived and tormented. I recognize the tactic. It's not new to me, but I gain a new insight that I've not had before.

I sense an opening within me. I'm thankful. As I walk into worship, I see the havoc the enemy is wreaking among the people. I'm not the only one who notices. A leader asks me to play the guitar quietly while he begins speaking. I walk to the stage and pick up the instrument. I am a warrior and I wield the sword. I reach for God's presence and begin to play.

It takes a moment to find the rhythm. I've never done this before and I learn quickly that application is different than theory. After warming up a chord progression, and finding my balance, I move directly into a song called Come In. I open to the Holy Spirit and ask for the presence of God to enter the room. I can sense the power moving.

My eyes are closed and I sing quietly. This is amazing. I feel the contact with God. I have been invited to play, but I invite God – the **source**. No drug will ever compare to the experience I am having right now, and this is only a taste of the power, peace, and strength God has waiting for me. He is allowing me access. I fall in love all over again.

Thank You Jesus.

As I play, I see one man walk across the room and start talking to another. He asks forgiveness for his anger, and the breach is repaired. I start crying. God is moving, bringing the change of heart and restoration that I can't. I'm being interwoven with spirit. I don't entirely understand it, but I love the process.

The leader has finished speaking and takes my place on the stage. I surrender the instrument, and he begins the worship service proper. By the end of the service, everyone has broken off into small groups and are praying for each other. Revival stands at the door and is calling us in. I walk through the room, in prayer. I understand why God changed my prayer life this morning. It was all for this moment.

Imagine what *could* be, what *will* be, when God decides to move in force.

Saturday

There are flowers on the plant in the common area. This plant blossoms in extraordinary beauty. The flowers last only a single day before they whither and fall from the vine. I have never seen so many flowers at the same time. Usually, it only has a single flower each day.

I may be the most stubborn person this farm has ever seen, but it is for a reason – this *must* be real for me. I am being offered the world, but I am turning it down for the sake of God. I don't understand what is happening. There have been several changes recently that confuse me. I am hesitant to examine these changes, as though by looking at them, I could upset something that needs to be left alone. There is a mechanism at work here that I don't want to interfere with.

But someone is. I can sense it. I must investigate and protect myself. There are no clear instruction handed down to me from history. The prophets are dead. They did not leave a book of instructions on how the gift works. I don't know of anyone that experiences what I do. Certainly no one in my sphere of influence.

I do not speak of the gift because I do not trust the people around me. Satan could easily use them to lead me off the path. Today, I nearly destroyed a man while he sat in his chair staring at me. I could see the condemnation in his eyes. He has consistently tried to steer me away from the path of God.

I have been **sanctioned** by a higher authority, one beyond this earth and realm. I am seeking to uncover what man has concealed. What am I saying? I am using language to talk all the way around what I truly mean, because this journal will be read by the leadership of the farm.

"Why are you such a target?" asked someone yesterday. He has recently come to the farm, less than a week ago, but he noticed something very quickly that I have blinded myself to.

I have adapted to being in the war *always*. So much so, that I have stopped noticing the constant assault of my enemies, both physical and spiritual. I have become a soldier. I must fast. It is the only requirement left. I do not fast to make my voice hear, but to hear his. I can't delay any longer. Nothing can stand in my way. Nothing can bind me to this world. Jesus showed me the way. I must follow. Lord, give me the power to follow you in all ways, always, as much as you will allow.

> "Is this not the fast that I have chosen? to
> loose the bands of wickedness, to undo the

heavy burdens, and to let the oppressed go free, and that you break every yoke?

Is it not to deal thy bread to the hungry, and that you bring the poor that are cast out to thy house? when you seest the naked, that thou cover him: and thou hide not yourself from your own flesh?

Then shall thy light break forth as the morning, and thine health shall spring forth speedily: and thy righteousness shall go before thee; the glory of the Lord shall be thy reward."

Isaiah 58:6-8

Sunday

I am supposed to be leading worship at a large church or gathering. I bring my guitar and all my song sheets. I am excited and ready for this. Suddenly, the director of the farm appears and informs me that he will be playing with me. In fact, he is taking center stage, and I will just be accompanying him. I am angry. I will not play with this man. I have created this entire venue: the concert, the crowd, the music. All of it has come from within me, and he is trying to steal it from me. He is trying to claim it for his own. I scream at him, and walk away. I will have no part of this. I will have no part of it, nor can he use my name.

I get into a vehicle and drive back to the farm. The founder's wife is driving. She is careless and reckless. As we travel a turn alongside the river, we plummet over the gravel edge of the road, and plunge into the water. The water surrounds the vehicle, and we must escape quickly, or be pulled under.

"Are you ready?" I ask.

I open the windows, as water pours in, escaping the vehicle, and rising to the surface of the river. We pull ourselves out of the cold water, and walk the remaining distance back to the farm, our clothes soaked.

When we arrive, I see the farm has fallen into a state of disrepair in several areas. It has aged and changed. There is a pathway leading deeper into the farm, but it has become a vertical wall. It is the only way to reach the next level.

My house leader appears and begins to lead the way, climbing the wall before me. I follow him upward. I don't understand why he has chosen this path because there are other ways to walk. Pathways that are far less dangerous. He assures me that this is the right path.

He reaches the top of the wall, where grass grows, and vines fall over the edge. Although the wall is made of interlocking concrete blocks, poured and then raised, there is a layer of soil at the top. He pulls himself onto the ledge, and disappears from sight.

When I reach the ledge, and place my hands on the soil, he appears. He is blocking the path. I begin to lose my strength, and ask him to move aside.

"Don't be afraid," he says. "Take my hand."

I remove my hand from the wall, and take hold of his wrist. Suddenly, his face changes, and his expression twists. He pushes me backward, out and away from the edge. I am betrayed. He has lured me into a place where he can murder me, and make it appear as an accident.

I begin to seethe with rage.

FLASH.

I am inside a large building in the city. I have come to play guitar, but I am rejected. I am furious. I give up on these people, and walk outside, walking

David Burton

quickly to a convenience store. While I am paying for a package of cigarettes, a notice someone standing behind me in the line. It is the man who offered me a $1,000 dollars just to cash his cheque for him.

"Do you still have the cash?" I ask.

"Yes."

"Well, let's go then."

We exit the store, walk the streets, and head for the darkest place I can think of. I just don't care anymore. I am sick of these people with their manmade concept of religion, their condemnation, and their betrayal. I have given up on them. I want to get high, and forget all of it.

As we approach the inner core of the city, I see people hiding in back alleys, and sitting on the city street. I approach a group of people, and attempt to score some crack cocaine. They are hesitant to sell to me because they don't know me. I am a stranger to them.

The money I give to the dealer changes as it leaves my hand. It doesn't look real anymore. He opens an egg shaped contained and places a very large amount in my hand – much more than I have paid for.

"Thank you," I say, trying to express my surprise.

"You think that's a lot?" He asks, laughing.

I take the white stone and load it into my pipe, but as I push it inside it becomes rotting wood. At first, I can still see flecks of white in the crumbling wood, but as I search for them – they disappear. I look to the dealer, questioning.

"Allow them to strike you," he says, gesturing to his minions standing beside him. "Only then will I give you the real thing."

I desperately want to get high, and gain acceptance from these people, so I allow them. One man strikes me in the face with his fist, and the other takes a picture. The dealer moves closer to me, and I see the expression of pleasure in his face. This is what he enjoys. It brings amusement and joy to his soul. He is a corrupt child.

I stand and walk away.

I awake in a disturbed frame of mind. I piece the dream together and find a horror story. The whole dream is a war against my spirit; and, in the end, when I seek release, I am denied. This dream appears to be designed specifically to attack trust in my waking relationships, using betrayal as the method. It is intricately and creatively woven. Why does God allow this!? Or, is this dream a very accurate warning of what is coming? Perhaps both are true. I don't know. I never examine the source. I merely record the vision.

I did something today I never do. I shared the dream with someone. He offered an insight which I had missed. He brought to my attention the repetition of certain imagery – something real becoming a forgery. It is possible that I am accepting some lie as truth in my life.

In the alley, the demons struck me in the face, while the person with me was barely touched. This could represent me having to face trial or suffering much stronger than those around me. This makes sense to me because knowledge comes with suffering.

In my life, I have sought after money and crack cocaine. Both represent freedom to me. In the past, I have believed that these two pursuits could bring me pleasure, purpose, and peace. I have sought after these things rather than God, but only God can truly offer freedom.

So, I have believed (*and still do to a certain extent*) that these two pursuits will bring me the freedom I want. **I HAVE BELIEVED**

A LIE. I am not of this world, and nothing in this world will give me what I need or desire. I have looked to the *physical* to meet a *spiritual* need. **FAIL**.

I'm all over the place today. Two more people walked out of here today, and another one is catching a plane next week. I don't think any other them will return. Sadness has taken hold of me because I know the life they come from. A dark place of sorrow, pain, and misery. A place of torment and torture. Why do they walk back into the darkness? I don't understand it. Why does this gift of God mean nothing to them? Or, can they simply not see its worth? What does it take to walk this path I have chosen? And, how many people will I watch fall?

In spite of the sadness, I have an overwhelming sense of thankfulness for the gift God has given me. Truly it is a gift, because I can do nothing to earn it, there is no way to buy it, and I can't forcefully acquire it. I am walking as a new (living) man in an old (dying) world. Does this make sense?

Perhaps I stay on the farm just so that I have something to write about. Then again, maybe there is a deeper reason than I let on here. I want to write the books I've been given, if nothing else.

I will leave this instruction manual for the next one of my kind.

Monday

> "The voice of thy thunder was in the
> heaven: the lightnings lightened the world:
> the earth trembled and shook."

Psalm 77:18

The crash of thunder shaking my house awakens me at two thirty in the morning. I am wide awake instantly and rising from my bed. I see flashes of light coming from all around me, without a sound. I am nervous. What is happening?

The flashes continue and I attempt to wake my partner. Something is going on. I am so sure, that I wake up everyone in the room. They hear me freaking out. Several of us walk outside to investigate. Lightning is flashing in the sky above us.

"Just a lightning storm," they say and return inside.

I stand in awe and confusion. Where is the rain? There is no storm in the sky, and the flashes comes without a sound. The lightning pulses in quick intervals around the house. There is no single source of the light. I return inside of the building because I don't want a fight to break out with the house leader in the early hours of the dawn.

This is my first mistake.

I am not supposed to hide from God. When I sit down on the edge of my bed, thunder crashes around the building and the room blazes with white light. He is calling me outside, but I refuse. Why? We are not allowed outside alone, and I don't want to get in a fight with my house leader.

This is my second mistake.

The light continues to flash and pulse on either side of the building. The 'storm' is not moving. It remains directly above me. I fear what lay outside and my imagination exalts itself against the knowledge of God, producing more fear within me.

This is my third, and final, mistake.

I can't sleep. I know the scriptures that speak of God and lightning entwined. I **know** this is God calling me, but I allow fear to keep me within the building. He wants me to understand the complete failure of my trust in him, in order to bring me to repentance this morning. How does he do this?

The lightning flashes all around me for the next two hours. It pulses over and over again, flooding the room with light. There is no sound *at all*. The lightning doesn't travel. It remains above me, until it finally stops and vanishes.

I used to play with the lightning when I was young. Now I have lost the connection I once had. God is restoring it, and the people around me are trying to interfere. I am finished listening to people who *nothing* of the power of God. Like I've said before, they wouldn't recognize God if he was standing right in front of them.

Or, in this case, **hovering above their house**.

What an interesting day. Many things transpired and I sought counselling to help me overcome my inner turmoil. It appears as though people are walking away from the farm in an absolute panic. I don't know why. What do they think is out there for them? I've heard all the excuses. I've used most of them myself.

The most obvious one, was a man who told me that he needs to leave because his wife and young daughter need him. He spun the story to deceive himself. The moment a cheque came for him, he left the farm in the middle of the night. Perhaps he left to find his wife, and support his daughter, you ask. No. A week later his wife called the farm, looking for him. She had no idea that he had left. He is missing.

It's the darkness in his eyes, and the anger in his soul, that betrays the truth. No matter what words he uses, his eyes always give him away. There is also some indefinable quality in the tone of his voice. He is out smoking crack. He may not survive this relapse, and will leave his daughter fatherless.

This is a very interesting school, if that's truly what it is – this farm. I see it more as a school of wizards. We come from all walks of life, and many of us from very dark places. Many have had contact with the demonic, even if unaware of it. Maybe if we all wore cloaks, and strapped swords to our belts, we would feel more comfortable. As it stands now, there is nothing that we identify ourselves with. Almost no one wears a cross, yet all profess to be Christian.

So, what changes us from being powerful in the dark arts, to being powerful in God? I don't want to pretend to be something I am not, instead of accepting the truth of what I am. I used to my life entirely on faith, yet now I find myself relying on reasoning. This is what the farm teaches. There is little faith here on the farm, and it is fading quickly.

When I was in the suffering of addiction I read the word of God. I believed it usually without question. It spoke to me, and taught me of itself. I used the power I found there to acquire faith and defend myself. Now, I have people trying to tell me *what it all means*. **They know nothing**. The word does not need a human translator to interfere, twist, and corrupt the message.

I hate the church because God has been reduced to an hour long ceremony with ritualistic overtones. Communion is a travesty. Let me explain. Allow me to show you the meaning of breaking bread and drinking wine. What is the one thing humans must do to survive? They must eat. They will always eat. It is fairly difficult to forget about eating, because it sustains life. So, if I embed a concept into a meal, the concept will never be forgotten. It will be passed down through the generations of human descent.

Every time I break bread, I remember the broken body of Christ. Every time I drink, I remember the blood Christ poured out to fulfill the law of God. I am now clean before God, brought into relationship, and restored. Communion is not a ritualistic act to be done once a month. It is every day, every time I use the sustenance of this world to continue living in earth. I don't have to wait until

Sunday communion to remember who Jesus died for, or why. I don't need to be in a room full of strangers, eating crackers and sipping juice, to be thankful for the freedom he has given me. I don't need someone teaching me about God because I am fairly certain he can do it himself. He is God after all.

When a human approaches me and attempts to convince me of some doctrine, I cringe inside. One group of people would have me believe the whole situation is about using God to acquire wealth and healing. I am disgusted. Another group would have me believe it is entirely about self-denial and righteous works. The 'do-it-yourself' method to acquiring heaven. I know nothing of these doctrines because they are created and taught by MEN, not God. I do not accept the teaching of men because it causes a loss of faith within me; and, therefore a loss of power.

Science is a doctrine of men, and when it gives an explanation of lightning as being simply static electricity grounding itself, it becomes "just lightning." God is removed from his creation entirely. In the same way, human explanation of the word of God turns it into "just a book." The power fades and dies. It is no longer the word of *a living entity that has a voice*. It becomes merely *words on a page*. And, words can be memorized and recited without ever understanding what they mean. Therefore, words can be twisted, changed, translated, corrupted, and interpreted without anyone noticing. I don't want to write about this anymore. It is overwhelming and disturbing.

I will give an example. This morning as I walked to the gathering, I looked out over the valley. The sun had risen minutes earlier. The sky was blazing with color and cloud. The sun was hidden behind the bright red-orange-blue opalescent clouds, and rays of light were piercing through, casting beams of sunlight to the earth below. It was an awe inspiring sight that no one seemed to notice as they walked to the gathering. God created a beautiful masterpiece painting of earth and sky. The people passed by without looking, walked into a dark hallway, arriving in a dark electric light room, where the blinds are drawn closed.

"Let's pray to God," they say, as they turn on the television, and the computer system used to power it.

Tuesday

Last night was frustrating on many levels. After speaking to a counsellor about the situation in my house, I spent the entire evening in the exact place I wanted to avoid. Our fifteen minute prayer meeting turned into an hour of argument. I don't understand it, yet I do I understand. It is obvious that there is no time during the day for people to deal with their issues, so we end up discussing it all at the end of the night. There is no flexibility in the daily schedule, in order to form close relationships with counsellors, and deal with problems as they arise.

I have attempted to change this because many days I am in desperate need of help, a sounding board, a question and answer time, a rock wall, an emotional release, a validation, or whatever. Without these times of sharing, I reach the end of my own ability to contain, and I explode in a fury of language interwoven with emotion.

I will explain the level I have reached.

Less than an hour ago, I was talking with a man about my life. At the end of our conversation, I felt lighter, some of the burden had been lifted, and he made several suggestions. As I walked away, I found myself smiling and feeling free inside. An hour later, I am sitting in a class ready to start screaming in rage.

There is a failing here. Something is amiss. It is ridiculously obvious.

Last night, I slipped into meditation, and *something* happened. As I awoke, crying out with my voice, I realized the **something** was still happening. I was 'seeing:' walking in vision. I could adjust and shift, unlike other times in my life. Although it was beautiful and amazing, it can't help but bring my attention to what I am lacking. The gifts I have are WASTING. I spend no time at all developing what I've been given, and in exchange, I invest in a useless schedule that provides nothing I need.

The men here teach ridiculous concepts that are contrary to the knowledge of God. If they knew him, they would not teach false doctrine.

> "Neglect not the gift that is in thee, which
> was given by prophecy."

> Timothy 4:14

After several hours of counselling, I have come to a conclusion. I am bringing Christ from heaven to earth through me. If Jesus needs a person to manifest within, I am willing to be that person. I am beginning to understand this in a new light. I am changing – entirely. I am a new creature. I don't have enough information to write about this. Expressing the concept is not as easy as I thought it would be.

Maybe because I am using another's language to describe it. I am an alien who forgot he was an alien. I lied to myself, and forced myself to be human. Now I am suffering the consequences of those choices. I am lost and tired. I want to have a shower and think about something else for awhile.

Please disregard the last paragraph.

Wednesday

I find myself in a difficult situation – unwilling to compromise my beliefs, while attempting to adapt to the structure put in place by men. I am extremely cautious in my decisions, and each choice has been agonizing. I am weighing the balance and walking a tightrope.

I am an ambassador. I never gave much thought to this concept until someone brought it to my attention yesterday. It accurately describes what I am doing here on earth. The prophets have left me a message that I am attempting to understand. Sometimes, I think I am here to negotiate the world's surrender, before they are destroyed. How am I to proceed?

Since arriving on the farm, I have done the impossible, but it still isn't enough. Until the people believe without question, the message is lost. I am tired of failure. I am tired of waiting. I am emotionally distraught, and the internal pressure is unbearable. I am noticing a clarity to my vision, a change in my perception, and an embracing of the truth. I am awakening slowly. My frustration comes from knowing that however fast I progress, it may not be quick enough to prevent the coming destruction.

I trust that God will complete what he has started within me, and awaken me fully when the time is right. One day I will be made whole. One morning I will return from the spiritual world with power and faith. My words are not given lightly. I've gone through long periods of time, clinging desperately to the hope within me, always standing in faith.

David Burton

I've hidden things even from myself, to prevent the enemy from taking them from me. Understand?

Last night I entered meditation and entered into a vision so crystal clear that I didn't understand that I was inside a vision. When I awoke I was confused. Was it a vision? Did it happen? I moved from one world to another without even knowing it happened.

I sought counsel all day long, but I still ended up in an argument with another resident, and it almost turned physical. Instead of engaging, I walked away, but the temptation was present. When the conflict arose, I voiced my words without hesitation. Truth can be painful. I will no longer bite my tongue, and spare someone's feelings. I will not lie, nor will I accept a lie in my life.

I haven't come to this farm to allow people to abuse me. I don't understand this place at all. I have boundaries, and I will not let people walk all over them. I have heard teaching on boundaries, from both Christian and secular sources. However, this farm completely disregards all information on the subject. Instead, they offer condescending comments such as, "you're picking up rights!?"

They have taught me here that **I have no rights**. When I express the reality that I do, *in fact*, have certain rights as a human being, they respond with, "you have a bad attitude."

Bullshit.

Wars have been fought, families destroyed, countries torn apart, and lives sacrificed, so that humanity could have *rights*. How about the human rights movement spread all over the world? Are we to allow oppression to reign? Are we to embrace slavery? Are we to teach our children to blindly obey without question? Am I supposed to allow someone to abuse me because I am a worthless drug addict with no rights!? This is insane!

Just because someone is given authority here on the farm doesn't mean they have *the right* to treat other people badly. A small taste of power usually goes directly to someone's head and they try to force their will on everyone around them.

I didn't come here to listen to people. I came here to seek God. I don't know what to do. I have come to the end of my understanding. I can't adequately communicate with leadership, and they aren't listening anyway.

Thursday

I am working as a cook in a restaurant, but being treated as a slave; being commanded to do disturbing things, corrupt and unclear. The person who has employed me, the person who owns the restaurant is standing beside me, asking me to do something with several creatures laying on the grill.

I refuse. I can sense the evil within this man and more importantly I understand that he considers me nothing. He is trying to enforce this upon me, that I am a slave and worthless. I am neither, and I am finished with allowing people to keep me captive or oppressed.

I walk away from the man, take off my apron and exit the building. I walk into the parking lot, step onto the hood of a vehicle and start jumping up and down, crushing the metal beneath my feet.

I walk from vehicle to vehicle, destroying them. I see a small set of stairs leading toward a door, and I know the restaurant lay behind that door. As I approach, I look for a weapon. I see a rake; it seems appropriate. I gather it in my hand and ascend the steps in a single motion.

I pass through the doorway and my eyes are assaulted with the image of a dining hall. The tables are covered in white cloth and set with silver cutlery, sparkling wineglasses intersperse the settings. I see money sitting on small black platters, but everything I see is a forgery.

David Burton

This entire restaurant is a lie; this is the window dressing that hides the evil from its patrons. My eyes see the truth, and the slavery behind it. I take my rake and draw it across the table, sending cutlery, glasses and cash flying into the air.

As I hear the objects crashing to the floor I leap onto the table and continue to work my way across the room; my decision is made: I have become resolute.

At the far end of the hall a boy is dining with his family. As I sweep away the lies set before him, he is offended. He looks at me with disgust and anger. He is indignant and he begins to speak – I stop him quickly with my reply. My eyes are on fire as I speak,

"If you consider this is an injustice, look at my life." I have silenced the child, and I have stayed long enough.

I awake in the process of seeing the message, but I don't commit the words to the page until later in the day. This is the power of God: Christ inside me. I belong to him, and we are in communion.

Another man has decided to leave the farm. A few days ago I had a vision of him leaving, and now it is unfolding right before my eyes. I spoke to him about his decision, but he is convinced that it is the right path to take. How can I stand in the way? God has given us all a choice. I can't make the decision for other people, and I refuse to enforce my will upon them.

Where does that leave me? I see what will happen to this man, but I remain powerless to change his path. I attempt to reason with him, contend with his heart, and warn him of the coming destruction. There is nothing else left to be done. If he will not hear me, then he will not hear me.

I am crying by 7:30 in the morning, weeping in the arms of a friend. I break down so completely that I can barely breathe. I am praying and he is praying. I had been trying to contain myself, but in desperation I reached out to a friend for help, and help me he did.

Friday

I am crying in agony on my knees before 7:30 in the morning. I've been awake for just over an hour, and already I have come to a place of desperation. People around me have no idea what is required of me in order to stay on the farm. If anyone experienced what I have, they would run away screaming in terror.

Many people leave this farm. Many leave for stupid reasons. Many leave to go relapse. Many leave to return to their old lives. Many leave because they simply can't stand the way the farm operates. I have the greatest reason for leaving, but I remain nevertheless.

The last person I saw break down emotionally was a young man. It was his first day in the program, and he crumbled under the first onslaught of emotion that surface. Many of us have repressed our emotions for years with drugs and alcohol, and having them resurface is overwhelming and often unpleasant.

I've read in the scriptures where "Jesus wept." I don't think he just teared up a little bit, coughed, and then wiped away his tears with the back of his hand. I believe HE WEPT with a heart wrenching cry, as agonizing emotional pain flooded his body until he was "moved to compassion," and resurrected a dead man.

When Jesus cries, the dead rise.

I will search for his method, not man's forgery. God strips away all the things of this world. I have chosen God and I will follow Christ. Wherever he leads, whatever he asks.

It is becoming insanely difficult to continue here on the farm. The restrictions on my time are unbearable, and the lack of understanding is torture. Many people aren't prepared to accept what I say, because the eyes of their understanding have been darkened, and I don't know how to open them.

God, I can't go another night without you showing up in power. I NEED contact – face to face, spirit to spirit. I fell asleep on my knees, praying. I never thought it would happen, but now it has. My standard has just risen to a new level, and it is at an all-time high. What now, Lord?

Cry, cry, and cry some more. My heart is being torn out in agony. My friend left at the exact time the vision revealed, within minutes, and nothing I did changed the outcome. I told the man what I had seen, and rather than changing his mind, it confirmed his decision to walk away.

"My mind is made up," he said.

A part of me wanted to leave with him. What is the point of knowing what is coming if nothing can be done to change the outcome?

In the vision, I left with him. "Might as well leave," I said. "I need a good humbling." The words were said with irony, and a touch of "This is ridiculous." Of course using alcohol is not humility. It is, in fact, the complete opposite. Relapse clears states to everyone around me that I am **no longer teachable**.

The only part of the vision I could change was the decision I was going to make. God warned me of what was coming, impressed the importance of my decision, showed me where my thinking was heading, and gave me a way out – a chance to make the right choice.

I didn't want to use drugs. I wanted to escape this prison I find myself in. Jesus Jail. That's what this place has become. Leadership uses Jesus Christ as a method of control and restriction, rather than hope and freedom. The people here don't have the ability to relate with me. Each person seems to have a piece of the puzzle, but they are blind to the complete picture. The pieces interlock to form an image, but no one except me is aware of this fact.

I find myself a science fiction life in a fantasy world. The prophetic vision has destroyed nearly all sense of reality. I used to understand life, but now that understanding has faded into a distant memory of the past.

The scripture teaching here on the farm leaves a lot to be desired. The teachers don't seem to understand the words or the concepts of the text. The continuously misuse the scriptures, twisting them to form doctrines that are corrupt. These people *believe* they are doing the right thing (*I think*) which makes them even more dangerous. A man who believes in his cause is harder to reason with. He becomes committed to his way of thinking, and is impossible to reach. Rather than examine his doctrine, he will defend it.

I find this lack of textual knowledge strange, considering anyone can go to the local bookstore and purchase a *concordance*. This would give them the ability to look up the Greek and Hebrew words that have been translated into English, and understand what they mean in the original language.

I think the truth of scripture remains hidden because they are intentionally deceiving people to further their own agenda, or truly ignorant and lack the knowledge.

I keep trying to explain to leadership that I am consistently seeing future events. These visions manifest over and over again, without fail, but when I communicate this concept with other people, I get stupid comments. Such as, "It's just a dream."

These responses only confirm the ignorance of humanity, and the validity of the scriptures.

David Burton

"Bring forth the blind people that have eyes, and the deaf that have ears." - Isaiah 43:8

I am beginning to wonder about this journal. Is it sealed? Someone could read a plain description in these pages, placed here by my hand, and still be unable to understand. Isaiah writes about the existence of such books. Sometimes, I forget that these types of books were written by men. I am not alone, I am not the first, and my condition is not unique. Someone *must* have the answers I am searching for. Contrarily, what I speak of so casually, is extremely rare. I am becoming convinced that I answers I require will not be found on the farm. I am surrounded by people who have **no understanding** at all.

Another acquaintance decided to leave. When I walked into our worship service, I noticed very quickly that he was gone. I could '**see**' that he was not in the room, nor anywhere on the farm. In the physical sense, I am a blind man who requires glasses to see. My eyesight is not very good. I was not wearing my glasses when I noticed the disappearance of my acquaintance. It wasn't because of my physical sight that I knew my friend was missing. Understand?

I was skeptical at first. When I '**saw**' that he was gone, I searched the room with my human eyes, walking from person to person, until I could no longer lie to myself. Upon confirmation, I wept quietly and gently.

I did not speak to anyone when I first arrived here on the farm. What did they have to offer me? I talked to God alone. He doesn't a human translator. The leadership here have ridiculed me for this. They continue to maintain that God speaks *through* people, but doesn't actually speak *to* people. They use this argument to force me into listening to their methods of Christianity.

I disagree with their conclusion. God has a voice.

In an attempt to appease leadership, and still stay true to myself, I have created an experiment. I've started communicating with counsellors, leadership, and other residents. Anyone who God draws into my path. I pour out my heart and mind to them, as I would to God, and allow them to speak. I do this consistently all throughout the day. The moment a situation arises that I don't have a solution for, I immediately seek instruction and answers from the people around me. When my emotions break forth and wreak havoc, I go to someone and share the emotional chaos. I **allow** people into my life and into my heart.

What is the result?

Leadership ridicules me because I am reaching out for their counsel several times a day. They are now irritated with my verbal communication, and have decided to tell me to, "Go to God for instruction."

I want to scream and tear my hair out. These people are insane. Nothing satisfies them. I begin to suspect that they are only interested in having someone to control, so that they can lie to themselves, and say, life is alright.

Anyway... *moving on*. I have discovered a method of explaining the dream world to these people. Ready? I will take a man into a room, just inside the threshold of the door, and strike him in the face. Then I will pull him into the adjoining room, and tell him it didn't happen.

"What's that, silly man? You're in pain!? Why? Stop being ridiculous! That happened while you were in the **other** room. Don't let it affect your day."

Saturday

I pray and ask God specifically for my wings. It's been awhile since I've flown. I lay upon my bed and fall asleep for several minutes. This is his response, and this is what I see.

I am standing in the grass near a building here on the farm. I am speaking another language. I start quietly, but increase my volume as I form the words. I spread my hands out to each side and I feel the power surging all around me. It flows through my outstretched hands. I can't see the world around me anymore.

Suddenly, the power manifests as two blazing white wings directly in front of me, lightning dancing around them. I am aware of what is happening. I know I am about to return to the physical world. I place my hands in front of me, opening and closing my fingers as everything around me passes into darkness.

My hands flash with opalescent color until I awake, opening my eyes and rising from my bed. My mind is on fire with the vision I have just seen, but God calls me again, and I fall asleep.

I awake in the air, in flight. I approach a house where everyone expects that I will land and walk among the people. Instead I rise higher, soaring above their heads, and entering the building from a balcony. I touch down for a moment, take a few steps, and leap skyward again. I crash through panes of glass, transparent windows, and fly over a large dining hall. The tables below are covered in white cloth.

I reach the edge of the balcony, the next opening, and cling to the ledge with all my strength. My flight fails me momentarily. I am caught unaware, but only for a single moment.

I pull myself to the ledge, run several steps, and take flight, crashing through another set of window panes. I reach the final balcony on the far end of the house. I stand for a moment, quietly looking out over the grass lawn, wooden fence and dull glowing streetlights, before stepping off the railing, and into the sky. I glide in the air.

FLASH. *I am inside a barn. I can see a demon nearby, standing next to the animals. At first, I think nothing of this demon, but it soon captures my attention. Satan suddenly manifests within him. I watch as the horns grow up out of the pasty skin and then wrap around the back of his head. The evil is increasing, and the demon is changing. At next glance, he is fully aroused and he starts fucking the animals. I am disgusted and horrified. I don't think this demon is aware of my presence. I walk around him and leave the barn.*

FLASH. *I am in a room, dimly lit. There is a single table in the center of the room with two chairs on either side. There is a metallic ball in the center of the table and I sit in one chair, facing another person. We awake at the same moment, somewhat disoriented: neither of us know why we are here or what is happening.*

The sphere in the center of the table has slots carved into it and from these cuts a red light begins to glow. As the light gets brighter it shifts through the spectrum, ending in a brilliant white light that I raise my hands to shield my eyes from.

The other person is terrified, even as I am fascinated.

"It is taking us somewhere," I say. I feel the shift, but it is quick, and without disorientation. I stand and examine my surroundings.

I am in another room, as empty as the first; however, there are two openings on either side of the room – doorways. I walk to the doorway and look through. There is a large empty area brightly lit with white light. It appears to be a large enclosed room, designed for practice or testing.

I see several objects, and I understand, but don't simultaneously. I turn and walk to the other doorway; peering through, I see the same area of containment, with several differences in the objects. The wall to my left is embedded with equipment and covered in strange symbols. I inherently know that this is a testing ground.

I blink only to find myself standing in the center of the room I was just looking at, as creatures materialize out of nowhere and attack immediately. I am

David Burton

surprised more than anything else. One creature attaches itself to my back. I pull, trying to remove the protective clothing I am wearing.

I toss it to one side, and I awake.

As I lay upon my bed, waiting for sleep to come, I heard a female voice call my name. Her voice was crystal clear. I could hear several other voices in the distance, but I couldn't grasp the words.

This day has been a nightmare. Following the intensity of last night, this day has delivered the same insanity. I was about to start playing guitar when I was informed of yet another two hour punishment in the greenhouse. The only personal time I have during the week has been stolen from me. I freaked out. I couldn't contain my emotions. I walked to the dormitory, and lashed out in fury as I packed my suitcase.

I've had enough of this punishing attitude here on the farm. I let go of all control. Words have failed me at this point, and actions have become a necessity. I bring my emotions to life. My house leader, and all other residents, scatter in different directions, trying to avoid my scathing rage. One man stays and attempts to talk me off the ledge, for the second time in the last week.

I don't understand why he wants to help, but he knows the right words to say, in a way that make sense to me. It's as though he expects my outbursts and is prepared for them. Everything I own is packed in my suitcase, but I calm down enough to go serve my sentence of pulling weeds.

I grab a can of pop on my way out the door, knowing it will be hot and I will become thirsty. As I am walking up the hill toward the greenhouse, I see my house leader in the distance. I am still lashing out, filled with resentment of all the past wrongs, and decide to hurl my pop at him. I don't even stop to consider the outcome, I simply act on impulse, and calmly watch the can soar through the air. My mind is shutdown, and I am operating straight from emotional fury. My body acts of its own accord.

The can hits the ground directly in front of him, and explodes, showering him in carbonated sugar water. My aim is exact, the explosion unplanned, but inevitable. He freaks out and comes running at me across the gravel, cursing and preparing for a fight.

I keep walking. I'm past the point of caring, and I'm not intimidated. I've dealt with people like him on the street for a long time, but now I am clean and my mind is clear. I won't fight him, which enrages him further. He hits me in the back of my head, but I turn and walk in a different direction.

"I won't fight you," I say. *Keep going and seal your fate*, I say inside my mind. *Show your true colors. You're only making it worse for yourself.*

I don't need to defend myself. He strikes me again, and pushes me hard. He is yelling. I am calm, quiet, and continue walking away.

People have noticed the conflict, and decide to intervene. I could care less. I once had a man wrap a steel chain around his fist and beat me with it. When he had finished, and started to walk away, I chased him down and asked him, "Is that all you have?" I lost my fear of men that day, and I learned something about myself.

I face demons on a regular basis. What is a man going to do to me? I am tired of playing games. I am an advanced student, and I'm sick of playing stupid for their sake. I can toy with their minds if I wish. It's simple. I have refrained until today because I live by one single principle: *just because I* **can***, doesn't mean I* **should***.* Being able isn't enough. There needs to be purpose and resolve, reason and compassion.

I seem to be lacking on the compassion side at the moment.

Another leader arrives. I've lost all composure. I'm out of control emotionally and physically. When I decide to be ME, I have no boundaries or limits. All action and speech is sanctioned. This makes me dangerous. I am a weapon, and my consciousness is the only aspect that holds back complete destruction of everything, and everyone, around me.

What if I had decided that throwing a can of pop wasn't enough of a statement? What then? I start crying while the leader talks to me. Surely this will end in disaster. They will ask me to leave. All of this work for nothing.

I've reached certain limits of what I can currently handle. The vision of the demon came crashing back into my mind during morning prayer, precipitating my entire breakdown. It caused me to cry out in horror. **I can't run from this war**. I must face it directly. I've attempted to explain. I am doing everything I must to survive the onslaught of spiritual concepts beyond the reasoning of man.

My statement is simple. Join me, or get out of the way, because annihilation is coming, and I don't have time to waste with stupid human perception. I don't have time to run around convincing people that *rain is coming*. I need to build the ship. I don't want to argue about what a boat is, or discuss why it must be built, or give lessons on design. **I JUST WANT TO BUILD**. Leave me alone. I'm building right now, and your interference is irritating me.

Sunday

I had absolutely zero time to myself this weekend. As I was starting to play guitar, I was informed that I had to cook in the kitchen. I cook all week for these men, and I don't want to do it on the weekend. I need a break.

I can't believe this farm. I'm not a staff paid position. I'm not a counsellor. I just live here. In fact, I *pay* to live here. I sick and tired of working all the time. Work, work, work. Volunteering is one thing, enforced slavery quite another. This work program is beginning to look more like slavery every day.

I will never be an ambassador for this program. I already have a realm that I represent, and I'm not interested in having a conflict of interest. I will not waiver in my belief, or bow before another master. Christ is my all in all.

My sleep was restless. The chain that binds my cross around my neck snapped in the pursuing tossing and turning. I found my cross on the floor beside my bed this morning, and the cross beneath it.

My perception is changing, and my world view with it. I feel myself awakening in a way I never have before. I want to awaken fully, and embrace the spirit within me. I am searching for spiritual contact, and removing everything in my life preventing me from doing so. I need help. I don't completely understand this process, and asking the farm is hopeless.

Two more people left this morning. They went to Hastings last night, and couldn't handle the experience. I knew these two individuals were struggling, but leadership allowed them to go anyway. Stupidity. Ironically, I was forbidden to go, even though I've passed the testing time and time again. It makes no sense to me, like so many other things on this farm.

Want some more farm insanity? My friend underwent heart surgery recently, and is now on medication. Leadership decided not to pick up his medication from the pharmacy this week. I can't fucking believe it! Do they want to be charged with negligent homicide!? This place is beyond insane sometimes. We confronted leadership about their failure to produce life sustaining medication, and they tried to pass it off as no big deal. In the same way they do every time they make a mistake. *People complain, leaders make excuses, and everything remains the same.* Honestly, this goes beyond comprehension.

My head hurts behind my eyes. Severely. It comes in waves, and the pain is powerful. In the shower, my mind is flooded with imagery of alien eyes. I see them clearly, and the pain is intense. I sing through the onslaught with my palms pressed against my face, covering my eyes and holding my head.

Just another day in my strange life.

Monday

I awake unrested. Although not as tired as previous days, I question why I am still here. I am facing another day of manual labour in the work camp. This weekend was full of activity, punishment, and still more work. Where was the rest, relaxation, quiet reflection of life, and contemplation of the future? Nowhere. None to speak of.

Why do I stay here? I remain because I hope situations will improve. I am lying to myself. It will not improve. More than likely, it will get worse as time passes. There is an internal conflict that can't be resolved by simply continuing. The conflict must be examined and addressed. My sobriety is contingent upon my spiritual condition. It has always been this way.

The farm is holding me back. They say I can't, when I know I can. They say God can't, when I know he can. I won't allow someone else's disbelief to rule my life, or dictate the terms I live on. A part of me hopes I will find a reason to stay, but nothing is emerging.

Today I discovered another addition to the work program. Now we will be working in the evening as well, cancelling the classes. It is farming season, and there is work to be done in the berry fields. I don't have anything personal against berries. I love them. The point is that this farm has turned into a full time job, and I'm still paying to live here. I didn't come here to work all the time, but that is what we do all day long.

I have little, or no time, to do the things I love. I haven't drawn a single sketch for duration of my stay. Not one. I'm an artist, and when I'm clean I always seize the opportunity to produce new images. Renderings that reflect light rather than darkness. I fear drawing, but I do it because I need to face myself and see what is within me.

I am a slave here on the farm. If I refuse to work, I am forced to leave. It is an ultimatum. They have no interest in helping me find work off the farm, in a profession of my choice. It is not allowed. I am not even allowed access to a phone directory. I am fenced in at every turn, but I see the obstacles, and I've been developing plans to avoid them.

My friend has a heart attack at supper this evening. He collapsed at his table. I went running to find someone with a cell phone, because none of us are allowed access to a phone line. The paramedics came and took him to the hospital. I am fucking raging. The combination of missing medication, being forced to work all day in the heat, and the stress of living here, *has taken its toll*. The lack of medication, and his collapse, are completely interwoven. I want to put my fist through a wall. I love this man. His heart is good, and his spirit beautiful.

Rather than being a place of healing, this farm has placed his

life in danger. No excuses. I've watched him speak with leadership, asking for rest, and help with his condition. All to no avail. No one listens, nothing changes, and this is the result.

The anger I feel is not just because of his situation. It is because of my own. I've approached leadership countless times for help, and nothing is done. I ask for help with my emotional explosions. Leadership ignores my request. I eventually explode. Leadership punishes me for my outburst. It's like withholding bread, and then punishing the person for being hungry.

I will leave this farm, and I will never return. I want nothing to do with it. I want to move on with my life, and forget I was ever here (to a certain extent). I need to remember my experience here, so that I won't leave myself an excuse to return. The farm is not the place I thought it was, and I will not allow fear to trap me here.

I used to walk away from bad situations at the sound of a pin being dropped. Gone before the pin hit the floor. I don't want go backward, I want to move forward – skyward. God has not abandoned me. Anyone who tells me that I can be separated from him is lying.

I want to tell you a story here today.

In my addiction, I fell in debt with a drug dealer. I was beaten, held hostage, and ransomed. At the cash drop, undercover officers arrested everyone at gun point, the house was raided, and people went to jail. All sheer stupidity, but very dangerous. The officers interviewed me, asking me *one* question.

"Why didn't you just run away?"

"Run where? I knew the people holding me captive. He, and every other drug dealer in town, knows where I live and where I work. My addiction is not a

secret. There was no running away for, and way of escape. They are evil. The debt was small, but they didn't care. It was the principle.

They don't care about the money. They feed off the power, control, and fear. The more they convinced me of how worthless I am, the better they felt about themselves. They enjoyed tormenting me.

I remember them discussing the possibility of taking me up a mountain and putting a bullet in my head, like they were deciding what to order from a take-out menu. When the dealer pointed a pistol at me, and the clip fell out, I was amused and terrified simultaneously. The gun was not a fake.

What got me into this situation?

The dealer came to me as a friend, and 'helped me out' by smoking some crack with me, and then fronting a small quantity to me. We sat together and got high until morning – until it was time to pay up.

He wouldn't let me leave his sight without first paying my bill. I didn't have the money to pay it because he decided to charge me five times what the product was worth. That's when another evil man arrived, and the talk about my death began."

I can't help but examine my existence at the farm, and notice the similarities. Why don't I just run away? This situation feels all too familiar to me: the setting, the players, the demand. All the externals are wearing different face, but the underlying theme is the same.

I feel sick to my stomach even considering these things, but I must. These people came to me, offering to 'help me out,' but they have twisted the dialogue, and now profess that *I came to them*. After fronting me a bed, and some food, they demand payment in labour. They attempt to convince me that slavery is a positive outcome. Making matters worse, I pay them for my stay. More accurately, social services is paying for my stay.

The money and labour is not enough, so they demand power and control – all in the guise of niceties. I've been lied to, intimidated, my life threatened, and physically assaulted during my stay. Leadership continuously berates me with their unhelpful comments and rational, trying to convince me that I have brought these things upon myself. *As if I could*.

They say I have an attitude, and that I am filled with rebellion because I will not submit to, or perpetuate, their evil ways. I don't force my will on people (even when I see their future), and I don't intimidate or manipulate them into serving my will. I don't threaten, or punish, the people I love and want to help.

This farm is a classic example or beating a child and telling them it's for their own good. The leader who assaulted me faces no consequences or reprimand for his actions. In fact, he has been given a promotion, imbuing him with even more of this made man power structure of authority. *I didn't come here for this shit*.

I came here to remove the distractions of the world, and build a foundation of belief needed to make a stand. I surface from my addiction once every few years. My time is precious to me when I am clean, because it is so rare, and I believe it is being wasted here. I have conditioned myself to stay here, in spite of how I feel to the contrary. I don't think this psychological hiccup is helpful.

I want my life! The farm is not the only thing life has to offer. I won't be held captive here, nor will I allow them to toss me in the street like a piece of trash. I sacrifice my well-being to stay here because I don't know how to approach the next stage of my journey. It's not going to happen here, that much is clear.

I want employment! Now. I don't want to be living off the government if it means existing like this.

When did I begin to settle for this life of captivity? I am FREE from my addiction. Thank You, Jesus Christ. I will serve God. I don't have to stay here to do that. Leadership will not help me move forward, so I will do it alone. How? I don't know. One thing is certain. I will not exchange the slavery of addiction, for the slavery of man. Understand?

The schedule of the farm is so invasive that I have stopped reading scripture entirely. The book that never left my presence is beginning to sit on my shelf and gather dust. I am not impressed, to say the least. I explain this travesty to leadership, they tell me I am hearing more of the scriptures than ever before in my life.

I tilt my head to one side, staring at them quietly and confused. Their response is laughable, but I become angry instead. They blatantly lie to my face, and then condemn me, because I refuse to accept the lie. Perhaps they are unaware of my history.

I **sleep** with the scriptures in my hands. I keep them close to me because I don't when an attack may come. I am a warrior that sleeps with his sword – ready at any given moment. How did I become this way? War. My 'normal' is to fall asleep reading scripture. I read until my eyes can't stay open anymore. I have even fallen asleep in a chair, the book still held in my hands. I travel, and awake, motionless. My relationship with the word is a far cry from the forgery they present here. I'm not sure whether to laugh or cry.

Why do I remain?

Sometimes I hope that my presence will change the farm, that the light within me will push back the darkness, that the fire within me will spread, and that I might find another one of my kind. I stay because I have hope that God will reveal himself to the people through me. I see it as a way of balancing the scale for all the injustice I have committed.

David Burton

Every day that passes without me picking up a pipe is a step in the right direction. If nothing else is accomplished, at least this still stands. I consider this segment of my life as a preparation for what is to come. One day, I will serve the meal, but for now, I gather the ingredients.

There is a flight I need to catch. I don't want to be late, and miss the plane. There may be a flight scheduled for a later departure, so not all hope of reaching the destination is lost, but the human part of me would like to be on time.

Note:

I am beginning to live in a strange state of constant psychosis. It is only comparable to maintaining a 'high' state, without the accompanying paranoia. Nice, eh? I no longer have to pay to experience this, but it causes me to wonder what exactly is happening to me.

Tuesday

I visit a place I once lived to acquire the books I left behind. I awake disappointed and unsure of my stay here. Many things are being brought to my attention that confirm this place is completely ignoring God.

They teach the same content over and over, but I'm not interested. I have heard the same story so often that I am closing my heart to their words. I am carefully considering what my next move will be. I love certain moments here on the farm, but the rest of my time is wasted. I could be doing something else.

I don't want my life to pass me by. I am thinking about leaving, and entering the society I have abandoned. The hardest obstacle to overcome will be the time between leaving here and finding employment. Working will occupy my time and keep me focused on moving forward with my life.

During my stay here I haven't had to consider cash flow. I make one payment a month, and everything is provided for me. If I leave, I will be employed quickly. Sitting on social assistance is not an option for me. It seems like a recipe for disaster. I envision myself sinking into a depression, feeling worthless, and then torching my life.

I'm angry with leadership because they refuse to help me transition. Furthermore, they continue to condemn me for writing about my dreams in this journal. The dreams are the most significant aspect of prophecy. I've been developing this area for several years, and learning how to record the visions. I don't do this because of my own understanding. I do it because God has asked it of me.

I wrote nothing except my dreams for two years, recording every vision upon waking in the morning. I did not comment or interpret, removing myself entirely from the text. The dreams stand independently, untouched, and the metaphors unrevealed. I do not want my own perceptions to bias the people who will read this book in the future.

This week, one of the residents had a dream. Not anything extraordinary by my standards, but a dream nonetheless. During our church service on *Sunday*, the pastor brought the resident to the front of the room, and asked him to share the dream. The pastor slapped him on the back, confirmed that God was indeed talking to him, and gave him several encouraging words.

I quietly watched from the back of the room, seething inwardly. Leadership fight against me, ridicule me, condemn me, and mock me; but this other resident, they exalt. They praise in this resident what they try to torture out of me. I wanted to stand up and tell the whole lot of them to GO FUCK THEMSELVES.

I held back, mustering some sort of self-control. I'm not upset with the resident who has begun to dream. I'm angry with the spiritual forces influencing leadership, causing them to punish me, but reward the other man.

I feel sad for these people. A depth of sadness that overwhelms my intellect, and connects directly with my heart. I imagine what it must be like for them, desperately wanting a connection with the God, but not being able to experience him. They continue to drink grape juice, all the while thinking it is wine.

SAD.

It's hard to remain angry when I consider these concepts. Imagine spending an entire life searching for someone, and not finding him. They spend years waiting for God to speak to them in a vision, or dream, but they reject me because I have the experience every single night.

My fate is sealed. The director stood up in front of the class moments ago, and said, "Nothing will change here on the farm." Things will remain exactly as they are, even if it means accidently killing the residents.

Wednesday

I have discovered a common misconception here. We are taught the grace is limited, and that it expires after a certain amount of applications. Apparently, God's grace has an expiry date and is only available in limited quantities. Once grace is exhausted, punishment must be enforced.

Thank you, Jesus. Thank you, God. Thank you, Lord. For I know that your grace is not like this at all. I know that your grace is amazing and powerful, unlimited and ever-present. We deserve nothing, but you give us everything. Thank you for being our Father.

Thank you for ending the war. I am exhausted.

This morning someone decided to bring the fight to my door. I refused to involve myself in the conflict. I resisted the temptation to respond, or engage the enemy. I allowed God to fight this battle for me, and I did not need to raise a hand in defense.

"I'm not interested," I said quietly. I meant every word. I walked away. The man did not get the rise out of me that he expected, so he conscripted an acquaintance and tried again. He made his comments personal, attacking my character, not just my supposed behavior. I ignored his words, and refused to play the game. I turned my back on him, and started laughing. Something clicked inside me, and I realized that I was free – finally free from the condemnation of men.

My eyes looked upward, staring into the sky, watching the birds fly across the deep blue expanse. I couldn't hear the man's words, or the evil pouring forth from his mouth. He didn't exist for me anymore. I started talking to God about the eagles I could see in the distance, how free they appeared to be, soaring above the clouds.

In a moment of clarity, I understood that I have become the eagle. The man cursing me can continue to do so, thinking whatever he wants about me, and it has no impact on me. It does not affect me. I am no longer a slave. God has taken his rightful place in my life, and I trust him with all of my being.

At the exact moment I am praying these words, a hummingbird

appears beside me, flying up the staircase. Its colors are a vibrant shimmering red and green, so beautiful. I open my hands, palms up, and starting thanking God aloud. The hummingbird hovers between my outstretched hands, turning its head to look me in the eye, before flickering away and continuing on its path.

I walk away, following its flight path, and still speaking with the Lord. I have completely forgotten about everything that is happening around me because God is speaking. I haven't seen a hummingbird in many years, and the timing is incomprehensible. The moment I surrender, turning away from the evil, closing my ears to the lies of men, and opening myself to God – he answers.

I realize that I am standing in the exact place where the vision of white wings appeared in my dream. There is no such concept as coincidence in this earth. Don't let anyone tell you otherwise.

Sadly, no one notices the beauty of the hummingbird, my verbal exchange with God, or transformation of my spirit. The man is still looking at me with darkness in his eyes, trying to tear my flesh with his verbal assault.

"I will never listen to you," I whisper.

I follow God, not men.

Epilogue

Epilogue

Write this page.

The End